Civilizing Security

Security has become a defining feature of contemporary public discourse, permeating the so-called 'war on terror', problems of everyday crime and disorder, the reconstruction of 'weak' or 'failed' states and the dramatic renaissance of the private security industry. But what does it mean for individuals to be secure, and what is the relationship between security and the practices of the modern state? In this timely and important book, Ian Loader and Neil Walker outline and defend the view that security remains a valuable public good. They argue that the state is indispensable to the task of fostering and sustaining liveable political communities in the contemporary world and thus pivotal to the project of civilizing security. This is a major contribution by two leading scholars in the field and will be of interest to anyone wishing to deepen their understanding of one of the most significant and pressing issues of our times.

Ian Loader is Professor of Criminology and Director of the Centre for Criminology at the University of Oxford. He is the author of *Policing and the Condition of England* (with A. Mulcahy, 2003) and *Crime and Social Change in Middle England* (with E. Girling and R. Sparks, 2000) and an editor of the *British Journal of Criminology*. Ian is a leading authority on contemporary transformations in policing and security.

Neil Walker is Professor of European Law in the Department of Law at the European University Institute, Florence, and (for 2007) the Tercentenary Professor of Law at the University of Edinburgh. He has made well-known contributions to questions of transnational constitutional theory as well as to the study of policing and security. He has recently edited *Europe's Area of Freedom, Security and Justice* (2004) and *Relocating Sovereignty* (2006).

Civilizing Security

IAN LOADER AND NEIL WALKER

CAMBRIDGE
UNIVERSITY PRESS

CAMBRIDGE UNIVERSITY PRESS

Cambridge, New York, Melbourne, Madrid, Cape Town, Singapore, São Paulo

Cambridge University Press
The Edinburgh Building, Cambridge CB2 8RU, UK

Published in the United States of America by Cambridge University Press, New York

www.cambridge.org
Information on this title: www.cambridge.org/9780521691598

First published 2007

Printed in the United Kingdom at the University Press, Cambridge

A catalogue record for this book is available from the British Library

ISBN 978-0-521-87120-4 hardback
ISBN 978-0-521-69159-8 paperback

Contents

Acknowledgements

We have been working together on this book, or at least on its themes, for almost a decade. During such a span of time one necessarily receives support, assistance and encouragement from a great many quarters, both individual and institutional, and we would like to take this opportunity to acknowledge our debts and thank those to whom they are owed. We wish to thank, first of all, our friends and colleagues at the three extremely collegial and stimulating institutions at which we have worked during the writing of this book: in Ian's case, the Department of Criminology at Keele University and the Centre for Criminology at the University of Oxford, and in Neil's, the Department of Law at the European University Institute (EUI) in Florence. Ian would, in addition, like to thank the EUI for the award of a Jean Monnet Fellowship in 2004 and for the subsequent hospitality which allowed us to give the writing of this book something of a 'kick start'.

We would, beyond this, like to thank all the seminar and conference participants who have over this period commented on our work in progress during the various presentations we have singularly or jointly given, as well as those friends and colleagues who have been kind or interested enough to respond to draft papers and chapters, or who have engaged in discussion of the book's themes. At the risk of omitting someone with a legitimate claim to be included, and in no particular order of importance, such thanks are due to the following people: Andrew Ashworth, Richard Bellamy, Grainne de Burca, Damien Chalmers, Bill Dixon, Benoît Dupont, Andrew Goldsmith, Benjamin Goold, Carole Harlow, Jef Huysmans, Martin Innes, Vivienne Jabri, Les Johnston, Susanne Karstedt, Liora Lazarus, Hans Lindahl, Tim Newburn, Jim Sheptycki, Richard Sparks, Victor Tadros, Jim Tully, Jeremy Waldron, Rob Walker, Michael Williams, Jennifer Wood, Lucia Zedner and three anonymous Cambridge University Press reviewers. Didier Bigo and Clifford Shearing are owed particular thanks for pointing out why we were wrong in ways that helped sharpen our argument, while reminding us in the process of the virtues and possibility of civilized intellectual and political dialogue. Thanks also to John Dunn for issuing a challenge that we hope to have gone at least some distance towards meeting. It should be apparent that the usual disclaimer applies.

John Haslam and Carrie Cheek at Cambridge University Press have been a model of professionalism – and were rewarded by not having to wait as long as we usually detain our publishers. Finally, and once more, we have drawn inspiration from the love and support of, respectively, Penny, Eloïse and Imogen, and Gillian, Ross and Lewis, and from the recent and joyous arrival into the world of Iris and Emilia. It is to them that we dedicate this book.

The authors and publisher would like to thank the following publishers for permission to reproduce material for which they hold the copyright: Sage Publications Ltd for sections of chapter 1 that first appeared as 'Policing as a Public Good: Reconstituting the Connections Between Policing and the State', *Theoretical Criminology* 5/1 (2001), 9–35; Cambridge University Press for a sketch of the overall argument that first appeared as 'Necessary Virtues: The Legitimate Place of the State in the Production of Security', in J. Wood and B. Dupont (eds.) *Democracy, Society and the Governance of Security* (2006); and Hart Publishing Ltd for an initial version of chapter 9 which is to be published as 'Locating the Public Interest in Transnational Policing', in A. Goldsmith and J. Sheptycki (eds.), *Crafting Global Policing* (2007).

Prologue
On writing about security today

Citizens of western countries are too ready to take for granted the relatively civilized political conditions they enjoy, forgetting that politics in most times and places has been thoroughly predatory. Achieving a type of politics that is less predatory, and geared to some conception of the public good, is not easy under any circumstances, and may be impossible in the absence of certain preconditions. One of these preconditions seems to be a collective people, sustained by myths and capable of generating and monitoring political power. (Canovan 2005: 138)

There comes a moment in the historical development of any field of social enquiry, or at least in the formation of one's own thinking about its objects, when it seems necessary to return to basics; to dig up the foundations in order to subject to sustained reflection elements of the field, and the relations between them, that have come to be collectively taken for granted, treated as the unexamined presuppositions of research programmes. We believe that this moment has been reached in the social and political analysis of security and its relationship to the modern state.

Support for this judgement lies all around us today, both in respect of the profound and perplexing transformations that appear to be affecting the state's capacity to act as the pre-eminent guarantor of security to its citizens, and in the competing responses that these have provoked. On the one hand, there seems plenty of evidence to buttress the view that the modern state's place as not *a* but *the* security actor is being eroded under conditions of globalization and its neo-liberal thematization, such that commercial operatives, and non-state actors within civil, or uncivil, society, assume a far greater role in promising or providing security within, and across, contemporary societies (Johnston and Shearing 2003; Krahmann 2005). This, in turn, has generated reactions ranging from celebration, to cautious endorsement, to plain confusion, to cries of concern about the likely, inegalitarian and illiberal, consequences (Wood and Dupont 2006a; Zedner forthcoming). On the other hand,

1

one can find no little – on the surface contradictory – evidence that, in the wake of 9/11 and the Bali, Madrid and London bombings, state authority is reasserting, reempowering and relegitimating itself under the sign of security in the face of the dangers posed to society by transnational political violence. Here debate is routinely joined today between those political actors and commentators who hold that liberal democracies confront unprecedented threats from 'Islamic terrorism' and that states must take urgent, decisive measures to do what they deem necessary to defeat it, and those who claim that under the cloak of a 'war on terror' governments are mobilizing and responding selectively to threats in ways that place hard-won democratic rights and principles in great peril. It is against this backdrop, one in which security has become a trope of everyday political discourse and exchange, that it appeared to us valuable to revisit one of modernity's most profound conundrums and reflect fundamentally on the idea of security, on what it means for individuals to be and feel secure, and on the complex, contradictory intersections that exist between security and the practices of the modern state. This book is the result.

The upshot of our reflections on this conundrum will become apparent soon enough. But it may perhaps be useful at the outset – so as to be precise about the book's purposes and avoid offering readers a false prospectus – to state clearly what we have *not* set out to accomplish. We have not, first of all, sought to offer a detailed empirical mapping of the plurality of actors and agencies who are engaged in practices of security across the world today or a 'state-of-the-art' survey of the theoretical paradigms and empirical enquiries that endeavour to make sense of them (cf. Terriff *et al.* 1999; Zedner forthcoming). It is now commonly accepted, and almost otiose to mention, that writing about contemporary security requires one to come to terms with much more than the nation state and its police, military and cognate security operatives. The private security industry – in forms ranging from small local companies to global corporations – now functions within and across national boundaries and is engaged in 'domestic' security, the protection of transnational economic interests, and the support and conduct of military operations. We must add to this the 'grassroots' policing and protective practices engaged in by non-state actors within civil society – especially but not only in poor communities in the developing world. We need to think about the development of the European Union as an 'internal' and 'external' security actor and about the role played by states, the EU, the UN and international NGOs in practices of post-conflict policing and social reconstruction. And so on and so on. Faced with such pluralized, fragmented, commodified and by no means state-dominated environments, we plainly require better empirical knowledge, whether of the operation and effects of new security actors on the ground, or their linkages with 'old' protective agencies within security networks, or of the overarching institutional pattern within different jurisdictions and across their territorial boundaries. This much cannot be gainsaid. But such descriptive mapping is not the only task that the pluralization of security confronts us with and it is not the one we have chosen to tackle in this book.

This is not, secondly, a book about the 'war on terror'. Since 9/11 the shelves of bookstores across the western world have been filled – in new, hastily arranged sections earmarked 'terrorism' – with text after text purporting to analyse some element of the apocalyptic danger posed to liberal societies and western interests by al-Qaeda and its offshoots, or to praise or censure the ways in which the American or other governments have defined and responded to that threat.[1] Many such texts can no doubt lay claim to being serious books on a serious topic written by serious journalists or academics, as recent efforts by, among many others, Benjamin Barber (2003), Jason Burke (2004), John Gray (2003), Michael Ignatieff (2004) and David Rose (2004) attest. But there is a standing danger in the publishing industry that has developed around the 'war on terror' of authors either chasing events in a manner that gives their work an all too imminent 'use-by' date, or else of falling prey to the kinds of spontaneous thinking that are, as Pierre Bourdieu was at constant pains to remind us, the enemy of the construction of social scientific knowledge and understanding. We will, as the book unfolds, have cause to make observations on the way in which the so-called 'war on terror' is permeating the contemporary politics and practice of security, just as we will at numerous points seek to describe the agents and agencies that comprise a pluralized security landscape that stands today in great need of more precise cartography and fuller explanation. But these are not, we want to emphasize, our principal purposes.

What follows then, and instead, is an essay on the idea of security and its relationship to political community. It represents an attempt,

---

[1] During a recent visit to the books section of Amazon.com (16 May 2006) a search under 'war on terror' unearthed no less than 1,177 items.

on our part, to take a step back from the practical immediacies and apparent security imperatives of the present in a bid to make better sense of the former and scrutinize the claims made in respect of the latter. It is as such, if one wishes to insist upon a disciplinary tag, an exercise in applied social and political theory, by which we claim no more than that it is an effort to think and write as coherently as we are currently able about the practice of security and its relationship to the practices of the state, in ways that are informed by relevant research and reflection in criminology, the sociology of policing and social control, political science, public law and international security studies. We shall, in substantive terms, outline and defend the idea that security – understood sociologically as a 'thick' public good – is an indispensable constituent of any good society and argue that the democratic state has a necessary and virtuous part to play in seeking to realize the good of security thus conceived – in seeking, in the words of our title, to *civilize* security and to release its *civilizing* potential. This, we believe, is an argument that has application and purchase not merely in 'settled' democratic societies with strong state traditions, but also in those settings where authoritarian states routinely act in ways injurious to the liberty and security of their citizens and in environments where 'weak' or 'failed' states lack the capacity to act as a security-enhancing political authority. By way of conclusion, we seek to extend and revise the argument still further by examining how best to conceptualize and promote security as a global public good.

In making this case, we remain acutely aware that we are writing about (and within), and in a modest bid to act upon, a world that is deeply inhospitable to the democratic, egalitarian and solidaristic security culture that it is our purpose to delineate and foster; one from which, as John Dunn (1993: 122) has argued, 'any reasonable and relatively concrete social and political hope' has been 'deleted'. It is a world in which the governments of liberal states increasingly accede to populist, xenophobic demands in ways that undermine the democratic liberties of their citizens. It is a world where neo-liberalism – and the 'order of egoism' that it champions (Dunn 2005: ch. 4) – has come to be ascendant in ways that have enabled policing and security resources to be captured by those with the greatest supply of economic and social capital and thereby distributed in inverse relation to risk, and hence need. It is a world replete with authoritarian regimes, and divided or post-conflict societies, where insecurities, inequalities and the absence of democratic governance go hand in hand. It is a world, in sum, in which the idea of politically constituted public authority recognizing the claims and seeking to coordinate the security interests of all its citizens appears remote and increasingly far-fetched.

Faced with such inhospitable conditions, one can easily lapse into fatalistic despair, letting events simply come as they will, or else seek refuge in the consolations offered by the total critique of securitization practices – a path that some critical scholars in criminology and security studies have found all too seductive (e.g. Bigo 2002, 2006; Walters 2003). Or one can, as we have done, supplement social criticism with the hard, uphill, necessarily painstaking work of seeking to specify what it may mean for citizens to live together securely with risk; to think about the social and political arrangements capable of making this possibility more rather than less likely, and to do what one can to nurture practices of collective security shaped not by fugitive market power or by the unfettered actors of (un)civil society, but by an inclusive, democratic *politics*.

Social analysts of crime and security have become highly attuned to, and warned repeatedly of, the illiberal, exclusionary effects of the association between security and political community (Dillon 1996; Hughes 2007). They have not, it should be said, done so without cause, for reasons we set out at some length as the book unfolds. But this sharp sensitivity to the risks of thinking about security through a communitarian lens has itself come at a price, namely, that of failing to address and theorize fully the virtues and social benefits that can flow from members of a political community being able to put and pursue security in common. This, it seems to us, is a failure to heed the implications of the stake that *all* citizens have in security; to appreciate the closer alignment of self-interest and altruism that can attend the acknowledgement that we are forced to live, as Kant put it, inescapably side-by-side and that individuals simultaneously constitute and threaten one another's security; and to register the security-enhancing significance and value of the affective bonds of trust and abstract solidarity that political communities depend upon, express and sustain. All this, we think, offers reasons to believe that security offers a conduit, perhaps the best conduit there is, for giving practical meaning to the idea of the public good, for reinventing social democratic politics, even for renewing the activity of politics at all.

These, of course, may prove to be naïve hopes, futile whistling in a cold and hostile wind. It is in addition true that the project of civilizing security is ultimately a question not of social theory but of political praxis. But if such a project is ever to be thematized as a politics it requires, or at least can be furthered by, some form of theoretical articulation; one which reminds us, as C. L. R. James (1963) might have said, that those who know only of security of security nothing know. It is with this overarching purpose in mind that we have been moved to write in the way that we have about security today.

1 | *Uncivil security?*

OUR argument in this book is that security is a valuable public good, a constitutive ingredient of the good society, and that the democratic state has a necessary and virtuous role to play in the production of this good. The state, and in particular the forms of public policing governed by it, is, we shall argue, indispensable to the task of fostering and sustaining liveable political communities in the contemporary world. It is, in the words of our title, pivotal to the project of *civilizing security*.

By invoking this phrase we have in mind two ideas, both of which we develop in the course of the book. The first, which is relatively familiar if not uncontroversial, is that security *needs* civilizing. States – even those that claim with some justification to be 'liberal' or 'democratic' – have a capacity when self-consciously pursuing a condition called 'security' to act in a fashion injurious to it. So too do non-state 'security' actors, a point we return to below and throughout the book. They proceed in ways that trample over the basic liberties of citizens; that forge security for some groups while imposing illegitimate burdens of insecurity upon others, or that extend the coercive reach of the state – and security discourse – over social and political life. As monopoly holders of the means of legitimate physical and symbolic violence, modern states possess a built-in, paradoxical tendency to undermine the very liberties and security they are constituted to protect. Under conditions of fear, such as obtain across many parts of the globe today, states and their police forces are prone to deploying their power in precisely such uncivil, insecurity-instilling ways. If the state is to perform the ordering and solidarity-nourishing work that we argue is vital to the production of secure political communities then it must, consequently, be connected to forms of discursive contestation, democratic scrutiny and constitutional control. The state is a great civilizing force, a necessary and virtuous component of the good society. But if it is to take on this role, the state must itself be civilized – made safe by and for democracy.

But our title also has another, less familiar meaning – the idea that security *is* civilizing. Individuals who live, objectively or subjectively, in a state of anxiety do not make good democratic citizens, as European theorists reflecting upon the dark days of the 1930s and 1940s knew well (Neumann 1957). Fearful citizens tend to be inattentive to, unconcerned about, even enthusiasts for, the erosion of basic freedoms. They often lack openness or sympathy towards others, especially those they apprehend as posing a danger to them. They privilege the known over the unknown, us over them, here over there. They often retreat from public life, seeking refuge in private security 'solutions' while at the same time screaming anxiously and angrily from the sidelines for the firm hand of authority – for tough 'security' measures against crime, or disorder, or terror. Prolonged episodes of violence, in particular, can erode or destroy people's will and capacity to exercise political judgement and act in solidarity with others (Keane 2004: 122–3). Fear, in all these ways, is the breeding ground, as well as the stock-in-trade, of authoritarian, uncivil government.

But there is more to it than that. Security is also civilizing in a further, more positive sense. Security, we shall argue, is in a sociological sense a 'thick' public good, one whose production has irreducibly social dimensions, a good that helps to constitute the very idea of 'publicness'. Security, in other words, is simultaneously the producer and product of forms of trust and abstract solidarity between intimates and strangers that are prerequisite to democratic political communities. The state, moreover, performs vital cultural and ordering work in fashioning the good of security conceived of in this sense. It can, under the right conditions, create inclusive communities of practice and attachment, while ensuring that these remain rights-regarding, diversity-respecting entities. In a world where the state's pre-eminence in governing security is being questioned by private-sector interests, practices of local communal ordering and transnational policing networks, the constitution of old- and new-fashioned forms of democratic political authority is, we shall argue, indispensable to cultivating and sustaining the civilizing effects of security.

Security and its discontents

Raising these possibilities is, of course, to invite a whole series of obvious but nonetheless significant questions: what is security? What does it mean to be or to feel secure? Who or what is the proper object of security – individuals, collectivities, states, humanity at large? What social and political arrangements are most conducive to the production of security? It is also to join – in a global age that is now also an age of terror – a highly charged political debate about the meanings and value of security as a good, and about how it may best be pursued. It is these questions, and this debate, that we want to address in this book.

Security has become *the* political vernacular of our times. This has long been so in respect of 'law and order' within nation states. Authoritarian regimes are routinely in the habit of using the promise and rhetoric of security as a means of fostering allegiance and sustaining their rule – delivering safe streets while (and by) placing their citizens in fear of the early morning knock at the door (Michnik 1998). Democratic societies too have over the last several decades come to be governed through the prism of crime – a phenomenon especially marked in the USA, Britain and Australasia, though not without resonance in other liberal democratic states (Garland 2001; Simon 2006; see also Newburn and Sparks 2004). But security has also since 9/11, and the 'war on terror' waged in response to it, become a pervasive and contested element of world politics, impacting significantly on the 'interior' life of states and international and transnational relations in ways, as we shall see, that escalate the breakdown of once settled distinctions between internal and external security, war and crime, policing and soldiering (Kaldor 1999; Bigo 2000a).

Today, security politics is riven by disagreements over the pros and cons of self-consciously seeking security using predominantly policing and military means; by disputes about how and whether to 'balance' security with such other goods as freedom, justice and democracy; and by conflicts between a conception of security as protection from physical harm and wider formulations of 'human' or 'global' security. In the face of these debates we are aware that the title and ambitions of this text are likely to meet with one of three possible responses. They will be seen by some as offensive to the benign intentions and purposes of governments and security actors. They may be viewed, alternatively, as the naïve, wrong-headed pursuit of an oxymoron. Or they may be dismissed – by those who share our broad ambition to civilize security – as too limited in their grasp of what the idea of security can and should mean. We want to probe a little further into each of these anticipated reactions.

In so doing, we can begin to pinpoint the limitations of certain established dispositions towards, and public discourses about, security, as well as indicating how the debate about security can be moved to a different – we think more fruitful – place.[1]

The first – currently hegemonic – response issues from a lobby that seeks fairly unambiguously to *promote* security and that takes exception to the idea that security needs civilizing. Security, on this view, is an unqualified human good. The protection of its people from internal and external threats stands consequently as the first and defining priority of government. Far from needing to be balanced with democratic rights and freedoms, security is a precondition for the enjoyment of such goods. Far from needing 'civilizing', security is the foundation stone and hallmark of civilization. Security, moreover, can and should be directly and consciously pursued using what Joseph Nye (2002) calls 'hard power' – by enabling, resourcing and enthusiastically backing the military, intelligence agencies and the police. It is these agencies that will protect the state and its citizens, and these agencies whose purposes and effectiveness must not be hamstrung by excessive legal rights and safeguards that give succour to the enemy, or by forms of democratic deliberation that obstruct decisive executive action. This – stripped to its essentials – is the discourse that has animated countless 'wars on drugs' and 'crackdowns' on crime and disorder in both democratic and authoritarian states over recent decades, and which since 9/11 has fuelled and justified what may turn out to be a permanent 'war on terror'.

This disposition towards, and identification with, security has long antecedents dating back to Jean Bodin and Thomas Hobbes, and is

---

[1] Our concern in this section is not principally with paradigms of scholarly enquiry and exchange with all their characteristic caution and careful qualifications but, much more, with the dispositions towards security that find expression in contemporary public and political discourse. The positions we discuss – those we term the 'security lobby', the 'liberty lobby' and the 'human security lobby' – are clearly more internally complex than the brief typifications which follow allow; there are few 'security lobbyists', for instance, who do not make some room for rights-based limitations, just as few civil libertarians fit the political caricature of their opponents as complacent about the safety of their co-citizens. But what we seek to capture here are the overarching orientations of each worldview, the claims and contentions that their proponents instinctively 'reach for' and find emotionally compelling, those which consequently tend to constitute the broad contours of, and lines of division within, security politics today.

deeply sedimented in the present (Robin 2004). It represents the clear-sighted and hard-headed outlook of a good many politicians and police officers. It holds – for anxious citizens – a deep emotional allure. But it is not without some serious shortcomings, two of which warrant an introductory note. It proceeds, first of all, in ways that gloss over the paradoxes that attend the pursuit of security (Berki 1986: ch. 1; Zedner 2003). It has little to say, and rarely pauses to reflect upon, the most profound of these; namely, that the state's concentration of coercive power makes it simultaneously a guarantor of and a threat to the security of individuals. Security, as Berki (1986: 13) puts it, is inescapably a problem *for* and a problem *of* the state – a condition we deal with more fully in later chapters (see also N. Walker 2000: ch. 1). Nor does the security lobby grasp clearly the implications of how human beings are mutually implicated in one another's in/security – as both an ever-present potential threat to the security of each, and at the same time a necessary precondition for giving effect to such security. Still less does the security lobby register and absorb the fact that security is, in an important sense, destined to remain beyond our grasp – 'more within us as a yearning, than without us as a fact' (Ericson and Haggerty 1997: 85). Not only does this mean that there can never – in a paradox rich with implications – be 'enough' security measures, which hold out a promise of protection while always also signifying the presence of threat and danger. It also warns us that responding to demands for order in the terms in which they present themselves (i.e. zero-tolerant police, tougher sentencing, more prisons, 'wars' against drugs, or crime, or terror) can be little more than a bid to quench the unquenchable.

The effacing of paradoxes such as these is closely connected to – indeed a key contributor towards – the second and most deleterious shortcoming of the security lobby. This is its tendency to make security pervasive, to proceed in ways that treat and thereby produce 'security' – or, more accurately, security rhetoric and activity – as a dominant, emotionally charged element of political culture and everyday life. Security – as Buzan *et al.* (1998) usefully remind us – is not only a condition of social existence, a description of social relations marked by order and tranquillity. It is also a political practice, a speech act, one way of framing and naming problems. To call something 'security' – to make what Buzan *et al.* (1998: 25) call a 'securitizing move' – is to suggest, and to seek to mobilize audiences behind, the idea that 'we' face an existential threat that calls for immediate, decisive, special measures. It is, in other words, to seek to lift the issue at hand – whether it is crime, or drugs, or migration – out of the realm of normal democratic politics, to claim that as an emergency it demands an urgent, even exceptional, response.

The security lobby – blessed as it invariably is with 'blind credulity and passionate certainty' (Holmes 1993: 250) – makes precisely this move. It connects with and articulates public insecurities about crime, or disorder, or terror in terms that institutionalize anxiety as a feature of everyday life and link security to a conception of political community organized around binary oppositions between us/them, here/there, friends/enemies, inside/outside. In encouraging 'emotional fusion between ruler and ruled' around the question of fear (Holmes 1993: 49), it generates a climate that inhibits – even actively deters – critical scrutiny of the state's claims and practices. By translating security into Security, into a matter of cops chasing robbers, soldiers engaging the enemy, it risks fostering vicious circles of insecurity (atrocity – fear – tough response – atrocity – fear – and so on) that ratchet up police powers, security technologies and their attendant rhetoric in ways that it becomes difficult then to temper or dismantle. In all these ways, the security lobby makes 'security' talk and action *pervasive*, or what we shall call *shallow* and *wide*, reproducing 'security' on the surface of social consciousness and rendering it dependent on the visible display of executive authority and police power. In so doing, it fails to get close to the heart of what it is that makes individuals objectively (or inter-subjectively) and subjectively secure – it is unable, that is, to understand, still less to create, the conditions under which security becomes *axiomatic*, or *deep* and *narrow*. For us, these are vital distinctions, ones that we revisit and develop as our argument unfolds.

The second response to our stated ambitions – the one likely to regard the enterprise as hopelessly misplaced – is concerned above all to *counter* security. This emanates from what we may call the 'liberty lobby' which disputes the suggestion that security can be civilized. Security, on this view, is a troubling, dangerous idea. Security politics – especially in the form we have just set out – is seen as authoritarian and potentially barbarous – 'contrary to civil well-being' (Keane 2004: 46). It is a politics that privileges state interests (and conceptions of security) over those of individuals; that is inimical to democratic values; that possesses a seductive capacity to trample – in the name, and with the support, of 'the majority' – over civil liberties and minority rights; that is, in short, conducive to the very violence that it purports to stamp out. Security, consequently, is something that must either be curbed in the name of liberty and human rights or, given its close police and military associations, abandoned as a value altogether.

Let us briefly introduce two strands of this critical disposition. The first – common to human rights movements across the globe – seeks to *constrain* the power of security by questioning its imperatives, and fencing in its demands, with an insistence on protecting or enhancing the democratic freedoms and individual rights that security politics is indifferent to, throws into a utilitarian calculus, chips away at, or suspends. From this standpoint, habeas corpus, access to legal advice, limits on detention and police interrogative powers, jury trials, rights of appeal and the like are the expression and tools of a desire to preserve a space for individual liberty in the face of the forceful demands of an overweening state and global state system – whether in 'normal' or 'exceptional' times.[2] A second stance – associated with those working under the loose banner of 'critical security studies' (Krause and Williams 1997) – deepens and radicalizes the impulse and insights of the first. This holds that security is irredeemably tainted by its police/military parentage, and by its authoritarian desires for certainty. On this view, security is a political technology that must 'continue to produce images

---

[2] An intriguing point of intersection between the 'security' and the 'liberty' lobbies can be found in the idea of a 'right to security'. This most often finds expression today in the political vernacular of those who claim that an innocent, peaceable majority have a forgotten right to live free of crime and violence – a right which purports to trump those which protect law-breaking minorities (Loader forthcoming a). But this 'right' has also long taken a juridical form – one that need not carry the same resonance. Article 3 of the 1948 Universal Declaration of Human Rights speaks, for instance, of the 'right to life, liberty *and security* of the person', a formulation repeated in Article 5 of the European Convention of Human Rights. In these cases, reflecting the anti-totalitarian impetus of the post-war human rights charters, the security right in question is a highly limited one, identical to or basically continuous with the right to liberty against state interference mentioned earlier in the same clause. However, as Liora Lazarus (forthcoming) has highlighted, there are jurisdictions, notably South Africa, where a constitutional right to security has recently assumed a more substantive form and one more in keeping with the expansive political rhetoric mentioned above – as the right 'to be free from all forms of violence from either public or private sources' (Article 12 (1) (c) of the South African Constitution) – and where it is has been successfully litigated as such. In the more expansive political and legal formulations of the right to security one cannot avoid thinking that rights talk and protections are being turned against the 'liberty lobby' in ways that seem likely to increase the tendency of security to become pervasive.

of insecurity in order to retain its meaning' (A. Burke 2002: 18) in ways that make it, at a conceptual level, inimical to democratic politics; or else it is a practice deeply tarred by its intimate empirical relation to the formation and reproduction of state-centric interests and xenophobic, anti-democratic political subjectivities and collective identities (R. B. J. Walker 1997). The conclusion in either case is the same. Security, it is claimed, has to be *abandoned*, the dual analytical and political task being to unsettle and deconstruct security as a category so as to find ways of thinking and acting beyond it (Dillon 1996; Aradau 2004).

There is much of value in this critique of uncivil security – a great deal, in fact, which we are sympathetic towards. But these critical stances also share certain lacunae. Each, in particular, expressly or implicitly intimates that security – understood as being and feeling free from the threat of physical harm – is a problem, a conservative sensibility and project that is all too often hostile to the values and institutional practices of democracy and liberty (Huysmans 2002). The result is that each operates as a negative, oppositional force, one that evacuates the terrain that the security lobby so effectively and affectively occupies in favour of a stance that strives either to temper its worst excesses, or to trash and banish the idea altogether – a stance that appeals in part because so few others appear motivated to defend the liberties which are being imperilled. There is, on this view, little or no mileage in seeking to think in constructive terms about the good of security and the kind of good that security is. There is little point in fashioning a theory and praxis that explores the positive – democracy- and liberty-enhancing – ways in which security and political community may be coupled; in reflecting upon what it means, and might take, to make security *axiomatic* to lived social relations. There can, in short, be no politics of civilizing security.

Proponents of the third – 'human' or 'social security' – response share with us both a desire to transcend this received security–liberty dichotomy and, in their own way, an ambition to civilize security. On this view, however, such a project requires that security be rescued from a taken-for-granted association with the 'threat, use and control of military force' (Walt 1991: 212), and *extended* to other domains of social and political life (e.g. de Lint and Virta 2004).[3] We can usefully highlight

---

[3] Huysmans makes a useful distinction here between those critics of how security language constitutes political identity and community that we have just discussed,

two variants of this position – one international, the other domestic. The former takes its cue from the United Nations *Human Development Report 1994*, which introduced, and sought to mobilize opinion behind, the concept of 'human security', an idea which has subsequently been taken up in further work conducted under the auspices of the United Nations and the European Union (Commission on Human Security 2003; Barcelona Group 2004; cf. Paris 2001). It seeks to decouple security from questions of war and peace and deploy it as a device aimed at urging governments to treat as emergencies such chronic threats as hunger, homelessness, disease and ecological degradation – the latter, for instance, being described by the Commission on Global Governance (1995: 83) as 'the ultimate security threat'. The domestic version of the argument draws from the insight that there is no policing or penal solution to the problem of order the conclusion that crime control – or harm reduction – is ultimately a matter of, and dissolves into, questions of economic and social policy more generally. This is a commonly held disposition within both sociological criminology and social democratic politics, one which has in recent years informed a critique of situational crime prevention, crime science and other forms of technocratic crime control, and underpinned the promotion of multi-agency, social crime prevention (Crawford 1997; Hope and Karstedt 2003). On this view, security conceived of in a 'shallow' manner as freedom from physical harm or threat is both inseparable from a more profound sense of 'well-being' or 'ontological' security and, therefore, also dependent upon the broader institutions and services of social welfare (Fredman forthcoming).

There is, once more, much to applaud in this attempt to extend the meanings and application of the idea of security. It reminds us that freedom from physical coercion is but a part of any rounded conception of human flourishing. And it pinpoints the limited and often counter-productive role that security politics and policing institutions play within this wider project. But there are difficulties with this attempt to broaden and extend security. It too – like the liberty lobby – tends to abandon the contest over how to render individuals and groups free from the threat and fear of physical coercion – in this case by a hasty

---

whom he terms 'framers', and those who seek to extend the language of security to other domains of public policy, whom he calls 'wideners' (Huysmans 2006: ch. 2).

and undue relegation of the significance of security in its 'shallow' sense. But it also, more importantly, transcends the security–liberty opposition in a fashion that risks *making security pervasive in new ways*. It does so, in respect of intranational crime, by connecting security to better education, full employment, or improved social conditions in a manner that tends to colonize, or 'criminalize', public policy such that the latter loses sight of its own values and objectives and comes instead to be thought about, funded and judged as an instrument of crime or harm reduction. The quest for ontological security, in other words, itself risks being 'securitized' in ways that render security pervasive in a more expansive sense than already indicated: as simultaneously *deep* and *wide*, such that any reconsideration of its preconditions is treated as a threat, prompting both parochial, xenophobic reactions and calls for more security in the shallow – police- and punishment-centred – sense. Internationally, human security discourse likewise risks extending the dynamics and dangers of 'securitization', with all its antipolitical talk of existential threats and attendant calls for emergency measures, from the military to the political, economic, societal and environmental sectors (Buzan 1991; Buzan *et al.* 1998). By extending the reach of security in these ways, this position evacuates the terrain of contemporary security politics (and with it the struggle to make security axiomatic) in favour of a politics that risks turning *all* politics into security politics.

In this book we take up the challenge of developing a fourth position – of thinking constructively about the relationship between security and political community through reconceptualizing security *not* as some kind of *eigen*-value embracing the whole of politics, but as a more modestly conceived but still 'thick' public good. We also indicate how – under conditions of pluralization and globalization – we may realize this revised conception of security in terms of institutional principles and design. In making good on these ambitions, we clearly need to counter the charge that 'civilizing' security (or anything else for that matter) inevitably carries with it a class and colonial baggage – amounting to a mission to bring 'our' standards and ways of doing things to a backward, barbarian 'them', whether at home or abroad. We try to do so as the book unfolds. For now it is sufficient to record the intuition that guides our enquiry: namely, that there is something to be gained from thinking through the connection between a family of words – civil, civility, civilizing, civilization – that have to do with taming violence and fostering respectful dialogue, and another family – politics, polity, policy, police – that have to do with the regulatory and cultural frameworks within which such democratic peace building may best take place (Keane 2004: chs. 3–4).[4]

Our aim is not to effect a banal compromise, or occupy some implausible middle ground, between the outlooks of the security and liberty lobbies. We want instead to step outside the terms of the confrontation in a bid to move discussion of security to a different place altogether. In his work on authenticity, Charles Taylor describes this as an 'act of retrieval', a phrase that captures well the activity we have in mind. A work of retrieval, Taylor says:

suggests . . . that we identify and articulate the higher ideal behind the more or less debased practices, and then criticize these practices from the standpoint of their own motivating ideal. In other words, instead of dismissing this culture altogether, or just endorsing it as it is, we ought to attempt to raise its practice by making more palpable to its participants what the ethic they subscribe to really involves. (1991: 72)

To engage in such retrieval in respect of security requires neither 'root and branch condemnation', nor 'uncritical praise', still less 'a carefully balanced trade-off' between the received ideas and practices of security and liberty (1991: 23). It demands instead taking security seriously as a 'moral' category and engaging in a struggle to define its 'proper meaning' as a 'motivating ideal' (1991: 73). This requires, or so it seems to us, that we recover and develop two somewhat buried or neglected meanings of security. We need, first of all, to emphasize, as the human

---

[4] We should make it clear at this point that our title is not intended to reference, or to signal an explicit alignment with, the work of Norbert Elias on the 'civilizing process' (Elias 1939/1978, 1939/1982). Elias's historical sociology of long-term developments in the cultivation of manners, regulation of passionate drives and the control of private violence clearly has some overlap with the argument outlined here, as will become apparent. But the idea of civilizing security is, for us, much more specifically about the practice of taming private violence by redirecting the passions that security and threats to it arouse into and through political and legal institutions and regulating the violent potential of those public institutions. Here our inspiration and debt lies rather more in Mahatma Gandhi's famous response to being asked what he thought of western civilization. In replying that 'it would be a good idea', Gandhi supplied an immanent critique of the claims of western governments to be 'civilized' coupled with the thought that 'civilization' remains, for all the atrocities that have been carried out in its name, a desirable and unfinished political project.

security scholars have rightly done, the idea of the individual as the basic moral unit and referent of security – an idea that originates in the political theory of modernity.[5] That individuation of security necessarily implies and so alerts us to the irreducibly subjective dimension of security, an idea that led Montesquieu to opine that 'political freedom consists in security, or at least in the opinion one has of one's security' (cited in Rothschild 1995: 61; see also McSweeney 1998: ch. 1). This in turn provides a cue for a second act of retrieval; namely, of the root Latin meaning of *securitas* as freedom from concern, care or anxiety, a state of self-assurance or well-founded confidence. What this recovered cluster of meanings indicates is that security possesses subjective as well as objective dimensions, and that in both dimensions the 'surfaces' of physical security are intricately connected to the 'depths' of ontological security. And it is this intimate link between security and generic questions of social connectedness and solidarity that elevates it above terms like order, protection and safety as an orchestrating theme for our enquiry. The sense that security is about the *relationship* individuals have to the intimates and strangers they dwell among and the political communities they dwell within, and that it may therefore be connected in mutually supportive ways to the values and practices of 'belonging' and 'critical freedom' (Tully 2002), is what inspires our attempt to construct an alternative theory and praxis of security.

The state of the state

Our introductory remarks also pitch us into a second heated and current global debate – this time about 'the state of the state'. This debate takes two closely connected forms that are relevant here. At issue most broadly is the question of whether under conditions of globalization the political and legal sovereignty of the state over its bounded territory, and the associated coherence of national cultures, is being eroded by flows of capital, people, information, goods and economic power that criss-cross and undermine territorial borders. The more specific variant addresses the way in which the state's monopoly over legitimate coercion, and its attendant promise to guarantee the security of its citizens from internal and external dangers, is giving way in the face of the emergent claims and competences of private security

---

[5] This idea is developed in chapter 2 below.

interests working beyond the state, forms of 'grassroots' communal policing below the state, and transnational security networks operating above the state.

In respect of both these debates, a range of competing positions can be discerned. The question of 'globalization' is contested between those who emphasize the perhaps terminal demise of nation states in the face of de-territorialized – and footloose – economic power (Albrow 1996; Bauman 1998; Beck 2000), those who deny the existence of novel global processes and stress the continuing capacity of states to steer their economy and society (Hirst and Thompson 1996), and authors who argue that while there is nothing unprecedented about global interconnectedness, the 'extensity, intensity, velocity and impact' of planetary networks and flows is nonetheless reconfiguring radically the nature and loci of political community (Held *et al.* 1999: 16). The debate on policing is divided in not dissimilar ways between writers who take the view that 'modern democratic countries have reached a watershed in the evolution of their systems of crime control and law enforcement' (Bayley and Shearing 1996: 585) and those who offer a less dramatic reading of current 'transformations' (Jones and Newburn 2002).

We do not aim in this book to arrive at any settled view on these matters – something that would lead us towards writing a different book from the one that we intend. It is nonetheless useful for our purposes to offer some assessment – in the specific field of policing and security – of what appears to be the contradictory state of the contemporary state. We mean by this that there appears, on the one hand, to be plentiful evidence of the persistence, reassertion and extension of state capacity and reach over matters of internal and external security in the face of both 'old' intranational forms of crime and disorder and 'new' transnational threats to the safety of citizens. Yet this coexists, on the other hand, with an emergent plurality of policing and security actors. Whether located in large and small commercial enterprises, locally based citizens' groups, or bureaucratic networks operating between and above nation states, these actors answer to demands for order that the state cannot or will not meet, and increasingly, it seems, compete with states in promising to offer security to anxious citizens. Let us, then, begin with a brief overview of these competing tendencies, offering, in each case, an initial indication of the issues they raise for the project of civilizing security.

In defence of the contention that the state's presence in the provision of security remains powerful and pre-eminent, one may point to the following:

- State police forces retain a massive material presence in the life of modern societies. Though their role and effectiveness is often now called into question, and they have in many jurisdictions been subject to market-inspired forms of managerialism, we have in recent years witnessed the proliferation and global diffusion of crime-control strategies that continue to afford the police a privileged place, whether in the form of zero-tolerance, 'quality of life', intelligence-led, problem-solving or community policing. And nor is this centrality limited to societies with strong state traditions. Even in weak or failing states with limited infrastructural capacity and competing power centres, the police remain the sharpest and most visible face of the state in daily life, often in ways that threaten the liberty and security of citizens. Across the world, the police loom large in the social imaginary of nation states and are ideologically put forward as *the* solution to the problem of order. Any account of policing and security that fails to register the presence and effects of the police will remain wholly inadequate.
- Recent years, it is true, have seen the diffusion of crime control responsibilities 'downwards' to subnational tiers of government and 'upwards' to new inter- and transnational institutions and networks. But this represents a shuffling of cards within the state rather than a diffusion of responsibility to non-state actors. This is apparent, for instance, in jurisdictions (such as Britain and France) where municipal government has recently come to play an augmented role in devising local policing and community safety strategies, as well as in federal states (such as Germany, the USA, Canada, or Australia) with established traditions of subnational responsibility for policing. In both cases, national and subnational levels of government today act in consort with the 'responsibilized' businesses, communities and individual property-owners *through* which the state governs security (O'Malley 1992; Simon 2006). Similarly, practices of transnational policing, whether in the form of bi- and multilateral cooperation between national forces, or in respect of new security institutions (such as Europol) created under the auspices of the European Union (EU), have largely been 'steered' by state actors and are 'rowed' by public police operatives.

- The policing and security institutions of the modern state (and their attendant discourses) continue to expand their powers, resources and technological reach, often in ways that cross territorial frontiers and established political and legal categories. One can point here to the recent reorganization of historically decentralized police systems (such as Holland and Belgium) or to the formation, in Britain for example, of new national police institutions such as the Serious and Organized Crime Agency. And one can highlight the involvement, since the end of the Cold War, of national security agencies in matters of law enforcement with all that signifies in terms of a blurring of the distinction between 'internal' and 'external' security. The creation by the EU of a civilian (i.e. police) peacekeeping force to manage crisis situations in conflict zones beyond EU borders points in a similar direction. These trends, evident prior to 9/11, have accelerated and deepened as part of the 'war on terror' waged in response to it. New state security agencies have been created, existing ones have seen their powers and budgets swell. States of exception have been declared and basic rights infringed or suspended. Forms of surveillance against citizens at home and abroad have intensified, as have intelligence gathering, exchange and cognate modes of cooperation between states. In a further blurring of the increasingly lame internal/external security divide, soldiers find themselves engaged in policing activities (hunting wanted criminals, carrying out order maintenance patrols in foreign cities), while the US and UK governments engage in 'new imperial' efforts to constitute administrations (and public police forces) in client, quasi-sovereign states such as Afghanistan and Iraq.

We will return to, and flesh out, these examples in the chapters that follow. For the moment, all this brisk schematic overview serves to do is to highlight the fact that state power is still very much with us. Far from 'withering away', as Marx prophesied, states around the world continue to adorn their 'shiny uniforms' (Castells 1997: 303) and deploy powers that can protect – but also imperil – the lives and liberties of citizens. But these brief examples point also to some important reconfigurations of public power. They indicate the emergence of multiple sites of rule both inside and beyond nation states. Security inside states is divided between national, regional and local agencies organized around new mentalities of governance and new 'extensions' to and 'couplings' with non-state bodies (Rigakos 2002: 42). Practices of transnational policing unfold in opaque governmental settings that empower a new coterie of security actors. Each, in different ways, obscures lines of transparency and accountability and gives a new twist to long-standing problems of democratic authorization and legitimation.

The project of civilizing security must, in the light of this, be oriented to posing certain antique but still significant questions pertaining to the control and direction of public power. It must engage – in the field of policing and security – with the theoretical and practical work of subjecting the state's power of physical and symbolic violence to democratic scrutiny and legal control. But it has to do so in a multi-site security environment that has been, and is being, refigured by processes of globalization. These processes have not only ' "unbundled" the relationship between sovereignty, territoriality and political power'. They have also, as Held and McGrew put it, made the 'proper locus of politics and the articulation of the public interest . . . a puzzling matter' (2002: 127, 129).

Yet this 'puzzle' does not only have to do with transformations of and within the state. Today it cannot be assumed that the state remains pre-eminent in either authorizing or delivering policing and security. Other non-state actors now lay claim to authority and competence in this field. In defence of the contention that what Johnston and Shearing (2003) call the 'governance of security' is conducted by a multiplicity of institutions, one can point to the following:

- Private security has become big business across the world. In Britain, the USA, Canada, South Africa and beyond it has long been acknowledged that those employed by commercial security outfits outstrip the total number of public police officers. Private security operatives are hired by corporations, national and local governments, and private citizens to guard office complexes, airports, universities, housing estates, schools, hospitals, shopping centres, civic buildings, courts, even police stations. People's access to, and conduct within, large tracts of urban space is regulated by private security guards, employed by commercial companies, enforcing property rather than criminal law. Such guards also, in some settings, engage in 'front-line' law enforcement and order maintenance policework (Rigakos 2002). Anxious citizens, in turn, rely on the security market for an array of protective hardware (alarms, gates, locks, CCTV systems), as well as resorting to forms of self-policing – often encouraged by insurance companies and neo-liberal governments. Some have formed 'private residential associations' or sought security inside 'gated communities', withdrawing their demand and support for public provision (including policing provision) in the process. In response, the public police increasingly act as market players, contracting-out non-core 'business', eliciting corporate sponsorship, and marketing or even selling their services to a public disaggregated into individual 'customers'.

- All this is happening in societies with strong, established states. In those with weak or failing states, or undergoing political transition, the public police are not the only or main security actor, nor can they lay claim to a monopoly over legitimate force inside their territory. Across many parts of the globe today – in Italy, Colombia, Brazil, Northern Ireland, Russia, Afghanistan, the impacted ghettos of US and European cities – one finds alternative power centres contesting state authority, 'shadow sovereigns' (Nordstrom 2000) operating their own codes of behaviour and mechanisms of enforcement (Gambetta 1993; Varese 2001). In these contexts, those who can afford to have, once more, fled behind walls, venturing from their residential enclosures only to make passage to other protected work and leisure domains. The dispossessed by contrast are left at the mercy not only of militarized, partisan police forces, but also criminal gangs, hired 'rent-a-cops' and urban vigilantes. Alternatively, in some isolated pockets – parts of South Africa and Argentina for instance – poor communities are striving to put in place non-violent, local capacity-building forms of non-state security governance.
- Nor are these developments confined within the borders of modern states. 'Security' has also become a multinational business, one that crosses territorial boundaries and further erodes the internal/external security distinction. Several private security enterprises now trade their wares across the globe (Johnston 2006). They sell security advice, equipment and personnel to anxious citizens and warring factions in weak and failed states. They claim to be filling the 'security gaps' left by the fall of communist rule in the former Soviet Union and eastern Europe. And they offer to serve and protect the interests of multinationals operating in disordered, crime-ridden locations. To this, one can add the 'privatization of violence' occurring in many conflict and post-conflict zones around the world, as 'private military firms' such as MPRI and Dyncorp – dubbed by Peter Singer (2003) 'corporate warriors' – promote and sell military

'know-how', equipment and intervention to beleaguered governments and other armed groups (Avant 2005). It is a telling symbol of these trends that one of the fastest-growing industries in post-invasion Iraq is private security.

These examples too we will flesh out in more detail below. What they serve for the moment to illustrate is the existence of a pluralized – market-driven – environment where the state exists alongside, sponsors and competes against a plethora of non-state actors in a bid to promise security to citizens. It is a field where the state is not only less and less involved in delivering policing and security on the ground – what Osborne and Gaebler (1992) call 'rowing' – but also often lacks the effective regulatory capacity to 'steer'. It is a field constituted by new sites of rule and authority beyond the state, one where market power or communal ordering escapes from the forms of public will-formation that only the democratic state can supply.

Against this backdrop, the project of civilizing security is faced not only (or even mainly) with the task of controlling the arbitrary, discriminatory exercise of sovereign force, or with the excesses of state power. It is confronted, rather more, with a notable absence of political institutions with the capacity and legitimacy required to prevent those with 'the loudest voices and the largest pockets' (Johnston and Shearing 2003: 144) from organizing their own 'security' in ways that impose unjustifiable burdens of insecurity upon others. Or, to put the same point more widely:

> These days, the main obstacle to social justice is not the invasive intentions or proclivities of the state, but its growing impotence, aided and abetted daily by the officially adopted 'there is no alternative' creed. I suppose that the danger we will have to fight back in the coming century won't be totalitarian coercion, the main preoccupation of the century just ended, but the falling apart of 'totalities' capable of securing the autonomy of human society. (Bauman and Tester 2001: 139)

This is the predicament we address in this book – one in which states appear overly intrusive and subject to insufficient democratic and legal constraint, on the one hand, yet unable to exercise effective regulatory control over non-state 'security' actors, on the other. Both dimensions of this predicament are, in our view, baleful in their consequences. The first gives rise to uncivil, liberty-threatening states of 'security'; the second to inequitable and decivilizing conditions of insecurity. This situation calls for new and imaginative thinking both about 'forms of effective political regulation and democratic accountability' (Held and McGrew 2002: 122) fit for the altered conditions we find ourselves in today, and about the sorts of political community that such institutional arrangements can help to generate and sustain. It is in seeking to advance such thinking that we defend the idea that security is, sociologically speaking, a 'thick' public good and argue for the necessary virtue of the democratic state in the production of security thus conceived.

The state in policing and security studies

We suspect that many will find this an unpromising line of argument to pursue – one likely to be dismissed as sociologically untenable and normatively suspect. For if one scratches below the surface of many a text in policing and security studies, and contemporary social and political thought more generally, one tends to encounter the signs of a more or less powerfully felt scepticism towards the state (e.g. Tilly 1985). On occasions this scepticism is explicitly stated, sometimes passionately and loudly so. But more often it lies buried, unarticulated and undefended, an implicit assumption that quietly guides enquiry and analysis. Generally what is being assumed is that sovereign state power is a dangerous presence in social and political life (an evil), or at best a presence whose force is only to be prevailed upon at moments of last resort (a necessary evil). In either case, the state is postulated as a standing threat to the liberty and security of citizens, an entity that requires eternal vigilance, oversight and control. Much less is it assumed that the state may play a positive role in producing the forms of trust and solidarity between strangers that are essential ingredients of secure democratic societies.

This, it should be said, is not true of the field of enquiry taken as a whole. The vast bulk of atheoretical, policy-focused work in policing and security studies (of the sort found in a mushrooming number of applied reports, books, journals and think tanks) continues to address questions posed by the state, whose place in the production of order it leaves uninterrogated. It tends, as such, to be a *de facto* champion of the security lobby's contention that there exists an instrumental policing or military solution to the security question, and to imply that the issue at hand is to locate and evidence the strategy – targeted patrolling, improved intelligence or technologies, better community relations, zero-tolerance or problem-solving policing, military assistance or intervention – that will bring it to practical fruition. But in those more sociological, theoretically self-conscious – and in these respects critical – parts of the academy one can, we think, find the traces of deep-seated state scepticism, one that generates among (especially Anglo-American) policing scholars a tendency to think about security in ways that 'either downplay the importance of the state form or denounce it altogether' (Ferret 2004: 50). It is worth pausing at this point to reflect on this state-sceptical habitus and to engage briefly in the kind of 'sociology of the sociology of policing' (Ferret 2004: 50) that may tell us why the intellectual field is structured in these ways.

To do this we may usefully consider three ways in which policing has since the early nineteenth century been coupled with the state (Loader and Walker 2001). The obvious starting point here is Max Weber. In his essay *Politics as a Vocation*, Weber argued that the state must be understood sociologically in terms of 'the specific *means* peculiar to it' (1948: 78; emphasis in original), namely, he suggests, the use of physical force. He then characterizes the modern state in the following terms:

A state is a human community that (successfully) claims *monopoly of the legitimate use of physical force* within a given territory. Note that 'territory' is one of the characteristics of the state. Specifically, at the present time, the right to use physical force is ascribed to other institutions or individuals only to the extent that the state permits it. The state is considered the sole source of the 'right' to use violence. (Weber 1948: 78; emphasis in original)

What Weber offers here is a succinct theoretical distillation of the sociohistorical processes that from the seventeeth to the nineteenth century saw the modern (European) state wrest the 'right' to use violence from dispersed local centres of power and authority and consolidate for itself the institutional resources required to secure both its external borders (the military) and civil peace within those borders (the police) (see, e.g. Elias 1939/1982; Tilly 1975; Liang 1992). By *monopolizing the means of physical violence* the state was, in short, able to assert and defend its own interests in the post-Westphalian world of sovereign states, as well as threatening and prevailing over alternative sources of violence (and forms of free-riding) in the domestic arena.

Upon these coercive foundations two further connections between police and state have been forged. The first is a symbolic one. As modern states sought to nurture or foster national identities, police forces became deeply implicated in the wider cultural project of nation formation. Police forces historically played a key instrumental and symbolic role in forging the boundaries and identities of *nation* states, marking out 'national territory' and in so doing cultivating 'national citizens' (Emsley 1993: 87; see also Walden 1982; Emsley 2000). The state, in other words, claimed for itself *a monopoly of symbolic violence*, and the police remain one of the institutions through which this identity- and community-shaping power of what Bourdieu (1987) calls 'legitimate naming' is administered and national communities are routinely imagined and reproduced (Loader and Mulcahy 2003).

The second concerns the connections that have been established between policing and the broader project of governing a population. As modern states during the course of the twentieth century assumed responsibility and claimed credit for the well-being of their citizens, the police came to be interlocked closely with other agencies – health, housing, social security, environmental protection, utility supply – involved in giving effect to that broader 'welfarist' project. To varying degrees in different times and places, the police have been required at the level of policy generation and implementation to act in coordination with, or to direct, support or 'stand in' for, other agencies in the supply of state-guaranteed goods and services. In becoming in these ways an *instrument of social governance*, the modern police retain the traces of the pre-modern conception of *Polizei* (Knemeyer 1980), wherein 'police' (and 'police science') were concerned with producing and administering a general condition of stability and prosperity (Foucault 1981; Pasquino 1991; Neocleous 1998).

The sociology of policing and social control has since its inception in the 1960s and 1970s been wary of the consequences of all three of these connections between police and state. Its practitioners have been animated by the tasks of explaining, understanding, unmasking, criticizing, campaigning against and finding (better) ways of constraining the concentrations of physical, symbolic and governmental power inherent in them. Why though has this sceptical disposition towards the coupling of state and policing so dominated the field? Three reasons suggest themselves.

First, Anglo-American policing scholars in particular, but also those operating within the western liberal tradition more generally, occupy a cultural and political space where 'government is deeply distrusted'

(Bayley and Shearing 1996: 585), one in which suspicion towards the state is a deep-seated and long-standing cultural sensibility capable of finding articulation across the political spectrum – by conservatives, liberals, socialists and feminists alike.[6] Aside from the general structuring effect of this secular disposition, we should recall, secondly, that the sociology of policing was forged in the cauldron of political and social upheaval that marked the 1960s and 1970s. Against the backdrop of student rebellion, anti-Vietnam protest and industrial strife, the state – and its coercive 'front line', the police – appeared to be in the illegitimate business of upholding an unjust political order by violently suppressing protest, and a bankrupt moral order in ways that radically failed to 'appreciate' and served only to 'amplify' deviance (J. Young 1971). As one commentator wryly put it at the time: 'Cops are conventional people . . . All a cop can swing in a milieu of marijuana smokers, inter-racial dates and homosexuals is the night stick' (Brooks 1965, cited in Skolnick 1966: 61). This was closely interwoven, thirdly, with a prevailing intellectual climate in social science (loosely organized in this field around organizations such as the European Group for the Study of Deviance and Social Control) that was in revolt against the discipline and conformity that the state – even, perniciously, the welfare state – was striving to inculcate and enforce. It was a climate in which (police) sociologists 'took sides' (Becker 1967) on behalf of the protestor, the deviant, the poor – in other words, the 'underdog' – against the overweening power and authority wielded by the state. The state was, in short, a large part of 'the problem'.

The social analysis of policing and security has, for reasons pertaining to its conditions of emergence, tended to be organized around the domain assumption that the state's monopoly of legitimate violence – its capacity, as it were, to act as a *bully* – lies at the core of the 'problem of the state'. The analytical and research task has thus focused on the – essentially liberal – project of uncovering and constraining the multiple ways in which this bullying tendency manifests itself. Hence the research agenda over the last three decades has been structured around questions of police power and violence; the abuses of police discretion; the ways in which 'police culture' subverts efforts to control police work; the rise of paramilitary policing; and discrimination against

---

[6] The reasons for this deep-rooted sceptical sensibility are discussed at length in chapter 2.

minority groups both inside and outside the police. Hence also prominence has been given to questions of accountability – whether in terms
of seeking effective redress for individuals who have suffered at the
hands of the police, or controlling the power of chief officers to determine – undemocratically – the shape and direction of law-enforcement
policy.

These are not trifling matters. Nor, for the reasons we have already
stated, have they ceased to be pressing or pertinent. Far from it. But a
state-sceptical habitus that addresses itself only or mainly to these
issues cannot serve us well – either sociologically or normatively – in
seeking to address the security question today. Sociologically, it
remains insufficiently attuned to the ways in which power is being
reconfigured within and between states, on the one hand, and flowing
away from states, on the other, as well as to the new forms of insecurity that these transformations instil. Normatively, it cannot address
itself fully to the ways in which the state remains an inescapable part
of the 'solution' to this predicament, a vital means of generating and
sustaining the 'public interest' over matters of policing and security in
a market society whose neo-liberal champions triumphantly proclaim
that no such thing exists (cf. Marquand 2004). Yet state scepticism
remains a pervasive, deep-seated sentiment, inside and outside policing
and security studies, on the right, left and centre of the political spectrum. The project of civilizing security needs to navigate a path
through and beyond it.

Plan of the book

It is for these reasons that we devote ourselves in part I to a sceptical
reading of state scepticism. For these purposes, we have assembled four
'ideal-typical' forms of scepticism towards the state that we believe can
be located in the social analysis of policing and security, in social and
political theory more broadly, and in much contemporary political vernacular. These overlap in significant respects, not least in the core
assumption that it is the state's capacity to act in various ways as a
bully that lies at the heart of its dangerousness. Each, however, coa-
lesces around a specific elaboration of the 'problem of the state' and an
attendant set of worries about the operation and effects of its physical,
symbolic or governmental power. We therefore, in chapters 2 to 5,
offer a hermeneutic reconstruction and critical assessment of forms of

sceptical thought that depict the state, in turn, as a *meddler*, a *partisan*, a *cultural monolith* and an *idiot*.

In chapter 2 we focus on the foundational image of the modern state as a meddler in individual rights and interests, and use this as a lens through which to introduce and explore the historical, sociological and conceptual linkages between security and the state that developed within the modern social imaginary – something that saw the state *and* the critique of the state emerge and take shape hand in hand. We then explore three of these conceptual linkages in some detail. In chapter 3, we describe and dissect the view which sees the state as a means of fortifying the interests of those advantaged by the present unjust pattern of economic and social relations, one that depicts the state (and its police agents) as an unwanted and unwelcome force that needs to be monitored, exposed, struggled against and, ultimately, transcended. Chapter 4 focuses on how the state, and the forms of policing connected with it, is bound up with a production and reproduction of *particular* forms of cultural order in ways that are inimical to minority interests, cultures and practices. In chapter 5, we turn to what many analysts see as the most intractable problem of the modern state – its incapacity to acquire the knowledge it needs to accomplish its purposes, including its security purposes. This is illustrated by a discussion of various problems of contemporary security governance, and of the theorists of nodal governance who claim to have found a way of transcending both these problems and the state problematic which generates them.

In respect of each of the above, we outline a 'best case' version of the strand of scepticism under discussion, indicating the intersections that are posited between the state, security and liberty, and the alternatives that are projected to the alleged dangers of state-centric conceptions of security. We also interrogate the interplay that exists between these structures of thought and feeling and current transformations in practices of state and non-state security. It is in this light that we consider once more, and in greater detail, the empirical illustrations sketched earlier in this introductory chapter. In so proceeding, our aim is to indicate the strengths of each of these forms of state scepticism and highlight the particular challenges it poses for the project of civilizing security as we understand it; not merely as a 'concession' to critics of the state (cf. Wood and Dupont 2006a: 6), but because many of these criticisms are ones that we share. But we will also, in each case, pinpoint important blindspots that our positive argument strives to make good.

In part II, we develop this more positive case, which factors in, and seeks to alleviate or remedy, the dangers that each variant of state scepticism alerts us to, while nonetheless maintaining that the state's place in producing the public good of security is both necessary and virtuous. The key to this, we argue in chapter 6, lies in developing a more rounded conception of security as a 'thick' public good. Such a conception contains three elements. It posits – relatively uncontroversially – that security offers a necessary platform for the production of other social goods, but contends further that this instrumental dimension is symbiotically related to a recognition, first, that security has irreducibly social dimensions and, second, that it serves to constitute the notion of 'publicness' that remains, or so we contend, a key component of the good *society*. In chapter 7, we specify in more detail the kinds of cultural and ordering work that the state, or some functional equivalent to it, is alone or best placed to perform in producing the good of security thus conceived and argue that this translates into what we term an anchored pluralism. We then, in chapter 8, explore the pathologies of modern security that today give rise to security practices in which the vices rather than the virtues of the state tradition are in evidence, before spelling out – in terms of a set of institutional principles – how a politics of anchored pluralism may break the vicious circles that render security pervasive and contribute, instead, towards creating the preconditions for it becoming more axiomatic. Finally, in chapter 9, we extend our argument to the international and transnational arena, and consider what it may mean and take to configure security as a global public good.

PART I

On state scepticism

To be a friend of the state has been made to
seem an index either of stupidity or of corrupt
purpose. To be a dependant or client of the state
has been made to seem odious and degrading. By
contrast, the state's enemies have vindicated
their enmity as a direct expression of their own
practical insight and purity of intention.
(John Dunn, *The Cunning of Unreason*, p. 246)

2 | *The state as meddler*

T HE image of the meddler – of the state as prone to interfere in
matters that are none of its business and to do so to the detriment of those whose business these matters are – is an apt place
to begin our enquiry into the various modes of state scepticism and the
cumulative critique of state policing they provide. This is so because
the meddling metaphor can be taken as foundational in three distinct
though interrelated senses. First, it is foundational in a historical sense.
As we shall see, and as is important to our overall argument, the origins
of the modern state and its coercive power are inextricably bound up
with the origins of critical thinking about the modern state and its coercive power. The development of the modern state is closely linked to
the secularization of authority, and in that very process of secularization we see both the intensification of the burden of justification of
political rule and the emergence of new forms of such justification. In
particular, one important new species of political justification, including the justification of the policing function of the modern state,
comprised those normative schemes which saw legitimate rule as conditional upon and limited by the interests of those individuals over
whom such rule came to be exercised – and which therefore contained
a strong sense of the illegitimate potential of the state form if, where
and when it did not respect these individual-centred limits.

Secondly, the meddling metaphor remains sociologically foundational. Far from being eclipsed by later developments, the broadest vernacular of state scepticism and state police scepticism remains tied up
with the perils and pitfalls of meddling. This fear of meddling comes
in two forms. On the one hand, the fear that the state and its police
will overreach themselves and prevent or curtail the exercise of fundamental liberties – the classic negative freedoms of physical integrity,
freedom from arbitrary arrest, freedom of movement, speech, assembly and conscience, personal privacy, etc. – is as resonant within political discourse today as it ever has been, and provides a critical premise

which, at least in rhetorical terms, is common across the spectrum of political ideology. On the other hand, the concern that the state, through a mixture of pre-emption and prohibition, will disable individuals and groups from exploiting their negative freedom in order to take positive control of their own affairs, and in particular their security affairs, is also a powerful theme of state scepticism. And if this has been a less constant and pervasive preoccupation than the fundamental concern with negative freedom itself, it has, as we shall see, certainly assumed a new intensity in the contemporary age. In both cases, the fear of meddling is fuelled by the ways in which the very state tradition that reflects and sustains a new concern with the moral status of the individual also carries or nurtures certain conceptions of security and policing which challenge and conflict with this individual-centredness.

Thirdly, the meddling metaphor is foundational in a conceptual sense. For it is difficult to make sense of the other brands of state scepticism we will discuss – partisanship, cultural imperialism and idiocy – without seeing these as analytically continuous with at least some of the strands of thinking which fuse in the meddling metaphor.

In this chapter, we examine, in turn, each of these different foundational arguments, the first two providing an independent contribution to the corpus of state scepticism and the third, as suggested, serving as a short bridge to those other aspects of the sceptical thesis which are the concern of subsequent chapters. Before we do so, however, we must say something about our general method of exploring the origins and resilience of state scepticism about security and policing in general and the meddling critique in particular.

A note on the study of the state

Clearly we cannot make sense of state scepticism without a working notion of what we mean by the state, but this immediately presents certain challenges. Like so many of the key ideas in the social sciences, the concept of 'state' is an essentially contested one. Indeed, even its essential contestation is essentially contested. There is no agreement on whether the state is one concept or many – on whether there is a single broad conceptual umbrella under which we can place city states, pre-modern states, modern states, post-modern states amongst many other variants, or whether they each have to stand on their own conceptual ground. Neither is there agreement on what the key constituent properties of the state or of its various subspecies are, or about the conditions and periodization of its (or their) development and decline. If we feed into the other side of the equation the observation that the concepts of policing and security present similar conceptual minefields, the difficulties in explicating some foundational connection between state and policing become profound.

Fortunately, however, our focus of analysis is sufficiently sharply defined to permit us to cordon off some of the more treacherous sections of this conceptual minefield. There are two elements to this definitional refinement, the second of which we shall introduce a little later. First, and most generally, our enquiry is temporally limited. What we are concerned with in essence is the history of modernity, and in particular the legacy, if any, formed by developments in a certain phase of state-security relations which remain recognizably continuous with present conditions. This immediately narrows our perspective to the very gradual and uneven development of the *modern* state from the sixteenth century onwards (Finer 1997: 1261). It allows us to concentrate on the kind of capsule the emerging state provided for the development of new security mentalities and policing forms (and for the criticism of these mentalities and forms), including the new specialized institution of professional police forces which emerged in European cities as diverse as Paris, St Petersburg, Berlin, Vienna and Dublin as early as the seventeenth and eighteenth centuries (Emsley 1996: 45) and which, in a more intense phase of development of the 'new police', were then consolidated at national level across Europe and the United States in the first half of the nineteenth century.

Even if we may legitimately confine ourselves to the history of modernity, however, it of course remains the case that different conceptions of the modern state and of modern policing stress different emergent trends and constituent properties. Some, notably in the Marxian tradition, stress economic motivations as paramount, while others, often influenced by Weber, give top billing to changing modalities of political power and the institutional forms that these take. Others still, such as J. G. Pocock, Quentin Skinner and other exponents of the contemporary 'Cambridge School', concentrate on the power of ideas and of language as a carrier of ideas. Certainly, there may be particular contexts in which it is possible and important to discern that one type of cause was primary or catalytic. But where we are instead dealing with general trends which are expansive across time and place – where we are concerned both with the *longue durée* of historical change and with a pattern of change which unfolds across quite different societal contexts – too insistent a search for causal primacy seems both methodologically vexed, and, more importantly, simply inadequate to the complexity of human affairs. As Charles Taylor, himself often associated with the Cambridge School, has remarked, '[t]he only general rule in history is that there is no general rule identifying one order of motivation as always the driving force' (2004: 33).[1]

This thesis of multiple and mutual causality is vital to our understanding of the dynamics and future possibilities of policing and security as thick public goods, as we shall see in part II of the book. But for now we are interested in how it helps to account for the formative role of the meddling metaphor in the emergence of the state and state policing. In that regard, mindful of the importance of avoiding the mistakes of excessive idealism, excessive materialism or excessive institutionalism, we may follow the example of Robert Cox (1987) in conceiving of the modern state as a variegated but internally coherent structure made up of all three properties – ideas, material capabilities and institutional forms. The ideational component revolves around the twin concepts of nationhood and citizenship. Nationhood involves the idea of a cohesive community of sentiment and attachment based on linguistic, cultural and historical bonds. Citizenship denotes membership of a political community – understood as a self-standing entity to which obligations are owed and from which rights are derived rather than as an instrument of dynastic power and/or divine will. The material component implies a relatively segregated and integrated national economy, one whose division of labour within an emergent capitalist model of mass technologically assisted production by formally 'free'

---

[1] This should not be seen as a lazy retreat from hard historiographical graft or as a failure of normative nerve. Rather, it amounts to a simple recognition that ideas always come wrapped up in practices which they both complement and help to shape, that these practices are also influenced by and pursuant to material needs and interests, and that, additionally, these practices are constrained and enabled by institutional forms which are themselves both independently causally significant and reflective of prior norms and interests. In other words, where we are concerned with long-term transformation on a wide scale – even more so on a trans-societal scale – rather than the contingent balance of causal forces at play in the unfolding of a discrete local episode, then we just cannot escape the explanatory 'levelling effect' of the intricate and deeply recursive mutual causality of ideas, needs and interests and institutional forms.

labour is both sufficiently complex and diverse to meet the majority of domestic demand (and to provide the terms of external trade necessary to meet residual demand) and sufficiently coordinated in all the factors of production to be capable of providing for its own *re*production. Finally, the institutional component is based on a centralized government constituted through and regulated by an impersonal legal system, claiming a monopoly of the legitimate use of force within a defined territory against internal and external threats and with an administrative, military and policing capacity sufficient to exploit that monopoly and so stabilize its rule (Schulze 1996: ch. 2; Finer 1997: ch. 5; Sorensen 2004: ch. 1).

The links and forms of mutual support between the various elements are of course close. Ideas of nation and citizenship cannot be sustained without an administrative and political infrastructure committed to their development and consolidation, and without an economic system providing the material wherewithal to sustain the welfare of the relevant collectivity – however asymmetrical the pattern of individual and class contributions and rewards. The material component in turn depends upon an ideational and normative framework which 'naturalizes' the pattern and contours of commercial exchange and a legal, organizational and coercive superstructure which both tracks and monitors that pattern and provides the taxing power and the distributive mechanisms to enforce the prevailing economic order and to compensate for its worst excesses. Finally, the apparatus of government cannot be sustained without a socially resonant model of the polity as an abstract embodiment of the national interest and as an instrument for articulating the rights and obligations of its members, nor without a fiscal base in productive economic activity.

Yet this kind of synchronic account of the complementary character of the parts can never provide the full explanatory picture. We need, in addition, a diachronic account of how the various parts, and the whole, have developed over time. Otherwise, we lack a proper appreciation of what is distinctive and original – as opposed to resiliently self-reinforcing – about the modern state and its security and policing capacity, and so of what is distinctive and original about its security concerns and about the susceptibility of these concerns to critique. In so doing – to introduce a second 'focusing' restriction of our explanatory framework – we will take as our point of departure the ideational element of our ideational/material/institutional triptych.

Does this choice, however, not immediately fall foul of our own methodological stricture to be ecumenical in the consideration of causes? It does not, for the simple reason that as we are primarily concerned with the *critique* of the modern state and its police – and in the first place with the meddling critique – our discussion must be centred in the realm of ideas, and in particular on how the meddling critique connects with and emerges from the novel ideas which contributed to and became embedded in the foundations of the modern state. In any event, as demonstrated above, the analytical division between the different dimensions *is* only analytical – a heuristic device for teasing out complexity – and, as we shall see, in invoking the core founding ideas we also necessarily refer to institutional context and material interest.

Historical foundations

A common, and for us particularly apt, place to start a discussion on the founding ideas of the modern state is with the seventeenth-century political philosopher Thomas Hobbes, and in particular his classic work *Leviathan* (Hobbes 1946). Written against the backdrop of the English Civil War, *Leviathan* is of central interest to any enquiry into the relationship between the modern state and security for two reasons, one very obvious and the other rather less so. The obvious reason concerns Hobbes's substantive political theory and in particular his brand of social contractarianism. For Hobbes, famously, the Civil War which he lived through was no mere pathological episode, but provided a vivid and chastening illustration of man's natural condition. All men were created free and equal, but were also prey to their base instincts and selfish motives, and, consequently, if left to their own devices in the state of nature, became embroiled in a war of all against all. Yet it was this pre-political state of nature, however unpalatable, which provided both the normative thrust and the strategic rationale for the form the polity should take. Natural freedom and equality meant that only by the active consent and compact of the subjects of these natural entitlements could they be renounced and transferred to another entity. The selfish and predatory aspects of human nature meant that the only terms on which such a renunciation would be considered by the contractors as being in accord with their rational self-interest were those which protected all against the instincts of all, promising peace and removing or containing the most basic instinctual fear – the fear of death. This could not be achieved, according to Hobbes, except through a construct which would combine in itself the terrible potential of all the contracting parties. The state was thereby required to assume the form of 'the biblical monster Leviathan, which alone retained the wolf-like potential of man's primeval condition, and was the sole arbiter over peace and war, friend and foe, life and death' (Schulze 1996: 51–2).

Hobbes, therefore, indicates a fundamental, indeed mutually constitutive connection between the state and security, and whatever policing forms are required to provide that security. The very rationale for the state and its most basic function, in his view, is to provide for the security of its subjects. But this security comes at a profound cost. The ineluctable logic of Hobbes's position is to invest absolute power in the sovereign. For him, there was not the acknowledgement of an immanent republican *virtu* within the community which had reined in the early Renaissance conceptions of princely power of Machiavelli and others. Nor was there the sense of constraint in accordance with a legacy of divine or natural law which had stayed the hand of his 'sovereigntist' predecessor Bodin, or the comparatively benign and dignitarian view of human nature which led his contractarian successors, Locke and Rousseau, to argue for the possibility and desirability of a more limited and responsive view of political authority. For Hobbes, there were no such moderating influences. Rather, the promise of security could only be kept if all political power was retained in a single and indivisible source. So much so, indeed, that it has been persuasively argued that Hobbes's hypothetical sovereign, mandated to dictate his subject's beliefs and practices *just however* was best calculated to maintain public order, aspired to be the most absolute ruler in all history – more powerful than in the dreams still less the practice of any king or emperor from the classical period to the Middle Ages (van Creveld 1999: 180). Any liberty left to the subject in such an uncompromising scheme of rule would merely be by the discretion or default of the ruler – in Hobbes's memorable phrase, no more than the cracks left between the laws that the sovereign chose to enact (Hobbes 1946: 139).

Small wonder, then, that Hobbes's contribution to the tradition of critical thinking about the state tends to be seen in *negative* terms, measured only by the reaction it provoked. By setting up the state as the all-powerful behemoth, of the kind beloved of the more extreme sections of today's 'security lobby', he makes us starkly aware of the excessive price of making security an absolute value, and so invites those many who would balk at such excess to seek out and remorselessly expose the most basic tension in his own position. For if the purpose of absolute rule is to protect the ruler's subjects from one another, what happens, as seems to follow inexorably from absolutism, when the power accrued to the sovereign comes to present as great if not a greater threat to these subjects as they did to each other in their original state of nature? Will the solution not prove worse than the problem? This, indeed, is the founding paradox of state policing and state security generally (N. Walker 2000: ch. 1).

Much subsequent theory of the state, starting with that of Hobbes's near contemporary Locke, can in fact be seen as an attempt to rebut the illiberal implications of Hobbes's contractarian formula. Tellingly, however, the basic concept of the social contract itself by no means met with the summary dismissal that was the fate of Hobbes's particular *conception* of that concept. To be sure, subsequent social and political theory did quickly repudiate the idea of the social contract, and the state of nature which supposedly preceded it, as *empirically* false, and of course rightly so (e.g. Hume 1951). However, the idea of the social contract as a hypothetical and aspirational benchmark for assessing the justice or otherwise of a statal order has proved much more resilient. It has retained a hold on the theoretical imagination, and, indeed, inspired by the work of Rawls (1971, 1993), has undergone a significant revival over the past fifty years. Politically, too, the contractarian message remains an important frame for normative understanding and projection, as exemplified in and promoted by many modern constitutional preambles. And if we ask *why* the social contract tradition upon which Hobbes was such an important early influence has proven so resilient, it tells us something important about the *positive* contribution of Hobbes, and indeed much of early modern thinking and theorizing about modern political order, to critical thinking about the very idea – the state – which it sought to construct and refine.

This takes us directly to the second, less obvious, but more fundamental reason for identifying Hobbes as a key point of departure. For it is Hobbes who is often credited as *inventing* the very idea of the modern state. This is not a question of nomenclature, and indeed, although he sometimes did refer to the state by name, Hobbes's own preferred term was that of 'commonwealth'. Rather, Hobbes's innovation lay in his

understanding of the state as a purely abstract entity – *a persona ficta* –
separate both from the sovereign, who may nevertheless bear much of
the authority of the state, and from the ruled (Hobbes 1946: 146;
Skinner 1989; Runciman 1997: 32; van Creveld 1999: 179; Loughlin
2003: 58–61). Prior to Hobbes, the notion of state or its vernacular
equivalent in various European languages, all deriving from the Latin
term *status*, had been deployed severally, and in rough sequence, to
describe a process of increasing abstraction from the immanent sociopolitical order, whether the focus be on the condition of the ruler or of
the ruled. In a most specific and grounded sense, it is used from the four-
teenth century onwards to refer to the king's status or quality of stateli-
ness and fitness to rule. Later in the same century, a broader meaning
conveying the stable and peaceful state or condition of the realm begins
to emerge. Over the subsequent two centuries, the term gravitates
towards the positive framework of rule itself, and what is required for
rulers to hold onto their *status principis*. In particular, we find the
concept of state spreading out to signify the prevailing political regime,
or the general area over which the ruler is required to exercise control,
or, crucially, the institutions of government and the means of coercive
control that serve to organize and preserve order within political communities (Skinner 1989).

Even with this last development, however, the process of abstraction
has not gone far enough to fulfil the modern definition of statehood. As
the persistence of the medieval doctrine of the 'king's two bodies'
(Kantorowicz 1957) demonstrates, the distinction between the private
property of the king, on the one hand, and his public responsibilities and
governing apparatus, on the other, is consistent with the retention of the
idea that the king or sovereign possesses or even embodies these institutions (Skinner 1989: 103). In order to complete the modern understanding of state, what is required, and what is duly supplied by Hobbes,
is a sense of the 'doubly abstract' or 'doubly impersonal' character of the
state (Skinner 1989: 12). Not only should the authority of the state be
distinct from the people and their entitlements in the 'state of nature' or
pre-political society, but it should also be distinct from the rulers
entrusted with the exercise of its powers for the time being. For Hobbes,
as a purely 'artificial man', the state is quite distinct from both rulers and
ruled, and is thus able to call upon the allegiance of both parties.

Now clearly the general idea of the state as social contract fits
very closely with this process of double abstraction. The contract is

an autonomous institutional construct, a set of binding normative requirements which emerges from the negotiation of the interests of all parties or constituencies but which is irreducible to the interests of any particular party or constituency. No section of the ruled, therefore, and *a fortiori* no putative rulers, can treat the state so constituted as a mere cipher or instrument for their quotidian concerns, even if all parties can claim that the legitimate authority of the state, or contract, depends upon the interests of each of them being taken into account.

But what is novel and importantly discontinuous with the past about this doubly abstracted idea of the state, and the contractarian metaphor which is so intimately suited to its articulation, goes beyond mere theoretical innovation. It runs deeper than the discovery of a new intellectual scheme through which people can think in a disengaged manner about their common life. To adopt an expression introduced by Cornelius Castoriadis (1987) and taken up by Charles Taylor (2004), the fullest significance of the kind of transformation about how we think of political community which reached its apogee in Hobbes concerns how it tracks and influences change in our very 'social imaginary'. For Taylor, the social imaginary refers to a set of foundational understandings and assumptions which are broadly based, rather than the preserve of an intellectual vanguard, concerning how people 'imagine their social existence, how they fit together with others, how things go on between them and their fellows, the expectations that are normally met, and the deeper normative notions and images that underlie these expectations' (2004: 23). The social imaginary, thus conceived, is of immense significance as the most basic grid of meaning through which we see the world, but also, for that very reason, something which tends to be taken for granted. As a new social imaginary gradually becomes established and sedimented in our everyday understanding, it is treated as natural and unremarkable. It becomes invisible to us, and only by rendering it visible again can we re-acquaint ourselves with what is axiomatic in the break between one epoch and the next – in this case between the pre-modern and the modern genus of social imaginary and their accompanying forms of political organization.[2]

---

[2] In many of the above respects, Taylor's take-up and development of the idea of 'social imaginary' bears close and suggestive comparison with both Raymond Williams's (1964) notion of 'structures of feeling' and Bourdieu's (1990) concept of 'habitus'.

For Taylor, as noted above, the most important and most deeply rooted part of the social imaginary is its normative dimension, or what he calls its 'moral order' (2004: ch. 1). The moral order of modernity is axiomatically a secular and progressive order in which political society is understood as established for the mutual benefit of its members. It thus marks a rejection of a previously dominant conception of hierarchy in which moral agency depended upon its being embedded in a larger social whole – one which is located in a sacralized domain of 'higher time' (2004: 158) and whose very nature is to exhibit the hierarchical complementarity which is the proper order of all things.[3] As in pre-modern orders, the individuals of modernity remain social beings, unable to function in moral isolation. Yet unlike pre-modern orders, modern political society is one which these individuals make for their own ends. It is based upon some pre-political conception of what these individual ends might be, rather than an overarching cosmic scheme which defines and locates these individuals in its own terms. The primacy accorded to individuals acting in and upon secular time as *authors* of political society, rather than to the reification of that society in a zone of higher time, in turn encourages the understanding that, as with Hobbes and other contractarians, the basic *script* of that society should reflect its human progeny and emphasize the mundane needs of individual life and their coordinated pursuit. It should concentrate on those capacities which are necessary to produce and reproduce the existence of individuals as free agents – in particular prosperity and, of course, security itself. Freedom, as a prerequisite of individual agency, and disciplined action, as the means by which this freedom is harnessed to the pursuit of that mutual benefit which is the justifying telos of such an instrumental view of political society, thus emerge as the twin political imperatives of this new moral order. And

---

[3] The model of sacrality here could of course be that of the great transcendental monotheistic religions – Christianity, Judaism and Islam. However, it is just as consistent with a Platonic–Aristotelian conception of cosmic order, in which society necessarily corresponds to certain basic Forms and a certain irreducible order of things. Indeed, as Taylor argues in his discussion of the 'great disembedding' of modernity, the great post-axial religions are much more ambiguously placed in relation to modernity than neo-Platonic philosophy. For by continuing to affirm a higher cosmology they call into question the correspondence between this ideal order and the actually existing social order – so opening up the possibility and desirability of one of the key assumptions of modernity, namely the conscious *remaking* of political society (C. Taylor 2004: ch. 4).

legally and constitutionally, these twin imperatives become crystallized
in a concern with individual rights – those entitlements which are constitutive and defensive of agency and which thus have to be secured to
all agents equally, as well as with the responsibilities entailed and the
institutional order required for this agency to be effectively channelled
towards socially beneficent ends.

   It hardly bears mentioning, of course, that the idea of the modern
social imaginary has to be treated with historical caution. It *can* tell us
something interesting and distinctive about modernity, but only if we
do not ask it to explain too much. In particular, three caveats should
be entered, and their cumulative consideration can help us to refine
what we mean by the modern social imaginary. In the first place, its
development was slow and uneven. It did not emerge fully formed as
a result of some seismic rupture, but evolved only gradually. Like
Hobbes's work itself, it cannot be viewed as novel in all its parts, but
rather as a new synthesis made possible once various discrete strands
of thought developed to a sufficient pitch of intensity. We have already
seen, for instance, that the idea of the modern state could only take off
once authority could be conceived of as sufficiently divorced from the
prerogatives and privileges of the sometime ruler. Equally – and referring to the other element in Skinner's 'double abstraction' – the idea of
the modern state required a similar distancing from the interests and
aspirations of the sometime citizens of the polity (Skinner 1989:
112–16), which in turn points to an earlier tradition of individual-
centred political thought. And indeed, if we look to the various traditions of republicanism, both in its Greek and Roman roots and in its
later Florentine variant, these strands of thought placed the citizenry
in their public affairs squarely at the centre of political life, even if the
status of citizen was confined to a narrow and self-propagating elite.
Yet what was absent from early republicanism, apart from a more
inclusive definition of citizenship, was a sense of the apparatus of government as anything other than the instrument of the interests of citizens in the here and now, and this necessarily curtailed what could be
thought of and done in the name of politics. Only with the idea of the
institutional autonomy of the state do we find a corresponding discursive autonomy of politics – a sphere of cumulative discussion and
immanent reflection about what should be done in the collective interest, neither in the *eternity* of sacred time nor in the *instance* of present
time, but *over secular time*.

Secondly, even if we put aside the unevenness of historical development and the existence of pre-modern precursors to the modern social
imaginary and treat the modern and pre-modern as ideal-types, we
should not exaggerate the difference between them. In particular, it is
not the difference between a world in which the only concern of politics
was celebration of and service to the sacred and one in which sacrality
was dismissed or merely paid lip-service. On the side of the pre-modern,
and as the tradition of early republicanism itself suggests, there was of
course much concern with the politics of the everyday, with systems of
authority or governance at every level of social organization. Indeed, as
we shall see in the next section, the ancient roots of the idea of police
power are central to the domain of everyday politics. However, in the
final analysis, within the pre-modern social imaginary the boundaries
of what was thinkable in terms of earthly structures of authority were
constrained by the requirements of fit with some more pervasive notion
of the hierarchical order of things, however indirectly that requirement
sounded in any particular instance. And on the side of the modern, we
are of course familiar with the idea of the theocratic state – dedicated,
at least rhetorically, to the achievement of some sacred plan in the
earthly domain. But, crucially, where the state aligns itself to the cause
of one of the modern salvation religions it does not do so by presenting
itself as in full and passive harmony with a settled cosmic order, but
instead tends to subscribe to a modern idea of human agency and to the
active transformation of society over secular time in more perfect
pursuit of the divine plan.

In the third place, the modern imaginary, in its detailed articulation,
is not one but many, and, indeed, Taylor would be the first to insist
upon this. It is a genus of which there are many quite distinct species.
In its very depth and generality, the basic moral order of modernity is
actually compatible with a bewildering variety of fuller flourishings of
the social imaginary and attendant sociopolitical orders. To return to
the triptych of ideas, material capabilities and institutional forms
unveiled earlier, we can see that not only have the bare ingredients of
the modern state form been capable of being produced to different
specifications and mixed in different forms, but that the recipe itself has
undergone certain adaptations and mutations. In the realm of ideas,
both nationalism and citizenship provide partial articulations of the
notion of a self-made political community. For such a community,
giving priority as it does to the claims and aspirations of its authors,

needs a well-developed model of the effective ties and qualifications of membership – of the integrity of the pre-political cultural community whose compact the state is – on the one hand, and of the incidents of membership, or the terms of the compact, on the other.

In crude terms, we can observe that while nationalism has supplied the first of these models, citizenship has supplied the second. As it developed in its modern form in the eighteenth and nineteenth centuries, national community, as we shall have cause to pursue in subsequent chapters, provided an understanding of a community of attachment *over time* (Yack 2003: 36), with an image of a shared heritage – whether based upon territory, language, ethnicity, mythologized historical events or confessional allegiance, and most likely a mix of these and other commonalities – passed and transformed from one generation to another and extending into an indeterminate future. For its part, citizenship is more concerned with the rights and responsibilities which set members apart from non-members and which provide the appropriate articulation of individual freedom and collective discipline for these members. What this makes clear is that nationalism and citizenship are not alternatives, but inevitably go hand in hand in the making of the modern state. Yet the ways in which these concepts coalesce can differ greatly. And in the great variety of their mutual articulations, ranging from a nationalism of 'blood and belonging' (Ignatieff 1993) and a form of citizenship in thrall to an exclusionary cultural identity, on the one hand, to a thinner conception of civic nationalism and republican citizenship, on the other, we already see one aspect of the diversity of the modern state.

In the sphere of material capabilities too, we see the diverse pathways of the modern state. We have already noted in general terms how the development of the modern state is tied up with the needs and possibilities inherent in a more complex division of labour. More specifically, the gradual emergence of the capitalist form of production, based upon formal freedom of contract and an unencumbered conception of property rights, provides both one image of a pre-political realm (of commerce) from which a more instrumental conception of political society might grow, and some of the very individual-centred values which would inform the new social compact. Yet in its tension between freedom and agency on the one hand and mutual benefit and the collective discipline required for its realization on the other, the modern state also retained the tendency towards a more collectivist ethic of production and redistribution, where this is what mutual benefit was deemed to require, and thus towards the various forms of public intervention in and control of the economy we associate with socialism.

Finally, in the area of institutional capacity, there are also many possibilities. Clearly, the emphasis upon the freedom and equality of each individual agent and on the importance of collective consent provide a route to modern forms of liberalism and representative democracy. Clearly too, the idea of political society freed from a cosmology of timeless hierarchy, and capable of being made over to conscious human design and the collective discipline necessary for its implementation, opens the way to more collectivist ideas and ideologies of human flourishing, and to an institutional machinery moulded to these purposes. At one extreme, then, contemporary totalitarian ideologies – often aided and abetted by introverted forms of nationalism, together with the repressive forms of law and administration necessary to their sustenance – are as much the offspring of the modern idea of moral order as more individual-centred and democratically responsive templates.

However diverse the concrete forms it takes, the modern state remains basically compatible with and recognizable as an outgrowth of a single underlying moral order. The tension between the freedom that the recognition of individual agency is deemed to permit and the discipline which that agency is deemed to require in the pursuit of mutual benefit may be resolved in radically different ways, but both extremes involve the same fundamental epistemic shift from an earlier notion of a vertically ordered political society in thrall to a timeless cosmology to a horizontally ordered anthropology from which political society could be constructed and which would provide its sole justification.

Thus we can see how the modern state, from Hobbes onwards, contained the seeds of its own critique, and, most immediately, that critique which centred on its illicit meddling in the affairs of its individual constituents. To take first the general part of this argument, in accepting that the political order was a human construct, to be judged only by its cumulative and resilient capacity to satisfy human needs, the emergence of the modern state and the idea of moral order that underpinned it brought forth the very idea of immanent critique – a form of criticism of the *polis* which need not appeal to some force or order beyond the *polis* and which, as such, can be seen to inaugurate the modern phase of properly *political* criticism. That is to say, as the ends and means of the political order are no longer sacralized in higher time, beyond the scope of human intervention, but instead begin to be seen as within the gift of the constituent people represented by legislators and administrators operating in profane or secular time, then it becomes in principle legitimate to subject these ends and means (and those responsible for them) to ongoing criticism and revision. The political order becomes essentially contingent and 'mutable' (Finer 1997: 1303), an institutional form which because constructed can also and always be *re*constructed.

To move to the specific part of this argument, because the new moral ontology is individual-centred, the most fundamental critical axiom is in turn the protection of individual agency, whether at the point of consent to the political order or in its maintenance and furtherance. Hobbes's absolute state, with its massive capacity for interference and constraint, provides a palpably easy target for any individual-centred moral sensibility, but that should not blind us to the fact that it is the emergence of the individual-centred moral sensibility itself which is the more important innovation. The absolute state might be the worst case, but any state which, through its police and other agencies, subjects individuals to discipline and constraint in the name of the intermeshing interests of these very same individuals – and all states must *by definition* do this – now becomes vulnerable to the charge of illegitimate interference – of meddling in affairs which remained within the sovereign power of individuals in their pre-political state of nature.

Of course, critique is one thing, dominant authority another. The other side of the modern state, as noted, is the tendency to compromise agency, to subject individuals to discipline in the name, or at least the furtherance, of some collectively defined project, to which nation-based, class-based, faith-based and various otherwise grounded ideologies, interests and structures contribute in complex combinations. And here, palpably, the other parts of the grand tapestry of historical explanation – the material and the institutional – are more prominent. It is the fate of the modern state, then, to be inherently double-edged, to generate both the object and its critique. The history of the modern police and the history of criticism of the modern police, as we shall see, are directly implicated in and by this double-edged character of the modern state.

Sociological foundations

How has the fear of meddling in the affairs of sovereign individuals, so closely implicated in foundational thinking about the state, insinuated itself into debates about the scope and legitimacy of state policing? As noted earlier, that insinuation has taken two forms. In the first place, and most obviously, policing has always been a special target of those fears and criticisms which see the Hobbesian impulse of the state to protect the security of the individual as a standing threat to all of his or her other 'natural' freedoms – personal liberty, movement, speech, conscience and privacy – as well as to the very bodily safety the Leviathan is contracted to ensure. The fear, then, has both a narrow and a broader dimension. Narrowly, the state which adopts its own dedicated police force may be or become a self-defeating construct – or, less charitably, a purely self-serving construct in terms even of the core Hobbesian aim, threatening to generate more insecurity than it provides security. More broadly, to the extent that state policing may be successful or at least not a manifest failure in this narrowest sense, the trade-off in terms of the loss of other basic liberties may still be excessive. In the second place, the establishment of a public police force, as one manifestation of the state's broader propensity to interfere, threatens to curtail or remove the possibility of individuals exercising their joint and several 'natural' freedom(s) to make their own security arrangements. Let us now briefly examine in turn the form that these concerns have traditionally taken in the history of modern policing, and certain contemporary manifestations of these concerns. In so doing, we seek to acknowledge both the resilient strength and importance of these critiques and to indicate their equally resilient limitations.

Insecure liberties

Given its core emphasis upon the importance of protecting or constructing a sphere in which individuals can act without interference in ways that reflect their understanding of what gives meaning and value to their lives, liberalism is a political philosophy which resonates closely with the 'agency' dimension of the modern social imaginary. So much so, in fact, that we best understand the role of liberalism in modern political culture not as a comprehensive descriptor of how particular societies operate or even as a general theory or model of a just society, but as a powerful strand of thought, or 'ideology', which is present in different variants and to greater or lesser effect in *all* modern social orders – even those whose dominant tendencies may justly be viewed as distinctly 'illiberal'.[4] One such variant of liberalism, and an important part of the history of liberalism as an active political idea which goes to the very heart of the meddling objection, is what Judith Sklar has famously called the 'liberalism of fear' (Sklar 1989). This consists of an apprehension of what may be done to 'weak' individuals in the name of the state and through its overwhelming coercive capability. As we shall see later, that fear is always liable to assume a more specific form, whether of systematic bias in favour of and against particular sections of the population, or of the shaping and sustaining of an intolerant moral or cultural orthodoxy, or of cognitive overreach – of the state's failure to know the limits of its own knowledge and regulatory potential. However, just as liberalism began as a difference-blind ideal, as one which asserted the equal gravity of every individual claim to freedom, much of the anxiety about state power in general and the power of state policing in particular has historically often been conceived of – and, given the rhetorical power of the liberal idea of freedom in the political cultures which grew out of the modern social imaginary, even more insistently *expressed* – in difference-blind terms.

Our discussion of how the liberalism of fear informs the meddling critique proceeds in two stages. First, and picking up where we left off in the previous section, we examine how liberal concerns about the overweening security capacity of the state became lodged in the social

---

[4] According to Michael Freeden (1996: part II), liberalism is in fact *the* 'dominant ideology' of modernity, if ideology is understood as 'those systems of political thinking, loose or rigid, deliberate or unintended, through which individuals or groups construct an understanding of the political world they, or those who pre-occupy their thoughts, inhabit, and then act on that understanding' (1996: 3). Freeden is concerned, with this definition, to distinguish liberalism as ideology from liberalism as political theory or philosophy, stressing its instantiation in the 'thought-behaviour' (1996: 2) of individuals and groups seeking to understand and/or shape the social world in which they are implicated rather than its status as a relatively disengaged body of imaginative speculation or creation. Note, however, that if, on the one hand, 'ideology' is more grounded than 'theory', then, on the other, it nevertheless remains less fundamental than and is parasitic upon the underlying 'social imaginary'. Ideology draws upon and contributes to a discursively realized body of thinking, while the social imaginary represents the deeply engrained set of common assumptions about the social world that makes theory and ideology possible.

foundations of the modern state. The liberalism of fear has to be understood as a double-sided phenomenon, the product both of a new and distinctive mindset and of certain objective forces which encourage that mindset. On the one hand, it speaks to a conceptual tension in the very foundations of liberalism, one which fertilizes the seed of immanent critique planted in the very social imaginary which makes the modern state possible. On the other hand, this anxiety also reflects and responds to certain tendencies secreted in the long-term development of security and policing. In the second place, we examine the development of the institutional form of the new police from the early nineteenth century onwards, and highlight how this new form has profoundly ambiguous implications from the liberal perspective – both intensifying the meddling concern and in some measure responding to that concern.

Let us begin, then, with the deeper foundations. The conceptual tension at the heart of liberalism finds its focus in the equivocal status of individual freedom in liberal understandings of the state, and in particular in the profound difficulty in fixing 'in principle' limits to the permissible encroachment upon individual liberties by the modern state. Liberals are not anarchists. For all that they rejected the absolutism of Hobbes, writers as central to the early liberal tradition as Locke, Smith, Paine and Condorcet concurred with his basic premise that freedom from the fear and prospect of personal violation was an indispensable precondition for the sovereignty of individual action.[5] Indeed, as Stephen Holmes has said, security is the 'idée maîtresse' (1995: 245) of the liberal tradition, the commonly agreed axiom around which various and diverse liberal systems of thought revolve. So liberal thought has the luxury neither of the wholesale endorsement of the Hobbesian security vision, nor of its wholesale rejection. Instead, the paradoxically self-defeating tendencies of the state which seeks to be both strong *and* freedom-endowing have to be squarely faced. Somehow security and liberty have to be reconciled.

[5] Historians of political ideas typically date the evolution of liberalism back to Locke, even though awareness of liberalism as an ideological tradition is subsequent to the political employment of the term from the 1830s onwards, and even John Stuart Mill, considered by many as the prime exponent of nineteenth-century liberalism, did not actually describe his own writings as elaborating a set of political beliefs called liberalism. Nevertheless, even though liberalism as a full-blown ideology is indeed a product of the nineteenth century, a basic continuity of concern and commitment – of diagnosis and prescription – justifies the location of the roots of modern liberalism in the earlier tradition (Freeden 1996: 139–44).

Yet there can be no easy route to reconciliation within the liberal sensibility. Security may be the precondition of that liberty which is necessary to discover and pursue what gives meaning and value to an individual life, and the pursuit of security may only be justifiable if it promises such a freedom dividend. But this close conceptual interdependence does not mean that trade-offs between security and liberty can be avoided. Both security and liberty are relational concepts. More security typically implies less of something else, and that something else is often one or other of our cherished freedoms. Equally, more liberty typically implies a reduction in something else, and that something else may be our capacity to provide security. As we shall see in due course, the modern state has at its disposal certain institutional devices which seek to provide a measure of practical reconciliation of liberty and security, and these may help to deflect or temper concern about the proper relationship between the two concepts, not least by providing deliberative fora within which the question may be aired. But for now let us pursue further the more basic conceptual abeyance at the heart of liberalism, and how the failure adequately to fill this vacuum feeds anxiety about the spread of police power.

As an attempt to square the conceptual circle, the idea of 'balance' has for long been prevalent in legal and political discussions over the reconciliation of security and liberty, the resort both of liberals determined to hold or restore the line of individual liberty and of those seeking to justify the latest qualification of that liberty in the name of enhanced security (Waldron 2003a; Loader forthcoming a). Balance implies the existence of values which, when mutually implicated, tend to pull in opposite directions; where the optimal solution – the striking of the appropriate balance – may involve a sacrifice of some dimension of one or other value. But balance between these competing goods, for all that it may be the predictable conceptual terminus of liberty's equivocation over security – of that concern with the secular reconciliation of collective discipline and individual freedom which is the deep puzzle of the modern social imaginary – can never be a comfortable metaphor for the liberal, for two reasons. First, and more specifically, liberals tend to be deeply uneasy about the invocation of consequential reasons for the erosion of liberties (Waldron 2003a: 194). Our most fundamental freedoms, whether of expression, assembly or liberty of the person, are considered too precious simply to be weighed on a social scale against competing goods and diminished in proportion to the intensity of the claims made on behalf of these competing goods. If, as the liberal would argue, there are compelling reasons flowing from respect for the individual for maintaining that people be free from the fear or prospect of arbitrary arrest and detention, then a mere circumstantial increase in the security risk of maintaining that freedom – whether, to take two familiar contemporary cases, the circumstance in question be the hosting of a high-level international summit attended by controversial political figures or a local wave of terrorist attacks – cannot be enough in itself to dispose of these compelling reasons. The language may be that of Nozickian 'side-constraints' or Dworkinian 'rights as trumps' or the Rawlsian 'lexical priority' of basic rights, but the moral instinct of the liberal is typically to give some special status (even if not an absolute priority) to the protection of basic liberties, which means that they cannot simply be traded away for other social gains. The idea of balance cannot easily acknowledge that special status. Rather, it implies the existence of a single metric for the weighing of all social goods, and as such sits far more comfortably with that genus of political thought which is liberalism's great partner and rival within the cadre of individual-centred modern political ideology: namely, utilitarianism.

This highlights the second, and more general, source of liberal unease with the idea of balance. Not only is balancing unable to accord special priority to core rights, but it lacks *any* clear, consistent and uncontroversial meta-rule or formula for resolving disputes between different values. The idea of a single metric for assessing social benefits turns out, on closer examination, to operate as an exclusionary device. It suggests, negatively, that no species of value can be exempt from the general weighing of values, but does not specify, positively, how that comprehensive weighing is to take place. As the history of utilitarian thought from Bentham onwards indicates, how we calculate a unit of the good and how we reduce different goods to a single scale is itself a deeply uncertain and contested exercise, one finally dependent upon a privileging of one of many rival general registers of value (aggregate happiness, aggregate welfare, minimum aggregate infringement upon or frustration of individual interests, etc.), all of which are both controversial in conception and notoriously unclear in application. Balancing, in short, promises a false objectivity and suggests an artificial precision in our attempts to devise just institutional arrangements and answer liberal concerns. Behind its cover of careful calibration of diverse interests and preferences, balancing is actually peculiarly lacking in certainty and rigour. Once liberty is fed into the utilitarian calculus, what comes out the other end is a matter of deep uncertainty and disputation. Whenever and wherever a new assault on liberal sensibilities is apprehended, and in the contemporary new global climate of unease following 9/11 the sheer pervasiveness of that sense of assault is perhaps unprecedented, the mantra of balance is unfailingly invoked in the law courts, in political debate, in public commentary and in the vigilant critique of civil society's state-watchers. But it is difficult to avoid the impression that it is a mantra often invoked either by critics of liberalism in complacent or cynical disregard of its historical inability to set absolute or proportional limits upon the encroachment of liberty, or, if by liberals themselves, merely for want of any more compelling formula for holding the line.

Whether rooted in cynicism, complacency, or fragile hope, what is certain is that the idea of balance can provide no guarantee against certain structural tendencies deeply inscribed in the social foundations of policing and security, which brings us to the second – and objective – element within the liberalism of fear. These structural tendencies, as we shall see, have been significantly sharpened and intensified with the development of the modern state and its dedicated policing capacity. Yet if we fail to appreciate their pre-modern roots, we cannot fully compre-hend the depth and resilience of their substantiation of liberal anxieties. So whereas in the previous section we stressed the *discontinuity* of the modern social imaginary in order to appreciate the novelty of a certain critical modern understanding of the political, here, by contrast, it is important to stress the *continuity* and the accumulation of the social forces which makes modern police power so formidable.

In a powerful recent study, Marcus Dirk Dubber (2004, 2005) has traced the roots of the police idea to Greek and Roman ideas of house-hold governance. In the original Athenian distinction, while politics was a matter of self-government by equals – or, rather, by the equally privi-leged – in the public domain, economics was seen as the art of govern-ment by these privileged public actors of their private household for the common good of the whole family.[6] This idea of a private domain of patriarchal governance underwriting a narrow sphere of public citizen-ship was carried forward in the Roman law notion of the *paterfamilias*

---

[6] The distinction between economics and politics closely mirrored the distinction in classical Greek between two dimensions of life – *zoe*, or natural life, and *bios*, or politically qualified life (see Agamben 1998).

exercising plenary power over the *familia*. So far, so familiar, but the innovative aspect of Dubber's genealogy lies in his linking of these classical traces to medieval and early modern conceptions of police science, and to the idea of the king or the ruling elite as the head of a larger and secondary unit of governance:

> Police marked the point of convergence between politics and economics, when one mode of governance merged into the other, and created the oxymoronic science of political economy. The police power was born when the governmentality of the private (micro) household was expanded, and transferred, onto that of the public (macro) household. (Dubber 2005: 81)

But how did this merger take place? Dubber seeks to answer this question through a mix of discursive analysis and assessment of the developing jurisdictional scope and depth of police power. Discursively, the image of the household, and the sovereign as head of a second-order 'public' household and so responsible for its social and economic well-being, is prominent in many of the foundational tracts of modern policing. It can be located in the general works of Rousseau and the Scottish Enlightenment thinkers, and also in the more focused works of key figures in the anglophone police tradition such as Blackstone writing in the middle of the eighteenth century and Patrick Colquhoun fifty years later. Further, all of these writers, as well as acknowledging the relevant classical roots, were explicitly influenced by (and exercised a reciprocal influence upon) the contemporary continental method of police science (*Polizeiwissenschaft*), which in turn drew upon an earlier French and German tradition of police laws, police regulations, police ordinances and, in due course, police officials dating from the fifteenth century (Knemeyer 1980). The commonalities across this body of thought are striking, and three themes in particular can be drawn out (Dubber 2004).

First, and most obviously, there is an idea of strict hierarchy, mirroring the categorical distinction between householder and household. Secondly, there is the 'defining undefinability' of police power. Indeed, in continental police science, reflecting the common etymological roots of *police*[7] and *polis*, police power was regarded as the root and rationale of

---

[7] The modern term *police* has French origins and from these origins was received into usage in the two other early major European 'policing' traditions – the German and the Anglo-Scottish.

all governance. No form of regulation was in principle to be denied the higher householder in his efforts to educate and discipline his extended family in pursuit of its common welfare, and, as is well documented in the history of crime and punishment, this capacious view of the power of the *pater patriae* was eagerly accommodated across the length and breadth of early modern Europe (Keane 2004: chs. 3–4). Alongside the recognized catalogue of criminal acts, matters as diverse as sporting codes, gender relations, vagrancy, night-walking, gaming, fair commerce, usury, animal husbandry, public sanitation, undue expenditure, inappropriate dress, excessive diet, eavesdropping, malicious gossip and impersonation were viewed as essential to the good management of the public household and were thus subject to police jurisdiction, and infringement often led to draconian punishment. Thirdly, and related, the idea of patriarchal police power is marked by its 'ahumanity' and 'amorality' (Dubber 2005: xv). It was not just a power 'to govern men and things' (2005: xiv), but a power the moral status of whose objects – men and things – was not clearly distinguished. Both were merely 'tools in the householder's hands' and, as such, prone to be worked, adapted, discarded or reappropriated as the macro-householder saw fit and in accordance with all the technologies of power familiar from the domestic household (2005: ch. 1).

Of course, it is possible to overstate the strength of the household metaphor and its successful transfer to the macro-domain of the polity in general and the modern state in particular (Loader and Zedner 2007). Indeed, in his own work, Dubber seeks to explore the tensions and contradictions which ensued when this patriarchal conception of police governance met the social contractarian architecture and self-governing rhetoric and aspirations of the new American republic of 1789 (Dubber 2005: part II). We will return to these tensions shortly, but first it is worth emphasizing two points about the household origins of police power which cumulatively underwrite the strength and tenacity of its influence on modern policing.

In the first place, we may surmise that part of its resilience as an idea capable of being borne, copied and adapted across the ages from the classical to the early modern lay in its resonance with a pre-modern notion of hierarchy. The patriarchal metaphor, especially as extended in a vertical chain of connections from various 'private' contexts, whether the Greek or Roman household or the English manor or the 'quasi-households' (Dubber 2005: 61) of the guild or corporation, the religious order, the military, or the slave plantation, to the 'public' household of the polity, was well capable of being accommodated within an earlier social imaginary of pre-ordained and seamless hierarchical order. Indeed, once relocated and viewed in the broader context of governance of which it was a part, the classical idea of republicanism itself, for all that it also served as a precursor of modern forms of comprehensive and comprehensively secular politics, is merely one horizontal plane supporting and supported by an otherwise vertically ordered framework of governance and social organization.

In the second place, its close fit with that earlier conception of moral order notwithstanding, we can also see how the extended household metaphor could be carried forward and reconfigured to meet the disciplinarian side of the modern social contract. Some of the most insightful work on the social history of the state, indeed, has been concerned with precisely this bridging of the pre-modern and the modern. Writers such as Norbert Elias (1939/1978), in his account of the 'civilizing process', and Michel Foucault (1984), in his analysis of the rise of an encompassing 'biopolitics', have eloquently demonstrated how taking individual freedom seriously and harnessing it to a collective production helped justify, in the era of the emergence of the modern state, continued investment in that sense of unity of order which sustained earlier and more 'natural' conceptions of hierarchy, now adapted to an altogether larger scale and more ambitious remit. Those calculations and devices that were deemed necessary and justified to civilize the macro-household of the state in the name of its sovereign collective utility were increasingly unconstrained by the demands of some transcendental conception of order or of harmony with or deference to other spheres and sites of social organization, and so could be more comprehensive in the extent, and remorseless in the intensity, of their regulatory claims. The new *raison d'état* was explicitly self-referential and all-encompassing in its moral and strategic vocabulary, tending to eclipse or subordinate the claims of other forms of reason or sentiment. As pointed out earlier, contemporary forms of totalitarianism may be the most pathological outcome of this dynamic, but this should not blind us to the disciplinary power secreted in *all* forms of modernity, and to the generosity and aptness of its inheritance from earlier notions of patriarchy.

So, it appears, just as no conceptual 'floor' of liberty can be guaranteed within the balancing act of modernity, so its countervailing principle, security, knows no objective 'ceiling' – no constraint on its potential pervasiveness. Rather, if the utilitarian calculus is in practice tied to the collective good, and if that collective good is in practice susceptible to paternalistic definition, then the policing of that collective good can become just whatever measures are deemed necessary to secure good order and just whatever instruments are deemed necessary to implement these measures by just whichever public authority stands *in loco parentis*. As one contemporary ethnographer of the police has noted, policing may in principle be 'concerned with *all* the manners of a society'; in that one pithy formula he traces a direct line back to pre-modern and early modern conceptions of police power, and to the liberal fear it has consistently provoked (Laurie 1972, cited in Manning 1979: 45).

But, to move to the second stage of our enquiry, how *are* these underlying conceptual concerns and social dynamics translated into the institutional forms of modern policing? Here we find conflicting tendencies. If, as is commonly agreed, the major distinguishing features of the 'new police' which emerged across the western and colonial world in the nineteenth century were their degree of publicness, professionalism and specialization (Bayley 1985; N. Walker 2000: ch. 2), then each of these three trends speaks eloquently to liberal anxieties. Publicness, first and foremost, because the replacement of diverse local or private suppliers by a central state supplier or licensor ascribes to the state for the first time a monopoly or dominant position in the direct provision of legitimate coercion within its territory, rather than simply in its overall coordination and last-instance authority. Professionalism, because the replacement of part-time amateurs by a full-time, trained and bureaucratically organized corps increases the effective capacity of police power. Specialization, because the gradual shedding of regulatory and administrative responsibilities across a wider sphere of governance – and thus a retreat from the broadest conception of police power of the early police scientists – and the concentration on core policing tasks of crime prevention and detection and the maintenance of public order, means that policing can be better focused on matters of security.

Yet, even if we accept this somewhat stylized conception of the transformation from 'old' to 'new' policing, each of the key three traits actually has more ambiguous implications for police power than may be immediately apparent from a state-sceptical perspective. Publicness may be as much a counter to local excess and a pledge of commitment to general and uniform standards as a central consolidation of power. Professionalism may be as much about new modes of internal regulation and investment in a distinctive occupational culture and honorific code – the emergence of new forms of other- and self-discipline within the police corps – as about refining techniques of social control. And specialization, as already suggested, purchases a greater intensity of concentration on core tasks – the very tasks which may increase the security of all sections of the population rather than simply bolster existing social hierarchies, in return for a stricter demarcation of jurisdictional boundaries and a renunciation of at least some of the older 'household' prerogatives.

Historiographical work on the origins of the new police remains highly polarized as to the causes and consequences of transformation, with 'orthodox' historians asserting the more benign interpretation and 'revisionists' preferring a more sceptical reading – one often closely informed by a neo-Marxist perspective on the new disciplinary challenges posed by the rise of a new urban working class (Reiner 2000: ch. 1). But here again, we must be mindful of Taylor's caution about the limitations of unicausal interpretations of history. The direct assertion and institutionalization of state authority can be seen neither as the fullest unleashing of Leviathan, now licensed to meddle in every nook and cranny of individual life, nor as its final capture. Rather, as Dubber portrays in his own work, in the ambiguous institutional implications of the new police we see conflicting projects and tendencies at work, with different forces prevailing or compromise achieved at different times and places. On the one hand, the new police, with their unprecedented manpower resources and ever evolving technology of coercion and surveillance, acquired and retain an unprecedented capacity for interference. On the other hand, the very liberal sensibility which feared the coercive potential of the state, and the underlying modernist sentiment that politics and the state be directed to humanist ends, provided a more or less effective countervailing power.

The strength of that countervailing tendency is most marked in those states in which the modern constitutional tradition, with its preoccupation with limited government, and in time also with democratically responsive government, has successfully taken hold. From Montesquieu onwards, modern constitutionalism sought to guard against the excesses of the state by a number of devices aimed at diversifying, checking and balancing institutional power. So from the original modern constitutional charters of America and France onwards, we are familiar with mechanisms both at the level of the general design of the organs of state and in the more specific context of police organization which seek to restrain the tendency towards the excessive accumulation of police power and its abuse (N. Walker 2000: ch. 1). At the general level, the division of power both horizontally, between executive, legislature and judiciary, and vertically, between central and devolved or federated units, guards against an over-concentration of power in one unit, and, crucially, the gradual development of the franchise over the nineteenth and twentieth centuries both permits a greater plurality of interests to be represented in the legislative and executive domains and guarantees electoral accountability of the representatives. The state constitutional order may also provide for a more or less justiciable charter of rights capable of overriding or qualifying legislative acts or executive action in respect of policing which is in violation of these rights.

Within the policing field more specifically, the articulation of state authority may, like the general institutions of state themselves, be more or less decentralized. If centralized, there may be one central force, as in Ireland or Poland, or several, and whether centralized or decentralized, the competences of the various forces in multiple systems may be coordinated and discrete, as in France or Finland, or uncoordinated and overlapping, as in Italy or Belgium (Bayley 1985: chs. 3 and 8). Furthermore, constitutional law may provide a scheme for the internal accountability of policing, through the specification of an organizational hierarchy and internal accountability relations backed up by a discipline code, and also for the external accountability of policing, whether to dedicated bodies such as ministries of justice, interior and defence, judicial or quasi-judicial complaints authorities, national or regional experts, elected or hybrid police authorities, civilian review boards and local consultative committees, or to more general agencies of accountability such as courts, prosecutors, ombudsmen or parliamentary assemblies and committees (Goldsmith and Lewis 2000).

This array of modern constitutional techniques for channelling, limiting and rendering police power accountable is of dual significance – both as a carrier and as a reflection of liberal anxieties and sensibilities, and as an objective methodology for curbing the meddling capacity of the state. Of course, as already intimated, how much difference institutional measures make in practice is a variable matter. For the concerned liberal, they can only ever be 'second-best' solutions, ways of mitigating rather than taming Leviathan. If there can be no stable and satisfactory balance in principle between security and liberty, then the constitutional arsenal can only ever provide particular and contingent solutions, opportunities for debate and publicity, and sites of vigilance and accountability. And since constitutionalism, too, is a form of power, we should not assume that the constitutional system is within the gift of a liberal, power-restraining worldview. Even where its basic framework is entrenched against easy reform, the constitutional system is far from immune from the influence of the government of the day, whose preference may lie more in bolstering its capacity to meet new or existing security threats than in self-limitation.[8] Moreover, the constitutional solution is more apt to 'take' in some policing and political cultures than in others, and in none is it proof against intrusive tendencies. In colonial and communist policing systems, for instance, policing has typically been an oppressive tool of an ideological elite – a licence for unlimited meddling – and post-communist and post-colonial systems have in many cases found it difficult to shed that legacy (Mawby 2003: 21–5). In the Far East, the continuing influence of older models of social discipline has led one commentator to conclude that, despite continental influence on institutional redesign, in both Japan and South Korea the contemporary police remain 'natural, hierarchical, authoritarian – respected and feared by the vast majority; opposed even hated by politically progressive minorities' (S. Y. Lee 1990: 91).

In the western cradle of liberalism and constitutionalism, too, where fears of meddling tend to be most vociferously expressed, contemporary anxieties can in some measure be traced to different traditions. So, although there has been some convergence in recent decades, continental systems remain on the whole more centralized and militaristic, more focused on administrative tasks, more associated with government and less publicly accountable than their Anglo-American counterparts (Mawby 2003: 20), and this reflects the abiding influence of

[8] This represents a paradox of police governance to join the more basic paradox of state policing as a potential threat to the very security it promises to deliver. This more specific paradox of police governance inheres in the fact that the national and local state is both an influential source of regulatory control over the police and, as one of the main beneficiaries of the police's ordering capacity, part of the problem that regulation seeks to address (N. Walker 2000: 4–6, 54–67).

continental police science and the *dirigiste* state tradition which complemented it. The Anglo-American model, for its part, tends to be more
localist and populist – particularly in the United States where the
republican and federal origins favoured local self-government. In
neither case, however, can institutional design remotely be considered
a liberal panacea. In the continental system, the fear of meddling is the
fear of intrusion by an aloof, unaccountable and politically interested
central authority. In the Anglo-American environment, recent central-
izing tendencies have stoked similar fears, but a more long-standing
liberal concern is with the interlocking of police with local political
elites, and the partial and uneven intrusion in the lives of different local
populations this threatens.

The liberalism of fear, then, retains a widespread resonance within
the state tradition. One of the paradoxes of globalization, moreover,
particularly in the light of 9/11, is that concern with the oldest of state
monopolies, as well as the state behaviour which gives rise to this
concern, is communicated more and more effectively *transnationally*.
As we shall see in later chapters, cross-border policing is also a burgeoning activity, and it gives rise to its own set of anxieties. But probably the primary impact of global interconnectedness on policing
remains the way in which the experience of elsewhere corroborates and
amplifies well-established intra-state forms of relations between police
and population and their attendant anxieties. Police meddling and its
fear, as we have tried to argue, is the original sin of the modern state
security tradition, the inevitable upshot of the founding tension
between individual freedom and collective discipline. Modern state
formations may be deeply diverse in structure and dominant ideology,
but we continue to recognize in them all, as they recognize in each
other, that common resilient tension.

Liberating security

Let us now deal more briefly with the second element of the meddling
concern – the desire to liberate security provision from the clutches
of the state. In recent years, we have seen a revival of interest in non-
state forms of policing provision (see, e.g., Jones and Newburn 1998,
2006; Johnston and Shearing 2003; Mazerolle and Ransley 2006) –
a revival which has had repercussions for our historical understanding of the stages of police development and which has also fed into a

contemporary sense that the phase of the centrality of the state-controlled 'new police' within the overall profile of policing may be coming to an end, or at least undergoing significant revision. From the historical perspective, there is now greater appreciation than once there was that non-state policing activities by no means disappeared with the onset of the new police. Rather, the new police have always been complemented, or at least supplemented, by a range of specialist security activities by non-police public bodies, by commercial organization, and through citizen initiative. In terms of contemporary trends, much current analysis of policing is concerned to identify, and in many cases encourage, an acceleration in the trend away from state policing, pointing to a diverse array of contributory factors ranging from the fiscal crisis of the post-war state and the rise of 'mass private property' (Shearing and Stenning 1987) in the form of office plazas, shopping malls, sports complexes, etc., to a more general commodification of security in response to an increased awareness of, and sensitivity to, the intensity and diversity of social risks and the inability of the traditional state police to address all such risks (Jones and Newburn 1998: ch. 8; Kempa *et al.* 1999; Loader 1999; Rigakos 2002).

Just as the background factors are various, so too are the range of predictive trajectories and normative hopes associated with this new school of analysis. Some of the more radical diagnoses and institutional suggestions have less to do with a concern with rescuing the private individual from the encroachment of the state and more to do with devising alternative forms of publicly sanctioned collective organization of security provision which avoid some of the other pathologies of top-down state provision – in particular its lack of responsive intelligence – and so are more appropriately considered at a later juncture (see chapter 5). For now, though, let us concentrate on that strand of analysis which retains the meddling theme, stressing the dangers attendant upon and damage caused by the state's undue interference with the entitlements and voluntary market exchanges of sovereign individuals.

This line of scepticism is of course rooted in the same modern social imaginary as the critical perspectives considered in the previous section. Its most obvious intellectual debt is to neo-classical (or neo-liberal) welfare economics, which, with its axiomatic insistence on treating the individual as a rational utility maximizer, closely overlaps the concerns of both liberalism and utilitarianism with the sovereignty of the individual agent and the reducibility of collective welfare to individual-centred concerns (Freeden 1996: ch. 7). Today, the sharpest edge of that scepticism is to be found in that brand of economic theory known as 'public choice economics' (Buchanan 1978), which applies the insights of neoclassical economics to the political decision-making process itself.[9]

Four charges are from this standpoint levelled at the state as a mechanism for producing and distributing social goods, including security. First, that as public bureaucracies (especially those of a monopoly kind such as the police) have no price signals to which they are required to respond, they have no incentive to be efficient and keep costs down. Second, that state provision tends to be colonized by vested bureaucratic interests, thereby subordinating consumer interests to those of producers. Third, that state forms privilege the interests of the knowledgeable, articulate, active or merely noisy over and above those of people who do not wish to make political participation central to their conception of the good (Seldon 1990: 99). Fourth, that public bodies offer consumers only the 'cumbrous political channels' (Friedman 1962: 91) associated with what Hirschman (1970) calls 'voice',

---

[9] Perhaps the contemporary thinker who most obviously bridges the two sides of the meddling critique is the libertarian Robert Nozick, who begins his opus *Anarchy, State and Utopia* with the arresting proposition that 'Individuals have rights, and there are things no person or group may do to them (without violating their rights)' (1974: ix). Unlike many liberals, Nozick rejects the social contract as an artifice which, lacking empirical credentials, is in danger of allowing all sorts of metaphysical assumptions about the source and proper trajectory of the good favoured by the author to contaminate the foundations of the state. Instead, starting from a strong premise of self-ownership (including ownership of property acquired from the exploitation of individual talents), he prefers to draw upon the classical economist Adam Smith's famous device of the 'invisible hand' to explain the emergence of the state from the destructive and unstable contest between 'protective associations' that the state of nature is assumed to generate. The resultant entity is only, however, legitimate in its minimal form, enforcing criminal law, punishing transgressors and prohibiting acts of 'self-exemption' (Holmes 1995: 27), as well as providing the stable legal framework necessary for market exchange. Any further extension of the redistributive or other regulatory functions of the state involves immoral acts of coercion – at worst the coerced removal of one individual's legitimate holdings in order to improve the lot of another and at best the forcible extinction of choice as to how to protect and exploit what is one's own (Nozick 1974: part II). Such a libertarian perspective is equally suspicious of the two aspects of meddling – both arbitrary encroachment on citizens' person and property and frustration of their desire to do as they wish with their person and property.

channels whose efficacy is hindered by the inability of consumers to 'exit'. This style of thought does continue to recognize a sphere of 'public goods' whose non-excludability (and the associated problem of free-riding) makes it necessary for such goods to be collectively financed and provided, and policing is generally held to be among these – a point we shall have cause to develop at some length in part II. But the necessary involvement of the state in security stands as but a pathological – and still dangerous and inefficient – exception to the liberty-respecting purity of the free market (Hayek 1979: 46).[10]

What are the practical implications of this brand of scepticism? In part, it generates the belief that state policing (or at least the non-coercive aspects of it) should be exposed to the full blast of competition from the private sector. But it also implies that sovereign individuals should be able to break free from their undignified dependence on the state and pursue their own self-determined security interests. They should not, in other words, be prevented from clubbing together with others to realize their freely chosen security goals (by, for example, forming private residential associations or gated communities) or seeking through voluntary market exchanges to purchase the hardware and services they believe will make them secure, whether they be burglar alarms, gates, CCTV systems or commercial security patrols. Indeed, one of the particular fears neo-liberals and libertarians have about the state is that its actors may seek to discourage, control or even prohibit (in short, meddle in) these voluntary acts of security seeking. Hence the efforts made by neo-liberal governments across the world in recent years to encourage their citizens to take more personal responsibility for the security of their person and property (Home Office 1994; cf. O'Malley 1992; Garland 2001: ch. 5). Hence also the attempts of some neo-liberal economists to urge that governments act to stimulate security markets by, for instance, offering tax incentives to individuals who 'improve the security of their own property and purchase private policing services' (Pyle 1995: 54; see also Elliot 1989).

---

[10] There are some 'anarcho-capitalists' – such as Murray Rothbard (1985) and Bruce Benson (1990) – who cut through the arguments about the necessary minimal role of the state offered by social contract theorists and by libertarians such as Nozick (1974), as well as by public choice theorists, arguing that the state – and its law enforcement functions – can be dispensed with altogether and replaced by 'a fully privatized enterprise of law' (Benson 1990: 357). For a fuller discussion, see Loader (1997a).

Limits of the meddling critique

Several – if by no means all – of the claims and concerns about the state to be found under both branches of the meddling critique have a resonance beyond the parameters of liberal and libertarian thought and welfare economics. This form of state scepticism quite properly, in our view, emphasizes that security is a basic good that serves as a precondition for the meaningful exercise of liberty, even if it holds security to possess no non-instrumental value beyond that. And it rightly concedes the necessary place of the state in offering minimal guarantees of security *to all*, even if it finds it difficult to specify and hold that minimum line, and even if it sees no legitimate security-enhancing place for the state other than that, and, indeed, is acutely concerned that it may injure both personal liberty and security and curtail the sovereignty of individual choice to expand the state's place in the production of security beyond the elusive minimum.

The liberal and neo-liberal/libertarian variants of state scepticism are, accordingly, quite properly alert to the dangers that arise from concentrating the capacity to exercise legitimate force within a given territory to a single entity – the paradox being, as mentioned, that the very monopoly of violence that exists to guarantee the security and basic liberties of individuals stands as an ever-present threat to that security and liberty. It highlights, in other words, the inherently 'double-edged' character of state police institutions (N. Walker 2000: 6), even in their capacity as upholders of 'general order' (Marenin 1982) – the maintenance of public tranquillity and safety that is the indispensable basis for social routines and the pursuit of individual purposes in which all sections of a society have a stake. In so doing, it pinpoints the propensity of state police forces to exceed or abuse their power in ways that directly impinge on the very individual rights and entitlements they are 'contracted' to protect – a tendency most glaringly apparent in weak, failed or authoritarian states (Goldsmith 2003), but which remains a feature of state policing even in more sustainably democratic settings. At the very least, this scepticism about state power – a scepticism apparent in the long-standing preoccupation of police studies with the (arbitrary, violent) operation of police powers and discretion (e.g. Westley 1970; D. Dixon 1997) – indicates the importance of forms of constitutional and political regulation within any schema that seeks to defend the proper place of the state in the just and democratic production of internal security, and even here it is rightly concerned with the bluntness and fragility of such protective instruments.

It should, of course, come as no surprise that much of the meddling critique commands widespread sympathy. As we have sought to argue, the secular and individualist tendencies of the modern social imaginary which underscore both the promise of the modern state and the concern with coercive state interference have permeated across all of contemporary thought, exposing tensions which it is literally unimaginable to dismiss. Yet this does not mean that the meddling critique should be accepted uncritically, or that it has closed off all avenues for alternative diagnosis and prognosis. Rather, the more expansive conception of the state-security nexus we want to defend in this book must also identify and address, and seek to transcend, certain shortcomings exhibited in the meddling mindset, and particularly in the more extreme neo-liberal/libertarian variants of this brand of scepticism towards the state. Let us briefly highlight three.

The first concerns the preconditions that are required to create and sustain limited, constitutional, rights-regarding states. There is, as Margaret Canovan (1996: 38) points out, a tendency in classical liberal theory to assume 'that any fool can establish a nightwatchman state' and a corresponding disregard for the forms of trust and solidarity between strangers that provide the cultural conditions of possibility for the minimal, rule-governed state that liberals find acceptable. But surely such states require citizens to care about, and be prepared to do something about, abuses of police power or, more broadly, to identify with belonging to a polity in which the police are held to account and the rights of all equally guaranteed? This, of course, raises some thorny matters pertaining to the affective dimensions of social and political life (to which we return in part II), issues that neo-liberal and libertarian writers have tended to steer well clear of. They have remained too preoccupied with the (problem of the) state and the threat it poses to individual freedom, and insufficiently attentive to the trust-building functions of political community upon which the liberty and security of citizens depend.

A second and related issue concerns the forms of individual security seeking that neo-liberalism is eager to promote (or at least prevent the state from preventing), and the conception of security upon which these rely. This conception, in using a pre-social state of nature as its reference point, is atomistic and unrelational. This has both conceptual and practical consequences. Conceptually, it helps explain the difficulties liberals have with the balancing metaphor. For if the individual side of the security equation contains no social dimension, there can be no prospect of reconciliation with an idea of collective security which sometimes challenges these individual conceptions in the name of some broadly shared social good. The two become literally incommensurable, and the liberal lacks any means of conceiving of deference to a shared good in terms other than loss. Practically, the atomistic and unrelational conception suggests forms of individual security-seeking practices that are self-defeating and in a profound sense oxymoronic (Loader 1997b), an 'expression of the desire for sovereign agency' (Markell 2003: 22) that depends upon and projects a semblance of security produced by lifting oneself out of coexistence with others in order to render one's own existence less contingently vulnerable and the future more predictable. These practices are often at the same time exercises of private power. They eschew democratic political life in order to achieve 'distributive outcomes according to one's assets, skills and preferences' (Offe 2003: 450) in a manner corrosive of the forms of trust and solidarity which any sustainable notion of the public good of security draws upon and, in its turn, replenishes. Neo-liberalism remains committed, in other words, to forms of security that 'organize the world in ways that make it possible for certain people to enjoy an imperfect simulation of the invulnerability they desire, leaving others to bear a disproportionate share of the costs and burdens involved in social life' (Markell 2003: 22).

The current proliferation of these private – anti-social – security practices raises the question, thirdly, of whether – as neo-liberals maintain – the state's always potentially intrusive and counter-productive attempts to 'insert some logic into the messy human predicament' (Bauman and Tester 2001: 137) are *the* source of social misery and insecurity in the world today. Might it not be suggested, instead, that the fragmentation and weakness of public political authority also lie at the heart of the contemporary security constellation, whether in respect of weak states whose repression of their citizens serves so often to mask their lack of effective infrastructural power, or in liberal democracies faced with growing market-induced disparities in the security resources available to their citizens? As we have seen, the state is no mere contingent product of the modern social imaginary, but the very frame of secular organization in which *its hopes and fears alike* are invested and reap their dividend. The state may contain certain ineradicable tensions, but if the only response is 'as little as possible', then that is to concede too much to the fears, with nothing to put in its place except other and more partial forms of the regulation (or deregulation) of secular affairs. The state is not the pathological message of modernity, but merely its (unavoidable) messenger, and, here as elsewhere, shooting the messenger can be no answer. Against this backdrop, neo-liberal and libertarian forms of state scepticism seem simply to be 'barking up the wrong tree' (Bauman and Tester 2001: 137). As Zygmunt Bauman says: 'Too much of the state is a catastrophe, but so is too little' (2001: 137).

Conceptual foundations

It should hopefully be obvious by now why we have started with the meddling critique, and why we must keep it constantly in mind while exploring the other brands of state scepticism. The meddling critique is inextricably bound up with the very idea of the modern state – with both its historical foundations and its social development – and we can and should no more dismiss it than we can or should seek to eradicate the state itself. The partisan, culturally imperial or idiot state – the respective subjects of the following three chapters – is always first and foremost a meddling state. Without the capacity and propensity to meddle, to act against the basic liberty and security interests of those whom it is supposed to serve, the state could not engage in these other pathologies; and, conversely, where or to the extent that it is innocent of these other pathologies, the meddling concern remains a live and pervasive one.

Yet it is not only the strength of the meddling critique but also its shortcomings which provide a bridge to later sections of the book. If the modern social imaginary lies at the source not only of the state, but also of the very notion of immanent political critique and the master ideology of liberalism, then we might expect the framework concerns of this mindset to surface again in our tour of state scepticism, and so should remain alert to the limitations of that mindset. We should be wary of the preoccupation with the atomized individual, and of the limits and dangers of the conceptual opposition of individuality and sociality. Most of all, we should be wary of any tendency to view the state as at best a necessary and at worst an expendable evil, rather than simply as the site within which the tensions of the modern social imaginary are inevitably played out – for good or for ill. This caution will by no means provide all the answers we seek, but, hopefully, it will allow our enquiry to be neither seduced by false utopias nor confounded by false dystopias.

3 | *The state as partisan*

W
E turn now to an image of the state, and a form of state scepticism, associated more with the political left than with liberals and the neo-liberal and libertarian right. It has deep roots in socialist and anarchist politics and through that pedigree line provides an exemplar of the anti-state thought which emerged hand in hand with the state tradition in the manner discussed in the previous chapter. As a disposition towards the state, it can, moreover, be argued to possess a contemporary relevance that stretches well beyond those bodies of deeply sedimented critical leftist thought, with proponents of this stance endorsing the broad concern of the liberal and the free marketeer about state violence and the paradoxes inherent in concentrating the power of legitimate coercion in the container of the state. But there the resemblance begins and ends. In contrast to liberalism, this leftist variant of state scepticism argues that the state's monopoly of violence is not merely a necessary precondition for the maintenance of a consensual 'general order'. The police are, rather, a vehicle for upholding what Marenin (1982) calls 'specific order'. They are a means of fortifying either the interests of the state itself, or those of constituencies favoured by the present configuration of economic and social relations. The state is, on this view, a partisan actor in social and political life, as are its agents the police. It is as such an evil, an unwanted and unwelcome force that needs to be monitored, exposed, struggled against and – depending on the particular variant of leftist politics – radically reformed or transcended.

In this chapter we present and scrutinize two instances of this radical critique of the state. The first has been a staple of work in critical criminology and police studies for some three decades or so. It posits the state as being structurally tied to dominant private interests, systematically directed towards coercing the weak and the poor, and integral to the reproduction of relations of inequality organized around class, gender, ethnicity, age and sexuality. This argument is most readily invoked in relation to authoritarian political regimes, as we shall see. But it also offers critical purchase on the operation of state power in more sustainably democratic societies, not least in divided societies or in states that have since the 1980s been captured and streamlined by neo-liberal governments. The second is associated more with work in international relations and critical security studies, though it too finds expression in current criminological writing. This focuses on the advent – both prior to 9/11 and as part of the 'war on terror' waged in response to it – of a 'new state of exception'. It addresses the presence today of a seemingly permanent and boundless emergency state, one whose securitizing practices lay bare the violence that underpins 'democratic' politics and represent a clear and present danger to democracy and political liberty – both at home and abroad.

Our aim is to review the respective claims of these two overlapping strands of radical state scepticism. We consider in each case the ways in which they illuminate current developments in policing and security practice. And we identify the issues that this state-sceptical disposition raises for the position we develop and defend in this book. Having done this, we conclude by pinpointing the blindspots of a stance that remains devoted to a critique of the state and, as such, unable or unwilling to grasp its indispensability to the project of civilizing security.

Partisan states

Critical criminology has since its inception taken as its leitmotiv the idea that the state and state power are a problem. This claim has over the last three decades been advanced in different theoretical registers, with contrasting degrees of sophistication, and in the name of various categories of oppressed groups. We cannot hope to detail here either the range of radical perspectives on the state or their application to questions of policing and security, and we do not intend to try. Suffice it to say that some of these are pressed in relation to social class, base their diagnosis and prognosis on one or other variant of Marxist state theory (cf. Miliband 1969; Poulantzas 1978; Jessop 1990) and are concerned, broadly, with how police institutions are conditioned by relations of property ownership and production which these institutions, in turn, help to reproduce (Spitzer 1981; Brogden 1982; Grimshaw and Jefferson 1987). Others develop critiques of the state from the vantage point of feminist (MacKinnon 1989) or critical race theory (Goldberg 2001), and have been concerned with the differential treatment that women, or ethnic minorities, receive either as police officers or as recipients of police attention or misrecognition and neglect (Scraton 1987; Cashmore and McLaughlin 1991; Westmarland 2001).

What can be said generally about these critical perspectives is that each is organized around some version of the claim that the state functions to protect and reproduce dominant interests and values. Each posits the police – an institution which is to the state what the knife's edge is to the knife (Marenin 1996a: 10) – as a vital force in the maintenance of prevailing political and social order. So too, more broadly, is the ideologically unifying appeal to 'law and order' that is mobilized to mask and sustain relations of domination in which marginalized populations are systematically subject to 'over-control' and 'under-protection'. In so arguing, this depiction of the state presents a wholesale challenge to liberal social-contract theorists who understand the state as being formed by equals to whom that state promises equal protection, and to the related self-image and ideological representation of the police as politically neutral state agents delivering an impartial, uniform service to all.

As a way into these issues, we may usefully borrow two now rather unfashionable categories from the Marxist philosopher Louis Althusser. It can be said first that the police function as part – arguably, to continue the knife analogy, the sharpest part – of what Althusser (1971) calls the *repressive* state apparatus. Under this heading, one might pinpoint several salient dimensions of policing practice in structurally divided societies. Firstly, we can point to the ways in which routine police deployments focus disproportionately on the economically and socially excluded so as to reproduce patterns of domination organized around class (P. Cohen 1979), race and ethnicity (Keith 1993), gender (Brown and Heidensohn 2000) and age (Loader 1996). This becomes most nakedly apparent in respect of those social groups (such as vagrants or migrants) whose disconnection from economic and social institutions renders their social control almost wholly a matter of policing – groups evocatively referred to by J. Lee (1981) as 'police property'. Secondly, one can highlight the manner in which police force is called upon at moments of socio-economic and political crisis to uphold the status quo by quelling the presenting symptoms of economic and social inequalities or development – whether in respect

of urban unrest, industrial strife or political protest. We return shortly
to these aspects of the relationship between policing and the social.

But policing and security institutions also function as part of what
Althusser calls the *ideological* state apparatus. They are one of a range
of bodies – the media, churches, the family, education systems – whose
practices seek to manufacture and sustain the consent of the ruled by
masking the unjust or oppressive 'realities' of prevailing economic and
social arrangements. Part of this involves finessing the coercive character of the state itself. Radical critiques have, in this vein, sought to
expose how the formal protections associated with the rule of law are
undone by the practical application of substantive categories of
inequality (McConville *et al.* 1991). Such critiques have similarly contended that various 'soft' policing strategies – notably community
policing – aim principally to win the consent of routinely policed populations by obscuring the 'hard' realities of the 'coercive state' – the
velvet glove covering and cushioning the iron fist (Bernstein *et al.* 1982;
Gordon 1984). But policing institutions also serve as an ideological
unifier in a more general sense. Through their socially authorized
power of 'legitimate naming', they are able to diagnose, classify and
represent the world in ways that apply forms of social glue at moments
of political crisis; articulating the crisis as one of 'law and order' and
highlighting and censuring assorted 'folk devils' as the cause of moral
breakdown and social malaise (Hall *et al.* 1978; Loader and Mulcahy
2003: ch. 7). This dimension of police power segues closely with the
state's capacity to act as a 'cultural monolith'. We therefore address it
mainly in the next chapter.

For now let us try to put some flesh on these claims by considering
several cases in which it may be argued that such partisanship is manifest. This argument is most readily applicable to authoritarian political systems. We mean by this systems which lack – or only weakly
embody – free and fair elections for political office, respect for the rule
of law and protection of human rights, systems in which 'efficacy'
becomes the sole criterion for judging the performance of policing and
security institutions. This, of course, is a more or less adequate description of a range of political forms both historical and contemporary,
including colonial systems, former and current communist regimes,
and military or patrimonial states (and, as we argue in chapter 8,
democratic societies, too, can harbour authoritarian tendencies). It is
also important to add that significant variation can be found both

between these different types of authoritarian rule and between states within each category (Marenin 1996b; Mawby 2003). Colonial rule admitted a range of styles of both administration in general and policing in particular (Anderson and Killingray 1991). China, Cuba and the former Soviet Union cannot adequately be treated as one for policing – or indeed other governmental – purposes. The parameters and dynamics of authoritarian rule do not amount to the same thing in Saudi Arabia, Indonesia or Zimbabwe; nor do the legacies left by dictatorship in 'societies in transition' such as Argentina, Brazil, El Salvador, South Africa and the former Soviet satellites in eastern Europe.

These differences are plainly important for any proper assessment of policing in authoritarian settings. For present purposes, however, we can fruitfully focus upon those features of authoritarian policing systems that most clearly reveal the partisanship of state power and its effects on the liberty and security of individuals.[1] Prominent among these recurring elements are a concentration on what Brodeur (1983) calls 'high' policing. Policing in authoritarian states is first and foremost about protecting the interests and ideology of the regime/leadership/party, as well as the private interests that it supports and that support it. The focus of secret and uniformed police agencies is on monitoring populations, the surveillance of political opponents and quelling dissident activity and public disorder, tasks for which they are given draconian powers. The flipside is that secondary importance is accorded to the prevention and control of 'ordinary' crime (e.g. Stanley 1996). The police in authoritarian settings function as the hierarchically organized, executive arm of the political centre, are subject to no independent oversight or control, and have little or no popular mandate. They tend to work in tandem with the security forces with

---

[1] There is a voluminous literature on policing in authoritarian states on which we have selectively drawn and condensed in order to advance our specific analytic purposes. We have found most useful the following: on colonial policing – Brogden (1987), Anderson and Killingray (1991, 1992), Ahire (1998); on policing in communist regimes – Michalowski (1992), Shelley (1997), Wong (2002); on policing in Latin America – Huggins (1998), Caldeira (2001), Goldsmith (2003); on policing in post-communist states – Łoś and Zybertowicz (2000), Kadar (2001), Uildriks and van Reenan (2003). We have also drawn upon Marenin's (1996c) collection on the intersection between policing and political change, and the tradition of scholarship on comparative policing (Bayley 1985; Mawby 1990, 1999, 2003).

whom – tellingly – they are often barracked. In authoritarian states no meaningful distinction is drawn between 'national defence' and 'internal security'. Fear operates as a central category of political rule (Łoś 2002).

Authoritarian states can be strong – or at least give the appearance of being so. But they are often today 'weak' or 'failed' states, either unable to provide basic social goods (including security) to their people, or competing with alternative power centres for the control of territory and the monopoly of the means of violence (Rotberg 2003). Weakness or failure seldom however signals equanimity. When states falter, police and military institutions are the last to display signs of weakness – though their strength can often inhere not in being directed from the centre but in an excessive autonomy to define and pursue their own interests. Indeed, violent repression of the population tends to exist in inverse proportion to the lack of infrastructural capacity (Goldsmith 2003), and in contexts of civil unrest or insurgency failing states frequently resort to brutal interrogation and the deadly use of force against their populations.

When authoritarian states are weak or have failed, or are undergoing processes of transition, crime and violence often spiral out of control, as do levels of public insecurity. This tends to generate degrees of popular identification with repressive policing – demands for states to crack down on new sources of fear. It can also give a lease of life, as in eastern Europe and the former Soviet Union, to new – often criminal – protection enterprises 'founded largely on the former secret security structures' (Łoś 2002: 181), or, as in Latin America, to anxious middle classes hiring armed groups to eradicate 'street kids' (Brazil) or *delinquente* (Colombia). The poor and dispossessed are thus often caught at the receiving end of partisan forms of both state and private violence. These, moreover, can come together in deadly symbiosis, as Michael Taussig's ethnography of violence-saturated Colombia – *Law in a Lawless Land* (2003) – so powerfully shows.

We are confronted here with states that are deeply violent and nakedly partisan – states that offend conservative and liberal sensibilities as well as those of state-sceptical radicals. But the latters' critique of the state does not only reference so obviously authoritarian regimes. It can also offer insights into policing systems in liberal democratic societies governed by electoral competition, the rule of law and respect for human rights – states with formally independent policing systems.

These states too come in different guises, as does their architecture of policing. Significant differences are to be found between policing systems in the USA (with its mix of federal, state, county, city and almost countless small-town police forces); England and Wales (with its common law ideology of the constable as 'citizen-in-uniform') and the military-based gendarmes found in continental Europe (Emsley 2000; Mawby 2003). We can again, however, concentrate on the commonalities. Foremost among these – the radical state sceptic maintains – is that policing in these settings remains tied to dominant interests (organized around axes of class, gender, race and age) and integral to the reproduction of unjust economic and social relations. Several claims are advanced in support of this proposition.

The principal charge is that even in formally democratic states the police form a constitutive element of a political order that allocates resources and recognition in ways that disproportionately benefit some social groups at the expense of others. And this includes the good of security, with 'over-control' and 'under-protection' by the police standing as a reliable indicator of one's marginality and powerlessness. Policing, in other words, operates in these notionally equal, rights-regarding societies in ways that are systematically biased. The police offer a *service* to the propertied middle classes, while being targeted disproportionately as a *force* at those located at society's margins – the destitute, the 'dangerous' poor – or those deemed to threaten its political centres – what former British prime minister Margaret Thatcher once called the 'enemy within'. These distinctions, moreover, find themselves embedded and reproduced in the working cultures of police organizations and in the practical categories of apprehension that officers bring to their social ordering and crime-control tasks (Shearing 1981).

As Margaret Thatcher's depiction of striking miners suggests, this systemic bias is 'revealed' most clearly at times of social conflict and political crisis, when the police are called upon to take on organized labour (e.g. Fine and Millar 1984; McCabe *et al.* 1988), or control political protest (e.g. Della Porta and Reiter 1998, 2004), or quell urban disorders (e.g. Skolnick 1969; Cowell *et al.* 1982) – often in ways injurious to the liberty and security of already marginalized populations. But it remains a recurring feature of capitalist democracies even at times of political calm. What forms of harm, violation and abuse pass unnoticed, lightly policed and rarely punished in such societies, the radical state sceptic asks? Those of the rich and powerful. And who – in liberal democracies throughout the world – is most likely to be stopped, searched, arrested, detained, prosecuted, imprisoned, even killed in custody? Answer: young, impoverished, ethnic-minority males.

Two examples can help to put some sociohistorical flesh on these contentions. The first concerns patterns of policing in divided – but nonetheless democratic – societies. Northern Ireland offers a good case in point here, though claims of state partisanship have also been pressed in polities with indigenous populations (such as aborigines in Australia and Canada) or minority groups seeking greater autonomy or secession (such as the Basques in Spain). Not only are the practices of indigenous or minority groups frequently subject to processes of cultural misrecognition and disproportionate police attention – as is strikingly evident, for example, in the case of Australian and Canadian aborigines (Royal Commission into Aboriginal Deaths in Custody 1991; Stenning and LaPrairie 2003). The demands of minorities are also often framed by states as threats to national security and responded to as such (Kymlicka 2005).

In the case of Northern Ireland, critics have argued that Stormont and – following the imposition of direct rule in 1972 – the British state have operated in ways that systematically protect the interests, culture and security of the Protestant majority at the expense of those of the Catholic minority. The partisanship and associated illegitimacy of the state exists, in turn, in a close and mutually reinforcing relationship to that of the police and security forces (Weitzer 1995; Ellison and Smyth 2000; Walker and Telford 2000). The Royal Ulster Constabulary (RUC), from its formation in 1922 to its replacement by the Police Service for Northern Ireland in 2003, was staffed overwhelmingly by members of the Protestant community whose interests (and state) it defended, and who in turn lent it passionate, often unconditional support. It has, conversely, been deeply suspected by nationalists who felt the grip of its coercive hand while being unable to call upon it as a service. In the context of 'The Troubles', the RUC operated in close tandem with the military, prioritized the suppression of political violence over the control of ordinary crime, and was alleged to have operated a covert 'shoot-to-kill' policy towards suspected terrorists and colluded with Protestant paramilitaries in the murder of Catholics. The police, in short, came in this 'democratic' setting to assume many of the features associated with forces in authoritarian states – centrally controlled, barracked with the security forces with whom they are entwined, focused on protecting the regime by suppressing political violence and dissent, and subject to little or no independent oversight. In the context of the current 'peace process', it remains an open question whether a democratic future can be forged out of this legacy of partisanship, and if so how (Patten 1999; Ellison and Mulcahy 2001; Mulcahy 2005: part IV).

But it is not only in situations of communal conflict that democratic states function as partisans. The leftist state sceptic can point, as a second example, to the rise of 'law and order' politics (and its attendant policing and penal strategies) in societies that have since the 1980s been ruled by neo-liberal governments espousing the very state-sceptical ideals we discussed in the last chapter. This principally means the USA, Britain, Australia and New Zealand, though, as Loïc Wacquant (2003) notes, free-market doxa is actively being 'exported' from the USA (often via Britain) and often enthusiastically 'imported' by governments and populations in western Europe, the former Soviet bloc and Latin America. What these societies have witnessed in the last two decades is a radical redrawing of the parameters and purposes of the state, with (supposedly initiative-sapping) welfare provision being elbowed out by the values and practices of the market. The social state and disciplined market have given way – materially, to footloose capital and the penal state (Gamble 1988; Wacquant 2003) and ideologically, to forms of 'authoritarian populism' (Hall 1980) that mobilize the demons and massage the fears of an anxious, discontented majority. As the state's 'left hand' (of public provision) has been withdrawn, so its 'right hand' (of police and penal force) has come to the fore in a bid to contain the social effects of the insecurities and exclusions that globalized market societies produce (Bourdieu *et al.* 1999; Parenti 1999; I. Taylor 1999).

The result is neo-liberal democracies dominated today by new policing strategies – zero-tolerance, curfews, anti-social behaviour orders – aimed at 'cracking down' on the disorder and incivilities of the urban poor in ways that are inimical to civil liberties and conducive to abuses of police power. Following the (it should be said, much disputed) 'success' of zero-tolerance policing in cutting crime in New York City, these strategies are now being trumpeted globally by a tireless band of police and political entrepreneurs (Dennis 1997; Bratton 1998). What is being promulgated is a new rationality for governing the 'outcasts' of the neo-liberal world (Bauman 2004), one which concentrates resources and powers on the police and accords ideological pre-eminence to a 'get tough' policing solution to the problem of order. Policing, by these means, has become tied up with a neo-liberal stream-lining of government – one that has seen forms of social support *for* the poor superseded by anti-social control strategies aimed by a partisan, minimal state *at* the poor.

What lessons may we distil from this dissection of the biases that attend policing and security practices in both authoritarian and demo-cratic states? There is little doubt that this leftist variant of state scep-ticism is valuable in highlighting the intersection between policing and security and various axes of social stratification; in pinpointing how in structurally divided societies the security of some groups is secured at the expense of others; and in its suggestion that the state is no mere neutral umpire holding the ring in conflicts between different societal interests. In all these ways, it poses a strong challenge to the position we want to defend. When confronted with the suggestion that security can be conceptualized as a public good it asks: whose security? which public? what good? It stands quizzically aghast at the idea that forms of trust and solidarity can (or indeed should) be fostered between con-stituencies with such structurally divergent interests. It asks: what is the point of democratizing security if the rules of the political game are stacked in such a way that certain groups find themselves losing time and again? And it questions the sociological wisdom and normative value of a perspective that places such a deeply biased entity as the state at the heart of a project to produce more equitable distributions of policing and security resources – whether in authoritarian or formally democratic contexts.

These are important objections and we will return to them shortly. First we must address ourselves to forms of policing and military prac-tice that have deepened still further radical scepticism towards sover-eign state power.

The new state of exception

The second strand of leftist state scepticism we consider in this chapter takes its cue from Walter Benjamin's essay 'Critique of Violence', orig-inally published in 1921 (Benjamin 1921/1985). In this piece, Benjamin takes issue with the idea that the police institution is connected to 'general law', still less subject to it. Rather, for Benjamin, 'the "law" of the police really marks the point at which the state . . . can no longer guarantee through the legal system the empirical ends that it desires at any price to attain. Therefore the police intervene "for security reasons" in countless cases where no clear legal situation exists' (1921/1985: 141). Law, Benjamin argues, can be located in a specific place and time that renders it open to critical evaluation. The police institution, by contrast, presents nothing solid, graspable, or controllable at all: 'Its power is formless, like its nowhere tangible, all-pervasive, ghostly presence in the life of civilized states' (1921/1985: 141–2). It, consequently, 'bears witness' – more so in a democracy than in absolutist systems that make no pretence of subjecting executive will to popular oversight – 'to the greatest conceivable degeneration of violence' (141–2). Police power is not violence fenced in and directed by reason and law, but violence beyond reason and law.

Benjamin's remarks offer an insight into the intersection between police power and sovereign statehood that has been developed in recent years by those working broadly in 'critical security studies' (e.g. Agamben 1993, 2004a; Campbell and Dillon 1993; R. B. J. Walker 1997; Neocleous 2000). Two sets of interconnected claims found within this literature are relevant here. The first is a leftist articulation of Carl Schmitt's characterization of modern politics and sovereignty. For Schmitt – writing in the context of the faltering Weimar Republic in the 1920s – the fundamental and irreducible element of what he terms 'the political' is the drawing of the 'friend–enemy' distinction (Schmitt 1933/1996). The task of the sovereign is to decide on external and internal foes and to adopt such measures as will protect the integrity of the state from them – in return for which he can demand obedience from a people 'terrified' by their own radical insecurity 'into the arms of authority' (McCormick 1997: 253). The political is, moreover, a realm of authority not law, one that calls upon firm, absolute decisions, not endless, polity-debilitating discussion. The sovereign state must decide and decide alone on both the figure of the enemy and what must be done to prevail over it, taking the necessary decisions with requisite speed unfettered by the kinds of parliamentary deliberation and legal restraint that may fatally weaken its capacity to perform this essential task. 'Sovereign', as Schmitt infamously put it, 'is he who decides on the exception' (1922/1985: 5) – by which he meant both when a situation is exceptional and what measures the exception requires.

What, though – for radical state sceptics working in the field of security – is the attraction of these authoritarian propositions? The answer, in short, is that Schmitt troublingly brings to the fore both the deep antagonisms that constitute political life and the role of extra-legal violence in constituting democratic polities that aim to be free of such violence – matters which liberal political thought is alleged to have effaced, or at least sought to (Mouffe 1999). In particular, Schmitt highlights the unlimited, violent decisionism that remains concealed during moments of political tranquility only to be unmasked when the state enacts its sovereignty by declaring an exception and exercising its will accordingly (Agamben 1998; see, also, Derrida 1992; Taussig 1997; R. B. J. Walker 2004).

The second – closely related – claim is that 'security' provides the discursive site though which claims to exceptionalism are mobilized and its practices enacted. As the 'principle of formation' of modern political order, security 'saturates the language of modern politics. Our political vocabularies reek of it and our political imagination is confined by it' (Dillon 1996: 12). It does so, moreover, in ways that tie it intimately and with deleterious effect to the state. By invoking security, the state calls forth an anti-political and anti-pluralist political practice wherein the problem at hand (be it terrorism, or drugs, or migration, or . . .) is declared to involve imperatives instead of trade-offs and political choices, to call for authoritative decision rather than democratic deliberation (or, in Schmitt's view, indecision), and to warrant the restriction of basic liberties as the price to be paid for the maintenance of public security. These practices are, moreover, fuelled by security's signification of an infinite and ever-disappearing horizon of possibility – its rhetorical self-presentation as a condition beyond our grasp that appears endlessly to require more 'security measures'. Security, in short, is the conduit through which a particular form of partisanship proceeds – one in which the state takes such extra-legal measures as it deems necessary to defend its interests and integrity. It is the paradigm of Leviathan unbound.

Understood thus, the state of exception plainly antedates 9/11 and the 'war on terror' that is being prosecuted in response to it. Indeed, this variant of state scepticism would identify exceptionalism in many of the quotidian acts of partisan states examined thus far. A consideration of the 'securitizing' practices that constitute this 'war' nonetheless help to further our understanding of this radical variant of state and security scepticism. Some care is needed here, however. There is a degree of overlap between the claims of this radical anti-statism and the concerns expressed by liberal writers about the liberty-eroding effects of the present security constellation – concerns that we in large measure share. The liberal worry prompts a discourse about the vexed but vital task of tackling terrorism democratically (e.g. Ackerman 2004; Golove and Holmes 2004; Ignatieff 2004; Rorty 2004). By contrast, the leftist critique of the 'war on terror' inspired by Benjamin and Schmitt insists that it reveals certain endemic features of sovereign violence in 'democratic' societies, such that 'in our age, the state of exception comes more and more to the foreground as the fundamental political structure and ultimately begins to become the rule' (Agamben 1998: 20; see also Agamben 2004b: 609; R. B. J. Walker 2004). There is no question here of combating terror democratically or, more generally, of civilizing security, as we shall see. Four elements of the current security landscape help to illuminate this particular state-sceptical disposition.

First, there is the advent of the USA as a self-appointed global hegemon in a unipolar world, a state that defines and pursues its own security interests either unilaterally, or with whatever 'coalitions of the willing' it is able strategically to assemble (Buzan 2004). The USA today operates in ways that bypass multilateral institutions or resort to them instrumentally (N. Walker 2006a; forthcoming a), treat international law as but one policy consideration among many, and refuse to be hidebound by constraints upon its freedom to act (such as the International Criminal Court, which the US government has refused to ratify on the grounds that it would gift to its enemies an opportunity for persecution of its 'good faith' warriors which they would ruthlessly exploit). The USA, of course, has throughout the period since 1945 engaged in – mainly covert – acts of 'regime change' and often sought to depict itself as 'the world's policeman'. But in the aftermath of 9/11, in the face of new and diffuse enemies, it has claimed the right to strike pre-emptively and unilaterally, not merely to defend its security interests, but – in the project for the new century proposed by the neo-conservative hawks in Washington – to spread liberal freedom around the globe (The White House 2002). In each case, the exercise of sovereign will is to be fettered not by any countervailing civilizing power, but only 'by its own sense of restraint' (Kagan 2004: 70). The result, critics allege, is the creation of a new imperial power offering the hand of protection to those it

deems friends in return for supine obedience, while intervening by force
of arms if necessary to reorder states which are, or which harbour or
otherwise assist, its enemies – states whose sovereignty has by the fact
of US power been rendered contingent.[2]

But what holds on the international stage also has parallels at home.
We have witnessed, secondly, in the name of protecting democracies
against terrorism, a strengthening of the executive and an empowering
of security institutions. New powers, bigger budgets and a much freer
hand of discretion have been granted to police and intelligence agencies – all in the name of enabling the kinds of lightly fettered, rapid-
fire, unilateral executive action deemed necessary to pursue and defeat
enemies at times of crisis (Scheuerman 2002). Prominent among these
measures are the following: (i) the extended powers of surveillance and
data-gathering granted by the USA PATRIOT Act 2001 and the
cognate provisions found in the Canadian Anti-Terrorism Act 2001
and the British Anti-Terrorism, Crime and Security Act 2001 and
Prevention of Terrorism Act 2005 – measures that have parallels in a
wide range of jurisdictions around the world (see, e.g., Roach 2001;
Lyon 2003: ch. 2); (ii) the formation of the new greatly empowered
Department of Homeland Security in the USA; and (iii) the enabling of
executive detention and military tribunals in the USA and the preventative detention without trial of terrorist suspects in the UK. The
former has suspended habeas corpus and due process rights for some
20 million non-citizens resident in the USA (Arato 2002: 458–9), while
the latter has required the British government to derogate from its
responsibilities under the European Convention on Human Rights.

None of this, moreover, is random or even-handed in its targets and
effects. While the daily life of the majority of citizens remains in large

---

[2] There is an expanding cottage industry on the question of American Empire
which presses this claim in a variety of registers. For radicals of the sort under
discussion here, American imperialism entails a new mode of planetary oppres-
sion and tutelage pursued in the name of protecting US economic interests and
disseminating neo-liberal doxa (Hardt and Negri 2000; Harvey 2003). For other
progressives, it stands as a dangerous temptation of America's hegemonic power
in the world (Barber 2003), or as an incoherent and fatal overreach of military
power (Mann 2003). There are, by contrast, some liberals and conservatives
who view US imperial rule – more or less enthusiastically – as an indispensable
ordering mechanism within the contemporary international landscape – the
attendant worry here being that the USA lacks the necessary domestic commitment to the long haul (see Ignatieff 2003; Ferguson 2004). For more detailed discussion, see chapter 9.

measure unaffected, surveillance is intensified against members of the very minority groups that partisan states have long since directed police attention towards. In a context where 'external threat' and 'internal contaminant' have become blurred (Newman 2004: 580), this has been particularly marked in respect of both resident Muslim populations and refugees/asylum seekers. Nor are these measures without their symbolic resonance and sociocultural spill-over, whether in terms of increasing lay enmity (and violence) towards minority groups, eroding the support of fearful citizens for democratic rights and freedoms deemed to protect 'terrorists' and imperil public safety, or in subtle but telling militarizations of mundane culture (as evident in sales of the civilian version of the US army vehicle, 'the Hummer').[3]

In these respects, the leftist state sceptic argues, we have witnessed a dangerous reassertion and extension of state power – one that has amounted in effect to a 'war on freedom and democracy' (Bunyan 2002). But the 'war on terror' has, thirdly, given a boost to new or intensified forms of security cooperation between states and to the micropower of transnational networks of policing and security professionals. The most telling developments here have occurred within the European Union (EU). In respect of the former, one can point specifically to the 'fast-tracking' – post 9/11 – of the European Arrest Warrant and the common definition of terrorism and, more generally, to an escalating frenzy of intergovernmental security activity under the rubric of the 'Area of Freedom, Justice and Security' – activity that has, among other things, deepened the tendency to posit areas of public policy such as migration/asylum as security problems (den Boer and Monar 2002; Gilmore 2002; N. Walker 2004; Bigo and Guild 2005; Huysmans 2006). In terms of the latter, one can highlight enhanced levels of police and judicial cooperation within Europe and intelligence sharing with the USA, a greater role for Europol in combating terrorism, and the empowerment of opaque professional networks such as the Task Force of European Police Chiefs and the now regular meetings of intelligence

---

[3] It is far from insignificant in this context that the USA PATRIOT Act is an acronym, standing for 'Uniting and Strengthening America by Providing Appropriate Tools Required to Intercept and Obstruct Terrorism'. This legislation extends a recent trend in the USA to name criminal legislation after high-profile victims, the most notable instance being the anti-paedophile statute 'Megan's Law' (Simon 2001). In the present case, of course, the named recipient is a collective victim, the act a sign of its determination to 'fight back'.

heads. To this one may add the formation of a standing EU civil (i.e. police) peacekeeping force with a mission to deploy 'humanizing' force in conflict zones around the world – notably thus far in the Balkans (Caygill 2001).

The charges in respect of each of these developments run broadly in the same direction: that the 'war on terror' has reinforced an already existing trend to privilege 'internal security' over 'freedom' and 'justice' in the development of the EU, such that it risks transmogrifying into an 'integrated law enforcement zone' (den Boer and Monar 2002: 27) targeting suspect populations in ways inimical to social justice and human rights; that it has buttressed and empowered what was already emerging as a bureaucratic transnational security elite of officials and security professionals – an elite that exercises micropower in opaque, informal settings at some remove from any kind of effective legal oversight and public scrutiny (Hayes 2002). A further charge is that the EU – like the USA – has developed the capacity and will to bring its moral order to peoples elsewhere in the world in a way that deploys violence in the service of morality and 'leads to the gradual abandonment of the territorial principle of modern statehood' (Douzinas 2003: 177).

This brings us, fourthly, to the blurring of certain key distinctions that once structured the field of security – a trend that pre-dates the 'war on terror' but which has been accelerated by it (Andreas and Price 2001). The first of these concerns internal and external security, policework and soldiering. Here one encounters a de-differentiation of once distinct worlds that have, since the end of the Cold War, been 'converging towards the same enemy' (Bigo 2000a: 173). External security agencies (notably, the army and intelligence services, but also customs and immigration officers) now seek out enemies at home and, in the case of the military, are called upon to secure domestic infrastructure – airports, bridges, utility installations – from attack. Soldiers, moreover, have since 9/11 found themselves engaged in manhunts for wanted criminals and conducting order-maintenance patrols of urban streets in Afghanistan and Iraq. The police, conversely, seek out 'internal' enemies – terrorists, organized criminals, drug traffickers – beyond the territorial borders of states (Nadelman 1993), while also finding themselves dispatched abroad on peacekeeping operations or to train indigenous police forces up to 'western' standards.

To this one must add – post 9/11 – a blurring of the related categories of war and crime (Feldman 2002; Huysmans 2004). The US government has since the attacks on the Twin Towers and the Pentagon been waging a self-styled 'war' against what it judges to be an unprecedented threat from international terrorism – and it is the circumstance of warfare that has justified the exceptional executive powers that states throughout the world have assumed. But this is no conventional war, perhaps not even a war at all. The 'enemy' is diffuse, unknown and composed principally of non-state actors. Its *modus operandi* is to commit criminal acts – however atrocious. Nor will it be clear when, if ever, the war has been won – something that raises the prospect of a more or less permanent assault on democracy and liberty. Yet, at the same time, the US government refuses consistently to apply the war metaphor (if metaphor it is), engaging instead in what Golove and Holmes (2004: 5) term strategic 'paradigm shopping' motivated by 'the desire to limit accountability and oversight'. This is most apparent in respect of the detainees held in the legal black hole of Camp Delta in Guantánamo Bay (Rose 2004). These are neither prisoners of war nor criminal suspects – both categories that afford a degree of due process and legal protection. Instead, they have been deemed 'enemy combatants' – a status beyond law whose consequence is that 'they are subject now only to raw power' (Agamben 2004b: 610). There can, for the radical state sceptic, be no more telling symbol of the new state of exception – a sovereign force exerting its will in a fashion that is simultaneously partisan and out of control.

These critical observations on the current security constellation impart some valuable warnings, some of which, as noted, are shared by liberal critics of the 'war on terror'. They suggest, first and foremost, that democratic societies risk spiralling into a vicious circle of terror–fear–repression whose all too likely consequence is the erosion, perhaps even demise, of democratic government and the rule of law (Rorty 2004). As political elites respond to acts of terror with 'security measures' that seek to assuage public insecurity (and anger) by further empowering police and military institutions, they do several things: not only do they direct the resources of the partisan state at already often unpopular and over-policed minority populations (both at home and abroad); they also institutionalize public anxiety in ways that make it difficult to envisage cultural conditions that will permit 'temporary' exceptional measures to be repealed, and leave themselves with little practical choice but to respond to the next terrorist attack with yet more – still tougher – 'security solutions'. As each 'ordering measure brings into being new ambiguities and ambivalences which call for further measures, the chase never ends' (Bauman and Tester 2001: 79; see, also, Dillon 1996: 127).

For liberals the practical task is to find ways of responding to terror (and the fear and loathing that it generates, or reinforces, or renews) in ways that break out of this insecurity-heightening, democracy-corroding spiral (see, for example, Ackerman 2004; Ignatieff 2004; Dyzenhaus and Hunt forthcoming). This too, more broadly, is the impulse that informs this book – one that holds that it is possible in this field to envisage and create virtuous circles that both civilize security and release the civilizing potential of security. The variant of state scepticism we have been concerned with here presses, however, a more disquieting claim – one that presents a serious critique of such possibilities. From this perspective there is no obvious route away from a world in which exceptionalism has become what Agamben (2004a: 2 and *passim*) calls 'the dominant paradigm of government in contemporary politics' – and certainly not one which travels under the banner of security. We are faced with what looks set to become an unceasing war against terror in which partisan, exceptional states name and chase new enemies, fortify borders as they violate them, suspend law in the name of law, and undermine democracy in an effort to save it. How, in such a world, the leftist state sceptic asks, can we speak meaningfully about, let alone begin to construct, a socially coherent project of collective security?

Against security?

The strands of radical thought outlined in this chapter offer a cogent critique of the state and its securitizing practices. It is a critique that appears able to capture important aspects of a historical record that has seen states time and again, in both authoritarian and democratic contexts, allocate the benefits and burdens of policing in ways that systematically protect the security interests of powerful constituencies at the expense of those of the poor and dispossessed. It supplies, in addition, a cogent account of the dangers of placing security at the ideological heart of government, of the capacity of security politics to colonize public policy and pervade social life in ways that threaten democratic values and sustain fear-laden, other-disregarding forms of political subjectivity and collective identity. In these respects, this variant of state scepticism offers a critique of the operation and effects of state power that in many significant respects we share (N. Walker 2000; Loader 2002). But it also poses what are undoubtedly some profound challenges to the position we wish here to construct and defend. If we are to make a persuasive case for both the good of security, and the indispensability of the state to the production of that good, then we need to find a means of rising to them.

These objections then are far from trivial, and we have not devoted this chapter to them simply in order to knock them down. But they nonetheless arise from a standpoint that is not itself without shortcomings, as we hope to show in meeting them. As a prelude to the more sustained effort along these lines that we offer in part II, let us consider briefly what these shortcomings are. For analytic purposes, they may usefully be put into three groups.

This radical variant of state scepticism tends, first of all, to underplay the openness of political systems and the theoretical and political prospects that this affords. It displays, in particular, a structural fatalism that overlooks the overlap between the production of specific and general order, such that disadvantaged groups and communities have a considerable stake not only in controlling state power, but also in using public resources (including policing resources) as a means of generating more secure forms of economic and social existence. It also remains insufficiently attentive to how the mix between general and specific order (the extent, in other words, to which policing is shaped by common as well as factional interests) is conditioned by political struggle and the varieties of institutional settlement to which this gives rise, thereby varying over time and between polities. Much the same point, moreover, can be directed at the radical critique of the violence that underpins liberal political orders that aim to be free of such violence. One finds here a quite proper insistence on the troubling conundrum that democratic polities ultimately depend upon coercion to enforce collective decisions and protect democratic institutions. But this point is hammered home in terms that are overly sweeping and reductionist – often, as in the writings of Agamben (2004a), as a philosophical claim that invites but resists sociological scrutiny. If 'there is always a violence at the heart of every form of political and legal authority' (Newman 2004: 575), upon what grounds can we distinguish between, or develop a critique of, the security-seeking practices of particular states – and why would we bother?

Radical anti-statism evinces, secondly, a preference for social and political criticism over social and political reconstruction. It favours a politics that privileges the monitoring, exposure and critique of the systematic biases of state power (as, for instance, in the indefatigable efforts of the British-based NGO Statewatch), one that implicitly or expressly holds that 'security' is so stained by its uncivil association with the (military and police) state that the only available radical strategy is to destabilize the term itself, while contesting the practices that are enacted under its name (Dalby 1997: 6; see, also, Dillon 1996: ch. 1). There can, from this vantage point, be no progressive democratic politics aimed at civilizing security. Rather, one is left with a politics of critique, and a failure of political imagination, that leaves radically underspecified the feasible or desirable alternatives to current institutional configurations and practices, or else merely gestures towards the possibility of transcendent forms of non-state communal ordering – as in George Rikagos's (2002: 150) claim that 'the only real alternatives to current policing practices are pre-capitalist, non-commodified security arrangements'.

Finally, one finds what we think of as a one-sided appraisal of the sources of inequality and insecurity in the world today. This leftist anti-statist sensibility tends, in the ways we have demonstrated, towards an account of social injustice that views it as the product of the state's malign and coercive interventions rather than of its impotence and neglect. Here one finds a curious parallel with the neo-liberalism considered in the last chapter – the state remains the problem. But one also encounters a critique of security politics that views it as tied to the production of authoritarian government – as if security is in some essential fashion inimical to democracy and human rights. Here the radical critic begins to inhabit similar ground to that occupied by what we characterized in chapter 1 as the 'security lobby'. They assess the landscape very differently and commit to diametrically opposed political purposes. But they cling commonly and tenaciously to the belief that security stands opposed to liberty.

Our aim, in part II, is to move beyond these positions and oppositions: first, by retrieving the idea of security as a public good that is axiomatic both to the production of other goods (most directly, liberty) and to the constitution of democratic political communities; second, by arguing that the production of this good demands not the wholesale critique and transcendence of state forms, but more robust regulatory interventions by democratized state institutions. We must first, however, factor into our positive case two further critiques of the state, starting with the claim that it is a *cultural* monolith.

4 | *The state as cultural monolith*

I N the previous chapter we saw how the state through its policing and security provision can be a powerful mechanism for the pursuit of special interests. The concern was with how certain general features of the security provision function of states are conducive to the articulation, consolidation and reinforcement of various asymmetries of power and forms of prejudice. In the present chapter we want to consider a complementary critique – one that is implicit in much scepticism about state policing but which finds less explicit theoretical expression than the other variants of scepticism considered in part I. This critique is concerned not with the state as machinery for the reinforcement of inequality and the amplification of bias generated elsewhere in the social and economic domain, but rather with the state as a site of cultural production in its own right, capable of generating meanings and of promoting orthodoxies of a certain type. Of course, the distinction between the state as material enforcer and as cultural initiator is sometimes artificial and never clear-cut. Frequently, as we will see, the state's ideological involvement in mobilizing or sustaining certain beliefs and sensibilities is in close synergy with its repressive function. To borrow another phrase from the old Marxist lexicon – the autonomy of the state from basic socio-economic forces and relations is only ever relative. Just as, in the argument of the last chapter, the forms of domination originating beyond the state will frequently rely upon the state and its security apparatus for their entrenchment or stabilization, so too the forms of meaning generated by the state and its security apparatus always owe something to broader social and economic pressures.

Nevertheless, the cultural critique of state policing is far more than a mere echo of the material critique. Rather, it supplies potent additional ammunition to the sceptic of state policing, threatening to check the counter-positions which we tentatively outlined at the end of the last chapter. To the criticism that the partisanship thesis is too fatalistic about the role of the state and too pessimistic about its emancipatory potential, the adherent of the cultural critique may deliver a considerable riposte. This begins by revisiting and refining and qualifying the distinction drawn by Marenin (1982) between general order and special order. For the core of the claim that the cultural work of the state in the domain of security has its own partial consequences lies in a refusal to accept that, unlike the specific order of those powerful public and private constituencies who succeed in manoeuvring the state in defence of their special interests, the generation and maintenance of the general order of everyday social tranquillity is somehow neutral between different security concerns or worldviews. From this broader critical perspective, there is *no* area of security work uncontaminated by some kind of bias. There is, rather, and however it may be presented, something *irreducibly* particular about the defence of general order (just as, conversely, given the cross-cultural familiarity of certain types of class, gender, ethnic or public bureaucratic bias, there is something general and recurrent about the defence of specific order). And in the irreducible particularity of even its broadest role we must understand state policing as the facilitator and defender of a kind of cultural orthodoxy which continues to privilege some ways of viewing and acting in the world over others. In the face of this additional set of objections, the argument of the proponent of state policing that the supposedly universal benefits of its quotidian security practices outweigh the disadvantages of occasional and episodic resort to the defence of specific interests threatens to be stillborn.

What does it mean to suggest that the cultural import of state security and policing, even when concerned with general order, is irreducibly particular? Just because, as already noted, this dimension of scepticism about state policing has been less explicitly theorized than the others, and tends instead to rest upon certain standing general assumptions about the culpability of the state, or upon the message of a wider body of work on the link between statehood and cultural monism, then, much more so than in the case of these other dimensions of scepticism, *we have to construct for ourselves* the best version of the cultural case for scepticism as it applies to the policing sector. Mindful of this, we assemble our argument in distinct stages. First, the basic conceptual building-blocks from which a more explicit theoretical argument might be constructed will be put in place. On that basis, the case will be made that the cultural particularity of the policing of general order is indeed irreducible and unavoidable, but that, crucially, just for that reason this characteristic must also be seen as logically prior to, and independent of, the state form of policing. Only subsequently will the way in which this cultural particularity tends to manifest itself in state settings be fleshed out and the question of the possibility of the state acting otherwise raised.

The particularity of police culture

The conceptual building-blocks take the form of a number of structural features or coordinates of the general policing role which shape the ways in which the police are implicated in the production of social meaning. These are the *singularity* of the police function, the tendency towards *uniformity* in the pursuit of that function, its highly *permissive* character, its *time-bound* quality and its *societal locatedness*. Let us examine these five features in turn, and suggest how their conjunction helps account for the tendency towards a monolithic cultural disposition.

First, there is the singularity of the policing function and its security objective. In an age when both the normalizing discourse of police management science and the self-presentational rhetoric of police professionals more and more emphasize the sheer diversity of police tasks, the versatility required to perform them, and the comparability and continuity of many if not all of them with other non-police tasks, this might seem counter-intuitive – think here of the abiding popularity of such disaggregating labels as policing by objectives and problem-oriented policing (Butler 1984; Goldstein 1990; McLaughlin and Murji 1997, 2001). Yet if we stand back from the 'profane' detail (Reiner 1995), it is arguable that policing remains a singular activity in two important and connected senses – one internal, the other external. Internally, it is striking the extent to which the many and various tasks of the police, even after they are bundled into very broad and loose functional categories, are further reducible to a unitary purpose, and indeed are treated in the final analysis as no more than means to the achievement of that overall purpose. Crime prevention, crime detection, the preservation of life and property, the prevention of public disorder, the regulation of traffic, and the myriad forms of assistance of other regulatory functions of the state in which the police are involved: this list is a typical catalogue of the mandate of modern policing, but all elements within the catalogue can without undue strain be gathered under the holistic umbrella of the generation and maintenance of those conditions of general order under which the citizenry are most likely both to be and to feel secure (Silver 1967; Bittner 1990; Reiner 2000: ch. 4). So much so, indeed, that while in the public politics of policing the question of the proper balance and trade-off between and within diverse police functions is often fraught with controversy, the idea that these functions be assessed in terms of their contribution to the overall purpose or meta-function of providing security tends to remain taken for granted.

This internal idea of unity – of holistic purpose – is linked to the second and externally directed sense in which policing can be viewed as a singular activity. The point can be developed in both a weak sense and a strong sense. In a weak sense, just as many particular policing functions are best viewed as instrumental to the general purpose of security provision, so too the security purpose itself is largely justified in its own terms, and *not* as a means to some even broader function or higher purpose. That is not to say that the general achievement of security *cannot* be viewed and treated in instrumental terms, but just that, for the most part, unlike some key areas of government activity, it is simply not viewed and treated in such terms, or at least not in a narrow sense.[1] Rather, to recall our discussion of the roots of the modern political order in chapter 2, security should be understood as one of the most basic, defining functions of the polity. And insofar as it can be viewed as linked to other major social functions, as we shall see in chapter 6, this is in a broad foundational sense rather than in a narrow instrumental sense – as a *sine qua non* of the achievement of a broad menu of other social goods rather than as something whose value is exhausted in the achievement of any particular such good. In this, however, perhaps security is not so unusual. Other areas of state activity such as health provision or education are also largely self-justifying, and if linked to other purposes are likewise viewed as broad foundations rather than narrow ladders.

Where security stands apart from other broad areas of public policy, and asserts itself more forcefully, is in its tendency in the name of urgency and indispensability, and so peremptory non-negotiability of

---

[1] Compare security provision in this respect with tax collection, whose purpose is purely instrumental to the achievement of other purposes.

its own imperatives, to evacuate other considerations from its functional domain (Wæver 1996). Not only is it the case that security is not merely instrumental to and so not parasitic upon any other distinct purpose, but, as suggested in our preliminary review of the critical security studies literature in the previous chapter, it tends to yoke the discourse of public policy to its own uncompromising purpose. The singularity of security, then, inheres not only in its (internal) unity of function but also in its (external) tendency to exclusivity. As we shall see, this has profound consequences for the ideological context in which security tends to be pursued.

One key aspect of this may be illuminated by tracing the close connection between the idea of a single all-encompassing meta-function of security and a second structural feature of the general policing role. This is the presumption that policing should be administered equally and uniformly – without discrimination between different contributors or beneficiaries. Most immediately, this appears to be a matter of organizational efficiency and of the necessarily diffuse effects of the production of some security 'goods'. General order is something that in any particular context has an indeterminate set of contributors and/or beneficiaries – whether this is the acceptable protocols of public behaviour at a football match, a public march, or a city-centre shopping mall, or the proper balance between preventative intervention and free circulation in a traffic network or in an airport security system, or the call-answering priority protocols of a fast-response mobile patrol unit, or the local prevention and reassurance dividend of a particular level of foot patrol, or the population range made more secure by the arrest of a murderer or the defusing of a terrorist bomb. It is thus simply often highly impractical for the police to act other than in accordance with broad and non-discriminating procedures or to other than non-discriminating effect. As with all contexts of mass and repetitive organizational performance, some degree of rule-following becomes a basic imperative of bureaucratic efficiency and operational coordination, and some equality of effect is inevitable given the non-assignable quality of many security benefits.

Logistics apart, however, there are also strong reputational reasons why the police either refrain from overt practices of discrimination in contexts where the operations of general order are on open public display or relatively easily discovered, or, in the frequent circumstances where public exposure is less likely, at least maintain a rhetoric of neutrality. In turn, these dramaturgical considerations rest upon a deeper and more fundamental platform of normative political theory, one that, significantly, reinforces the pressure towards uniformity not only *within* particular general order contexts but also *between* different such contexts. This strand of political theory, and the social imaginary with which it is associated, recalls our discussion in chapter 2 of the founding justificatory promise of the modern state, and in particular *the individuation and hence equalization* of the standard justification of political rule under conditions of political modernity. If each citizen is accorded formal equality *ab initio* then the terms of the hypothetical social contract should be the same for all – and never more so than as regards the foundational and singular contractual virtue of security. It follows that the conclusion of that social contract should not discriminate between individuals or classes of individual either as regards the value to be attributed to their security or as regards the basis on which their interests may be interfered with – including coercive interference with their own security interests – in order to protect the security of others. It also follows that, in order to ensure such uniformity or equality of treatment, the liberal state should have a monopolistic or, at any rate, pre-eminent role in the provision of security – there should be only one standard social contract with one state in the case of each territorial population. Of course, the most vigorous manifestation of these promises lies in the idea of formal equality before the law itself – the idea that the law should as a general presumption, and in the absence of special justification, be blind to differences between different categories of subjects in its specification of the terms and conditions of security (D. Dixon 1997; N. Walker 2000: ch. 2). Yet for the rule of law to achieve practical vindication it requires to be underpinned by an ethic of executive endorsement and bureaucratic fealty, of uniform – and disinterested *because* uniform – application of the legal mandate on the part of the officials of the polity, and in particular those officials charged with the singular function of security maintenance (Bittner 1983; Grimshaw and Jefferson 1987).

At root, then, the promise of uniformity can be seen as the ideological flipside of the claim to singularity. So much is staked on the idea of general order as encapsulating the police mission and as the trump of non-security considerations precisely because it is so central to the very justification of modern political community and the purpose of the social contract. Accordingly, the promise that this enormous power will be wielded *sine ira et studio* typically becomes axiomatic to its social acceptability.

That notion of uniformity, however, stands alongside and in some tension with a third structural feature of the general policing role: namely, the extent to which the police are nevertheless permitted, and indeed required, actively to shape their general role. For while there may be strong logistical, prudential and moral reasons for uniformity in the pursuit of the singular virtue of general order, the police also retain a high level of discretion in the performance of their function (Jefferson and Grimshaw 1984; H. Cohen 1985; Klockars 1985), one that both challenges the very idea of a transcontextual or 'uniform' sense of uniformity and strongly influences the content of any sense of uniformity that does prevail.

The first point flows from the notoriously high level of latitude allowed to officers 'on the street', at the operational cutting edge of the police organization. Such practical discretion is only superficially about the open texture of legal language and the ample scope this allows for the discovery and creative interpretation of 'hard cases'. At a deeper level, it is attributable to certain inescapable practical exigencies of policework; to the fact that, once we discount the high-profile rituals of mass public order, much policing takes place in dispersed 'regions of low visibility' (van Maanen 1983: 377) and in contexts which may require uncorroborated decision-making. It has to do as well with the sheer diversity and unpredictability of the situations of disorder which police officers may be required to repair and the immediacy with which such repairs may be required. In Egon Bittner's famous formulation, 'the policeman, and the policeman alone, is equipped, entitled, and required to deal with every exigency in which force may have to be used to meet it' (1990: 248). The police officer, therefore, is licensed to paint on a wide canvas, with bold and urgent brush-strokes. Even if it does not exclude rule- or recipe-based solutions entirely, this combination of variety and immediacy implies that, certainly at the level of the detailed encounter, any such solutions will be less than fully adequate to the task. In other words, the idea of a universal template from which a uniform practice of general order can be generated is already stretched thin by the very operational logic of day-to-day policework.

At the level of general policy, too, the legal framework is a permissive one. The idea of the police as servants of the law, and as keepers of the law's liberal promise, can at best be only a partial guide to the meaning of general order. Simple allegiance to the law may, subject to the caveats suggested above and within the bounds of common inter-pretation of often vague textual formulations, encourage an even-handed approach to individual cases once addressed by the police. But in a context of scarce resources and unavoidable choices as to the pri-orities to set both within and between discrete policing tasks, the legal text, however plain its meaning in addressing particular behaviours and decoding particular encounters, cannot provide criteria to decide which encounters should be sought and which cases should be identi-fied and treated *as* cases in the first instance.

Yet it has been observed of many western constitutional cultures that, despite the law's structural inability to provide a comprehensive directive to policing – to supply all the guidance the police officer (of whatever rank) needs in pursuit of general order – inflated claims to that effect continue to be made on its behalf (Jefferson and Grimshaw 1984). As already noted, the public image of the neutral uniformity of the police in pursuit of general order is a precious reputational prize, and so whatever can help anchor this belief, including the notion of the comprehensive authority of law, will remain rhetorically attractive. Paradoxically, however, by obscuring the problem of discretion, the idea of law's directive capacity tends only to exacerbate it. What this threatens, and often delivers, is a 'policy vacuum' (Goldsmith 1990: 96), where, under the cover of the supposed sovereignty of law, a con-ception of general order is allowed to flourish in which the cultural preferences and sensibilities of the police are required to fill the gap.

While uniformity, therefore, is a theme that is central to the legiti-macy of state policing in its pursuit of the singular objective of general order, it is also one that may be confounded by the obstinate reality of police discretion. The meaning of general order threatens to frac-ture into as many particulars as there are diverse contexts of police action, and to the extent that this may be resisted or mitigated it is only through the signifying or meaning-shaping interventions of the police themselves (Fielding 1984). What kinds of factors influence them in this cultural work, bearing in mind that it remains tied to the ideological discipline of a uniform mode of self-presentation? It is here that the last two structural features of the police pursuit of general order – its time-bound and societally specific quality – assume importance. And crucially, as we shall see, as they flow from certain irreducible features of policing as a distinctly or particularly *located* practice, it is these structural features that provide the fundamental explanatory key to the irreducible particularity of their cultivation of the idea of general order.

By asserting that the policing of general order is time-bound, we seek to convey two meanings and messages that are apparently in tension, but, on deeper reflection, can be seen as mutually supportive. The first is that the policing of general order is a backward-looking and conservative activity – one bound to the past. The second is that the policing of general order is a temporally contingent activity – tied to and shaped by the circumstances of a particular time.

The first of these characteristics – the conservative quality of mainstream policing – has been widely remarked upon (Reiner 2000: ch. 3). Often the focus of this kind of analysis is the substantive political allegiance of police officers – whether or not, and the extent to which, they favour parties and programmes of public policy and morality associated with the political right (Reiner 1980). While the fact that police are often drawn from working-class backgrounds may suggest a degree of sympathy – if not solidarity – with the relatively disadvantaged, a stronger and countervailing set of socializing factors is provided by the self-selection of those who seek to join the police as well as by the patterns of interaction involved in everyday policework. As noted in the last chapter, the routine clients of the police are typically the economically dispossessed and the culturally marginalized. This, together with the fact that in their public order and state security role the police are often set in opposition to the organized and disorganized forces of the left, tends to encourage or confirm police officers in a political worldview that looks sceptically both on the relationship between socio-economic deprivation and crime and on political resistance.

Rather than focusing on the question of who makes or can be 'made into' a good police officer, another and complementary type of research into police conservatism – one that allows us to begin to forge the connection between the two distinct senses of policing as a time-bound activity – has at its centre of gravity the structural question of what is generic to general order. Here, the emphasis is upon how the police, in Richard Ericson's (1982) term, are inevitably '*reproducers* of order' (emphasis added), and how it follows that 'their sense of order [is] . . . that of the *status quo*' (1982: 7). Their function is to *restore* order where it has broken down, whether because the normal authoritative practice which guarantees the security of social relations has failed, or because absent the normal authoritative *practitioner* – be it ambulance or fire service, teacher, social worker or priest – a 'stand in' is required (H. Cohen 1985: 37). Moreover, it is not just the reactive quality of much policework and the ensuing episodic, symptom-treating shallowness of the typical police intervention that encourages the occupational prejudice that how things ought to be should be closely modelled on how they have been until now. Preference for restoration over innovation is also one further consequence of the self-presentational imperative of uniform neutrality. An entity whose principal charge is simply to mend the tears in the existing fabric of security, rather than to treat the general quality of that fabric, will typically seek to make an ideological virtue out of that occupational necessity. It is likely to remain publicly indifferent to those deep causes of (in)security over which it has little leverage and less mandate, including the asymmetries of power and resources between different groups, and in so doing to style itself as the mere editor rather than the author of public policy.

Yet this very detachment from the underlying causes of disorder can also reinforce the conviction with which a very particular version of general order is pursued. On the one hand, in seeking to restore the existing order regardless of its social foundations, police officers also inevitably act so as to preserve these foundations. On the other hand, however, and paradoxically, a sense of general order that is unflinchingly and unreflectively tied to the *status quo* also tends towards its own reification. For a mechanical fidelity to the current security settlement implies either simple disregard for its underlying terms or the assumption that these terms are natural and unassailable – in either case encouraging an additional perception of general order as a timeless aspiration and imperative. It is here, then, that we can see the strength of the connection between the perennial and the quotidian – between the sense of being bound to the 'eternal' past and being bound to the present. Just because of the taken-for-granted, relentless priority of the everyday imperative of preserving the peace, it may be presented and self-understood by police officers to be about prevailing in an unending and essentially unchanging struggle. The idea, prevalent in many police cultures, of policing as a 'thin blue line' (Reiner 2000: 89), on whose resilience the maintenance of social order depends, gains resonance and derives its motivational power from the way in which today's problems, in being decontextualized and divorced from their roots, may be seen as but the continuation and latest manifestation of an eternal narrative of order and chaos. In a nutshell, the temporal variation of the patterns and priorities of mainstream policework tends to be masked by deep cultural understandings of general order as both a conservative virtue and a timeless preoccupation; yet this very masking supplies much of the motivational and legitimating background that makes such contextual adaptability possible.

If one way of grounding the particularity of general order is temporal, the other is spatial, and this brings us, finally, to the societally specific quality of policing. General order is never universal order. It always pertains to a specific territorial social order – an appeal to a particular place as well as to a particular time. And like the temporal appeal, its persuasiveness lies in its combination of objectification and contextual fit. Just as the appeal to the *status quo ante* apparently places the policing mission beyond the prejudice of the police themselves and locates it in the 'timeless' demands of the present, so the appeal to the needs and aspirations of a particular society holds a similar objectifying promise. Likewise with the locationally sensitive content of the objectified standard. Just as the appeal to a particular path-dependent construction of general order situates and domesticates the police task in historical terms, the appeal to a particular society and territory situates and domesticates it in geographical terms.

The allure of the 'here', then, is just as strong as the allure of the 'now' in the 'common sense' through which the preservation of general order is constructed. This is seen perhaps most spectacularly in the resilient attractiveness of 'community policing' ever since it became a designer label in the 1970s – one which has seen it marketed in many contexts beyond its Anglo-American origins (Brogden and Nijhar 2005; Ellison forthcoming). There is a larger story to be told about the success of community policing discourse, to which we will have cause to return, but its elemental attraction as a discourse about territory and about the social bonds associated with territory should not be underestimated. Indeed, if we look a little closer, we see that police talk is suffused with the language of place and place-centred social attachments – so much so that we often barely notice. From Neighbourhood Cops and Watches to local beat officers, from Apache Territory to 'skid row' (Bittner 1967), from Area Patrol to the European Union's 'Area of Freedom, Justice and Security', we find metaphors of spatial location – secure and insecure – central to characterizations of general policework. And between the local and the supranational, of course, lies another key site of policing, the nation state. It is to this key site that we now return.

The cultural partiality of state policing

The very idea of general order, then, can only be realized in a culturally partial manner. The singular and politically foundational quality of the core police mandate, the enormous power and responsibility implicit in the project of order maintenance, means that the stakes of social legitimacy for police organizations are set very high. One of the key ways in which the police seek to address this challenge is through the legal and organizational discipline of uniform neutrality. Yet the various and multitiered features of police discretion entail that a juridical model of compliance is never enough. In addition, and reflecting the fact that police practice is always a located practice (even if occupational self-understandings and self-presentations may often suggest otherwise), the police will situate their general role in the contingencies of time and place. In other words, they seek – and indeed have no option but to seek a contextually appropriate, and hence partial, sense of general order.

The relationship between these basic coordinates or characteristics of general order policing and the state form is a complex one. On the one hand, as already noted, if general order is always and necessarily coloured by its spatio-temporal particularity, then the state form cannot in principle be indispensable to such particularity. We must maintain instead that such particularity, just because it is a necessary feature of general order, could have emerged and could develop otherwise. On the other hand, as state-sponsored policing has been the dominant form of policing in the modern age, and as the concentration and specialization of resources on policing in the modern age are unprecedented, the irreducible particularity of general order and the cultural bias associated with this concentration and specialization have undoubtedly found their most powerful and eloquent articulation in the state context. That connection, moreover, is much more than circumstantial – it is not simply a case of the species 'state' being one indistinct or unremarkable carrier of the paradoxes and tensions of security associated with the genus 'polity'. Rather, we must see the state form, if not as inevitable and indispensable, as nevertheless the constitutive and the sufficient, or – in Aristotelian terms – the 'efficient', cause of the development of particular conceptions and manifestations of general order. Indeed, this is true in a double sense. For as we observed in chapter 2, we must understand the modern state both as decisively conducive to the development or maturing of a new social imaginary which stressed individuality and formal equality within a separate public or political realm, and as distinctively responsive to the new problems of general order and political rule associated with the maintenance of that new realm. The contemporary state, in short, is deeply implicated in both the problems and solutions of general order, and in the contribution of the police to these problems and solutions. If we examine this a little more closely, we can discern three cumulatively significant links between the particularity of the state and the particularity of the preservation of general order through policing. These are in turn structural, instrumental and symbolic.

In structural terms, we can see a deep homology between the situation – or rather the 'situatedness' – of the state, on the one hand, and of the maintenance of general order, on the other. Any political community will have its own distinctive spatio-temporal situation, but the form that this takes in the context of the state and the 'system of states' (Falk 1995) more broadly suggests a strikingly close fit with the basic coordinates of general order. For just as the so-called Westphalian framework of sovereign states 'locates' and articulates political community within a configuration of territorially discrete sovereigns, so too the policing of general order, with its emphasis upon singularity or coherence of function and uniformity of standards, and upon the monopoly power or pre-eminent authority required to achieve such singularity and uniformity, presupposes a mutually exclusive demarcation of the domains within which its various particular writs run. In both cases then – the state and the general policing function – a premium is placed on the construction of distinctive communities defined in terms of the two boundary coordinates of space and time.

If we continue for a moment longer to bracket the question of the specific (instrumental and symbolic) connection between state and general order, and instead pursue the general idea of their being homologous structures, we can already glimpse the basic outline of the cultural monolith thesis. For there is a considerable literature, much of which is hardly concerned with the policing function of the state, which attests to a strong causal connection between the nation state's need to provide an authoritative political space for a particular community at a particular time with a particular history, on the one hand, and its tendency to create and sustain what Jim Tully (1995: ch. 3) calls an 'empire of uniformity', on the other (see, e.g., Vincent 2002). As Tully indicates, nationalism is by no means the only code through which the unitary tendency of the state operates, yet the theme of one nation, one culture, one people is a decidedly powerful one. In particular, the emphasis on the role of the state as a mediator of belonging in ways that bring to the fore the affective dimensions of social and political life plays strongly on the idea of common nationhood – an active identity forged through some combination of common history, myth of origin, language, religion, territory, political bond or other sources of attachment and belonging. Often this argument is pursued in a critical spirit, indicating that the nation state tends to foster forms of 'imagined community' (B. Anderson 1991) that are unitary and homogenous, that rest on an unreflexive conception of political membership, and which 'admit only one – although largely abstract – identity, in relation to which struggles among all other identities are expected to take their proper place' (R. B. J. Walker 1997: 73).

And even where nationalist ideology is less prevalent and not viewed as hegemonic, those structural features of the state which flow from its authority-in-the-last-instance can still encourage cultural imperialism. For Pierre Bourdieu, for example, the state is the point of intersection of enormous symbolic and instrumental power, the place where both meaning and interests are authoritatively if always provisionally arbitrated. It is the site where, in series of meta-struggles over the very basis of political power, the mutually dependent questions of the 'the dominant principle of domination' and 'the legitimate principle of legitimation' are contested, negotiated and resolved, with the relatively open rules of contestation by no means compromising the unitary logic of resolution (Bourdieu 1996: 376). Moreover, the modern state's title to cultural domination can be assumed and exercised in a subtle rather than a strident manner; managed at a distance rather than hands-on; administered through the 'conduct of conduct' (Foucault 1978) rather than through primary regulation; elaborated in a thousand micro-edicts rather than in a discursively explicit and coherent ideology, advertised as common sense rather than political theology; cultivated through the detailed aesthetic and incremental seeding and weeding of the 'gardener' (Bauman 1992: 178) rather than contained in the static blueprint of the architect. Yet the message from this, as much as from the more explicitly nationalist literature, is equally one of the formidable quality of the state's role in cultural production.

Whatever their precise source, the monolithic tendencies of the state in the cultural sphere have two potentially deleterious effects. The first is an illiberal posture towards minority groups whose practices and values do not (or are deemed not to) accord with the dominant articulation of national culture. The consequent failures of cultural and political recognition, and the attendant calls for assimilation of those who do not share 'our way of life', may foster multiple forms of symbolic – and on occasions physical – violence against the minority cultures concerned (C. Taylor 1994; Levy 2000: 25). The second is the elevation of national boundaries (and associated distinctions between inside/outside, us/them, here/there) in ways that, at best, limit or undermine forms of solidarity and moral concern towards others and efface or refuse the mutual interdependencies that obtain under conditions of globalization and, at worst, generate forms of xenophobic hostility towards those marked out *by* territorial frontiers as foreigners or *within* territorial frontiers as strangers. These two claims form the cutting edge of a deep-seated scepticism within political theory towards the nation state as an appropriate symbolic mediator of political community. It is a critique, indeed, that is capable of reaching across a wide politico-intellectual spectrum, embracing both cosmopolitans – profoundly suspicious of a nationalist politics that 'substitutes a colorful idol for the substantive universal values of justice and right' (Nussbaum 2002: 5) – and those who would eschew the national particular in favour of other kinds of particularism (Vincent 2002).

But how significant, if at all, is the field of policing, and the practices and discourses associated with the general maintenance of security, in contributing to the culturally monolithic tendencies of the nation state? To what extent is the suggestiveness of the structural 'fit' vindicated through actual instrumental and symbolic links? The answer in both cases would appear to be strongly affirmative. The instrumental or functional link is an obvious one. Even in pursuit of their general-order function, the police possess the singularity and priority of purpose, the pre-eminence of authority, the legal means, the bureaucratic wherewithal, the irreducible discretion, the eternally urgent mandate and the contiguity of territorial jurisdiction to bolster and sustain the form and the content of the cultural orthodoxy of the state – both the very idea of a single orthodoxy and the particular substance of that orthodoxy. Whatever monolithic, anti-pluralist predilections are present within the political culture of the state, therefore, the police are invariably well placed to articulate and reinforce them. This is so whether, and most obviously, we are talking about discrimination against national minorities, or whether we are talking about any other orthodoxies and positive moralities which favour some ascriptive or affiliative categories and the behavioural codes associated with them over others (based on race, gender, class, physical handicap, ethnicity, regional identity, local habitat, age, sexual orientation, dress, etc.).

The symbolic link is also strong and multifaceted, and serves to reinforce the instrumental link. From the outset the structural correspondence between the state and the general-order function provided much material for mutual signification. Most obviously, this has been true of the way in which the policing of general order, with its emphasis on particularity and exclusivity of jurisdiction, tends to fix the very co-ordinates of statehood in particular spatio-temporal locations. That tendency is vividly demonstrated in Emsley's work on the importance of the gendarmerie in continental Europe in the eighteenth and nineteenth centuries in marking out 'national territory' and 'turning peasants into Frenchmen, Italians, Spaniards and Russians' (Emsley 1993: 87). Coming as 'the man praising order' (Emsley 2000: ch. 15), on arrival the gendarme was often the most tangible manifestation of the particular source and version of general order associated with this or that nation-state project, his symbolic flying of the flag having a quite literal foundation. Furthermore, the singularity and uniformity of the general police function, the idea of its providing an indispensable floor to effective political community, means that even in those countries, such as England, where the police were less directly involved in the initial consolidation of national territory and forging of national consciousness, the police and the police function in due course came to be associated with the continuing viability of the nation and with the preservation and refinement of national mores and authority (Gorer 1955; Emsley 1992).

In turn, this points to the importance of policing in the political fabrication and cultural forms of national memory. If, in the context of nation building, our common narratives do not simply record who we are and what we have in common but actually help to construct these marks of identity, then such narratives provide important sources of mythologization. Tradition itself becomes a rich source of invention. The structural centrality of the police makes them a key object of explicit fantasy and, as in the case of the Royal Canadian Mounted Police, they may be accorded an imaginary role in the founding of the nation (Walden 1982; I. Taylor 1999: 25). Perhaps even more importantly, at the 'paleo-symbolic' (Gouldner 1976: 224) level of unstated beliefs and feelings and the stock of meaning tokens and fragments that service this 'mundane culture' of everyday life (Loader and Mulcahy 2003: ch. 2), the centrality of the police to the 'timelessly timely' task of preserving order against chaos and providing protection against manifold social vulnerabilities means that the association of the police with the sense of the continuity of the national societal order within which such sentiments are framed is often deeply entrenched and highly implicit. The iconization of the police and their status as a 'condensation symbol' (Turner 1974) around which various concerns about social order are organized is achieved and sustained as much if not more through songs, jokes, paintings, photographs, fiction, comic books, films, TV series and the production and circulation of memorabilia as through more deliberatively coded forms of communication (Loader 1997c).

The forms of symbolic affirmation described above can of course help furnish the police with the authority to execute the tasks through which their instrumental role in sustaining the state and its general order is performed. However, this self-fulfilling vindication of their instrumental task is a double-edged sword. The various and cumulative forms of operationalization of the structural correspondence between nation-statehood and general order as situated and irreducibly particular activities that we have set out certainly underscore the enormous power of policing, but not always in ways about which we can be sanguine.

The key position of the police and their general-order function within a web of security-signifying beliefs and practices – one that tends to 'saturate the language of modern politics' (Dillon 1996: 12) and set the limits of our political imagination – operates in this regard to do four things. First, the massive assumption of security as a holistic and exclusionary discourse tends to privilege and cement the state itself as the guardian of security, and by extension the police as the guardian of the guardian, in ways that naturalize their 'tangible, all-pervasive, ghostly presence' (Benjamin 1921/1985: 141–2) in the life of modern societies and, with it, the institutional violence-in-the-last-resort that underpins 'democratic' politics (see also Taussig 1997; Neocleous 2000).

Secondly, by invoking 'security' as its foundational purpose and the policing of general order as the basic measure of that purpose, the state gives most tangible form to what in Schmittian terms (1922/1985: 5) may be viewed as its sovereign right to 'decide on the exception'. At best, then, security operates as *primus inter pares* in its claims on public policy as against other potential goods. At worst, security threatens to operate as an anti-political political practice wherein state actors declare the problem at hand (be it terrorism, or drugs, or migration, or . . .) to demand imperatives rather than involve trade-offs and polit-ical choices, to call for decisive decision instead of democratic deliber-ation, and to warrant the restriction of basic liberties as the price to be paid for the maintenance of public security (Huysmans 2004). Whichever is the case, what is crucial to underline is that what may be claimed to justify exceptional treatment under the banner of security need not be the threat to any identifiable special interest or specific strain of order itself of 'exceptional' importance, but rather the threat to the 'normal' standard of general order, however defined. And along-side and underpinning the privileging of security discourse there is a privileging of the key 'securitizing' (Wæver 1995) actors who partici-pate in that discourse and in its relevant politics of definition. As iconic figures in the production of national security, the police, despite their lack of democratic credentials, often acquire 'the right of legitimate pronouncement' (Loader and Mulcahy 2003: 46) – the reputational standing necessary to identify problems and deviations from the 'normal' standard of general order and make reckonable claims to their diagnosis and solution.

Thirdly, building on these formidable symbolic foundations of 'natu-ralness' and exceptionalism, securitizing state practices and state actors serve in particular ways to rally and reify a 'unitary people' whose social existence is fragile and deemed to be in need of authoritative 'protec-tion'. Here we reach the key insight of the cultural monolith critique. The state, with its security apparatus deeply complicit, can thus become a site in which individuals and groups practically and emotionally over-invest as a means of transcending their own vulnerabilities as individu-als and groups. They see in the state and its sovereign force a vehicle for producing the fantasy of total security that they lack the resources to secure alone. The state on this view becomes an obstacle, in Markell's (2003) terms, to producing a conception of security based upon an acknowledgement of our mutual vulnerability to and dependence upon each other. This is so because the generation of political community around the idea of danger tends to foster forms of solidarity that cohere around common enemies, such that national life is re/constituted through an antipathy towards those outsiders (whether within or beyond territorial borders) represented as hostile to 'our' freedom and 'our' security – something that has been ever more discernible in the USA and many other western states in the aftermath of 9/11.

More particularly, the fantasy of total security – of security 'deep' and 'wide' – is harmful to the extent that it seeks to, and does, generate an affectively charged, close to unconditional identification with those institutions – notably policing institutions – that through the process of symbolic affiliation we have discussed come both to embody the 'way of life' under threat and to be tasked with keeping the dangerous other at bay. The resulting investment in a policing solution to the question of 'deep' or ontological security (and often within that to particular repressive police strategies) can all too easily coexist with a tendency to overlook or condone abuses of power committed by 'our' police and turn a blind eye to practices that undermine the liberty and security of unpopular minority groups (see Loader and Mulcahy 2003: chs. 5 and 9; and, more generally, S. Cohen 2001). Security, accordingly, becomes not a precondition for the exercise of critical freedom, but a standing threat to it. And, especially when it is coupled with an overt politics of belonging in the broader public arena – as is most obviously the case in many so-called 'divided societies' (Brewer 1991; Mulcahy 2005), but is also in some measure true of any state with a dominant national tradition – there will be an illiberal, anti-pluralist price to pay. The more comprehensive in reach, and the more majority-indulgent and orthodoxy-affirming the publicly aspirational and broadly received understanding of the good of security, the more implausible and doomed to anxiety-fuelling disappointment it is likely to be even for those in whose name such an approach is pursued. Yet that very over-investment in orthodoxy can, at the same time, generate more acute harms of misrecognition or non-recognition for those constituencies deemed 'unorthodox' – increasing their sense of public inhibition and vulnerability, of precarious belonging and, perhaps, of frustrated disengagement or confrontation (Giddens 1991; C. Taylor 1994).[2]

Fourthly, and finally, we also have to be alive to the external effects of the development of culturally partial forms of nation-state policing. At the macro-level, one obvious consequence has to do with the very development and sustenance of the 'international' and of the related distinction between 'internal' and 'external' security. If policing and security are foundational to the nation-state project, and the nation-state project in turn remains fundamental to the Westphalian global order, then the very idea of a realm of inter-sovereign and so 'undomesticated' external order, with all of its instabilities and susceptibility to an 'anarchistic' (Bull 1977) and zero-sum security diagnosis and a military mode of treatment, is but the flipside and consequence of the proliferation of particular 'general orders' at the state level. We will have much more to say about this in the final chapter, but for the moment there are other potentially damaging external effects of the cultural particularity of national policing to which we should attend. These can be summed up under the twin themes of imperialism and mistranslation.

Policing, of course, has always been a key part of strategies of imperial domination, whether we are talking about the overseas colonies of

---

[2] The example of contemporary France is instructive in this regard. In the course of a remarkable few months between the autumn of 2005 and the spring of 2006, many French cities experienced two distinct waves of public unrest – in the first wave a series of clashes between young second- and third-generation members of ethnic minorities and the police and security services, and in the second wave a series of demonstrations led by middle-class students protesting against new laws which they deemed threatening to their capacity to begin and pursue a life-long career. What is most interesting about this case is the fact that both waves were so strongly defined and coded in security terms, and the connection between the two waves that this shared coding hints at. The first wave dramatized the sense of social and political exclusion of young members of ethnic minorities, and the intensity of the threat their disorderly and property-damaging behaviour was perceived to offer to a political establishment who subsequently stood accused in many quarters of over-reaction. The second wave was organized around the theme of *précarité* – in the first instance certainly *précarité de l'emploi* (job insecurity), but gradually widening to signify a deeper range of insecurities about the disappearance of a certain received understanding of the French 'way of life' – economic and cultural – under conditions of globalization. In the first wave, therefore, we see some of the symptoms and secondary effects of the harms of misrecognition caused to minorities, while in the second we see the dangers of reifying a particular conception of ontological security – one that is closely related to the minorities' sense of exclusion and misrecognition – for the very majority whose needs it purportedly serves (see, e.g., Pfaff 2006).

various European states (Brogden 1987; Anderson and Killingray 1991, 1992) or, from the very cradle of modern policing, the spread of the French gendarmerie over Napoleon's European empire (Emsley 2000). For present purposes, however, we are not concerned with the more directly repressive motivational edge of imperial policing which was highlighted in the previous chapter. For whether we are dealing with classical forms of colonialism or with the kinds of post-colonial imperialism implied by national or (increasingly) international interventions in failed or transitional states (Oakley *et al*. 2002), the development of a specifically and nominally *policing* solution in place of or in supplement to a military solution is always in some measure about the attempted routinization and normalization of rule, and in turn about how the idea of general order is utilized in that process of normalization. On the one hand, various features of the idea of general order, in particular the commitment to uniformity and the sense of involvement in a timeless war between order and chaos, encourage the view that general-order solutions appropriate to one context and culturally inflected by that context may be equally applicable to other contexts. This is especially so where the key agents of change begin from a position of imperial conceit – a sense of the superiority of any solution developed on 'home' territory and a paternalistic assumption that any translation problems are best handled by those expert in the source rather than the destination language. On the other hand, the irreducible particularity of general order – the uniqueness of the material and cultural conditions under which such order must be negotiated – means that such an approach always risks hubristic failure.

Whether we are talking about the globalization of community policing over the past thirty years, fuelled by its promise to supply 'a value-free commodity unencumbered with the trappings of economic and political interest' (Brogden and Nijhar 2005: 9), or the efforts of the United Nations peacekeeping capacity's civilian policing arm – CIVPOL – to use an internationally recruited policing force as a key catalyst in the 'nation-(re)building' activities of transitional administrations in Bosnia, Kosovo and East Timor (Bellamy *et al*. 2004: ch. 12; J. M. H. Wilson 2006), the manifold problems of mistranslation have been well documented (Linden *et al*. forthcoming). General order, in short, despite superficial appearances to the contrary, always travels with culturally specific baggage, and because of this can never adapt easily to its new environment.

Lessons and limits of the monolith critique

The variant of state – and security – scepticism set out in this chapter teaches a number of salutary lessons. It is highly attentive to the powerful, if often understated or misstated symbolic and emotive dimensions of security and community, and possesses a sharp sensitivity to their pathological consequences. In so doing, it warns those, such as ourselves, who wish to draw democratic virtues from the inescapable presence of cultural identity and political affect in the politics of security that they are 'playing with fire'. It supplies, further, a cogent account of the dangers of placing security even in the supposedly neutral and innocent form of general order at the ideological heart of government, of the capacity of security politics to colonize public policy and social life in ways that are injurious of democratic values, and of its propensity to foster and sustain fear-laden, other-disregarding forms of political subjectivity and collective identity. In all these ways, it reminds us that security 'cannot be dissociated from even more basic claims about who we think we are and how we might act together' (R. B. J. Walker 1997: 66; see also Dillon 1996: 34).

Yet critical work in policing and security studies remains, in our view, skewed in its account of these associations. It concludes too easily from the above that there can be no progressive democratic politics aimed at civilizing security, that security is so stained by its uncivil association with the (military and police) state and its monolithic affects and effects, that the only radical strategy left open is to deconstruct and move beyond it (e.g. Dillon 1996: ch. 1). In so doing, this strand of state scepticism commits two mistakes, both of which flow from its failure to appreciate or at least sufficiently to acknowledge what we tried to demonstrate in an earlier section of the chapter; namely, that state policing, however culpable it might be in *exacerbating* certain of the tensions involved in applying general order in any particular context, is not the fixed and fundamental *source* of these tensions. It forgets, first of all, that while the affective connections between security, state and nation are deeply entrenched, they take no necessary or essential substantive form. They can, in other words, be remade and reimagined in ways that connect policing and security to other more inclusive, cosmopolitan forms of belonging – to political communities that 'do not necessarily equate difference with threat' (Dalby 1997: 9). It tends, secondly, to forget that the 'pursuit of security' through general order is not only the product of forms of technocratic, authoritarian government that impoverishes our sense of the political (Dillon 1996: 15). Security, in the sense of a broadly responsive and acceptable conception of order, can also be, and indeed – if we examine the political aspirations which preceded and have survived the modern state – *must* also be, conceived of in a prior and abstract sense as a valuable human good, one that in concrete application is a key ingredient of the good *society* as well as being axiomatic to the production of other individual goods (most directly, liberty). It is our contention that security can be rethought along these lines, and that the state through its ordering and cultural work continues to possess a central place in the production of security thus conceived; we develop this argument in part II. We must first, however, consider one further critique of the modern state tradition.

5 | *The state as idiot*

ET us suppose for a moment that one could minimize or eradicate the shortcomings of the state we have examined thus far – its propensity to meddle, to be biased, and to privilege majority over minority norms and practices. Suppose one could build a benign, well-intentioned state that consistently acted in ways that respected individual rights, and was impartial between competing interests and protective of minority cultures. According to the sceptical stance we consider in this chapter, one would still be faced, even under these conditions, with a deeper, arguably intractable, *tragedy* of the state. The state is, on this view, an idiot. Its bureaucratic remoteness means that it lacks the situated knowledge and therefore the capacity to deliver security across a diverse array of local settings. Nor can it easily acquire such knowledge without resorting to authoritarian, diversity-threatening means. The state, moreover, is not merely deficient in the knowledge of local circumstances that is prerequisite to the production of security. It also tends towards obduracy – being both unreflexive about its own cognitive limitations and determined to press on with its purposes, including its policing and security purposes, in wilful disregard of its own ignorance. The state, or so it believes, 'knows best'.

Idiocy and obduracy are, according to this view, characteristics even of strong democratic states operating within their own national boundaries – in conditions, that is, where they at least possess the sovereign capacity and authority that enable them to generate knowledge of 'their' territory and populations, however imperfectly. But these traits are more radically marked in respect of 'weak' or 'failing' states which lack either the infrastructure and legitimacy that enable mature democratic states to 'know' their societies, or the control of territory that is a minimal precondition for administrative knowledge production. Knowledge deficits are, furthermore, a chronic feature of states operating in the international and transnational arena, whether in cooperation with other states, or when trying to resolve conflict, keep the

peace or otherwise intervene in environments overseen by other sovereign authorities – something US and British 'intelligence' failures in the
run up to the second Iraq War demonstrated once again.

The 'state as idiot' critique overlaps with all three of the sceptical outlooks we have addressed thus far, as we shall see. It is also protean in the
political form that it assumes, taking aim at the state from divergent
standpoints in the name of alternative institutional solutions. Several
variants of this stance can be found on the political right. It is implicit,
for instance, in Michael Oakshott's (1949/1991) withering attack on
'rationalism in politics', his fire being directed at the view that Reason,
and its practical manifestation in state planning, can be put to work in
solving human problems. On this view, the state is posited as the pur-
veyor of the 'sovereignty of technique' (1949/1991: 21) deploying its
bullying power to trample over practical knowledge in a bid to impose
'uniform conditions of perfection upon human conduct' (1949/1991:
10). One encounters it – even more explicitly – in Hayek's case for the
benefits of markets over administration as mechanisms for producing
and allocating goods. Hayek's starting point is that knowledge in human
societies is inescapably partial, widely dispersed and necessarily fragmented – in short, imperfect. Knowledge, he says, is contingent and temporary information about particular times and places, and 'not given to
anyone in totality' (Hayek 1948: 78) – a condition of ignorance that
chronically limits the coordinating and allocative potential of the state.
The 'data' needed for such coordination cannot, Hayek argues, be collected by a single authority, nor will such an authority be able to discern
its necessary implications. We must consequently abandon the idea that
'everything must be tidily planned and made to show a recognizable
order' (1948: 27), as any such deliberate organization of society from
the top 'smothers spontaneous formations which are founded on con-
tacts closer and more intimate than those that can exist in the larger unit'
(1948: 28). For both Oakshott and Hayek, this culminates in a profound
distaste for the state and the forms of political decision-making associated with it: in Oakshott's case out of a preference for the authority,
traditions and local craft-ways of practical knowledge; in Hayek's, as we
saw in chapter 2, in favour of decentralized and autonomy-enhancing
decision-making that he believes can only exist in market forms.[1]

---

[1] We should be careful here to note the dissimilarities between these two positions.
Oakshott clearly saw Hayek as having fallen victim to the very rationalist

We will have cause to revisit Hayek later in the chapter, as his work looms large in the attempt of Clifford Shearing and other champions of local initiative to think about and deliver security beyond the state. But our principal purpose in this chapter – as this brief mention of Shearing and his collaborators indicates – is to address those versions of the 'state as idiot' critique that emanate broadly speaking from the left – conceptually, under the banner of communitarian or pragmatist philosophy; politically, in the name of 'bottom-up' community politics and democratic experimentalism. As a way into this strand of state scepticism, we may usefully consider James C. Scott's influential *Seeing Like a State* (1998). Here one finds, as with Oakshott and Hayek, a critique of top-down rationalist planning, along with a parallel effort to pinpoint the cognitive deficiencies of the state – these forming, for Scott, a large part of the explanation for the tragic failure of 'so many well-intentioned schemes to improve the human condition' (1998: 4). Scott documents the disasters of what he calls 'authoritarian high modernism' across fields as diverse as city planning, scientific forestry, collectivist agriculture and vanguard politics. In so doing, he argues that modernist self-confidence in the capacity to deploy scientific and technical knowledge in an effort to change people's 'work habits, living patterns, moral conduct and worldview' (1998: 4) is doomed to fail because it rests upon 'thin simplifications' about societies generated by remote state actors in ways that gloss over the diversity, complexity and unpredictability of the social and disregard competing sources of local knowledge upon which the success of state projects depends. 'Formal schemes of order', he argues, 'are untenable without some elements of the practical knowledge that they tend to dismiss' (1998: 7).

Scott's critique of the idiotic and obdurate state is not, however, launched in the name of the sovereign individual and untrammelled market forces – he argues, *contra* Hayek, that markets generate their own 'heroic simplifications' (1998: 8).[2] His point, rather, is that the

---

patterns of thought that he believed had been the ruin of modern European politics, describing Hayek's *The Road to Serfdom* as 'a plan to end all planning' (Oakshott 1949/1991: 26). Hayek, for his part, explicitly distanced himself from the English conservative tradition of which Oakshott was a prominent representative (Hayek 1978).

[2] Scott similarly distances his position from that of Oakshottian conservatism. While he applauds Oakshott's 'astute and telling' critique of rationalist planning

state possesses a deep incapacity to recognize, understand and learn from the 'practical skills and applied intelligence' (1998: 313), the fine-grained awareness of local circumstances and contingency, that make up informal knowledge – or what he calls *mētis* (1998: ch. 9). This failure, Scott argues, is bound up, as cause and effect, with a twofold statist hubris: states regard themselves as far smarter and more far-seeing than they really are, and their subjects as far more stupid and incompetent than they in fact are (1998: 343). It is in response to this posture of *cognitive* imperialism that Scott advances the case for 'mētis-friendly institutions' that are plastic, diverse and adaptable in the face of constantly changing environments (1998: 352–7).

Our aim in this chapter is to consider the application of this critique of the state, and promotion of local knowledge, to questions of polic-ing and security. We do so, first, by examining the problems and failings of some recent top-down, state-sponsored policing and crime-control programmes through the lens of the 'state as idiot' problematic. In so doing, we highlight the trend towards multilevel, 'networked' security governance that these programmes are said to signify and the express or implied 'theory' of the relationship between the state and the social that they mobilize. We then offer a critical reconstruction of one influ-ential 'left-Hayekian' attempt to conceptualize and practically promote across various jurisdictions the possibilities of communal security beyond the state; namely, the work of Les Johnston, Clifford Shearing, Jennifer Wood and others on 'nodal governance'. We conclude with some brief remarks on the limits of bottom-up, non-state practices as vehicles for civilizing security.

Problems of security governance

We have, in recent years, witnessed a shift in crime-control practices away from the police towards policing and, more broadly, from gov-ernment to governance (Loader 2000; Pierre 2000; Mazerolle and Ransley 2006). These terms signal a repositioning of the state in rela-tion to the plurality of agents and agencies now involved in the 'gov-ernance of security' (Johnston and Shearing 2003). They attest that the

Footnote 2 (*cont.*)
  and his appreciation of the contingency of practice, Scott goes on to dismiss him as a complacent apologist 'for whatever the past has bequeathed to the present in terms of power, privilege and property' (1998: 424, 431).

state is no longer the sole or even pre-eminent player in efforts to control (rather than punish) crime, but, rather, exists today as part of loosely coupled security networks comprised of state, commercial and lay actors (Dupont 2004). This, in turn, has been accompanied by new mentalities and technologies of rule. The state – to cite again Osborne and Gaebler's (1992) familiar nautical metaphor – has become less oriented to 'rowing' (actually delivering policing on-the-ground) and more focused on 'steering' (setting the strategic framework within which delivery takes place). Far from displacing the state, however, the practice of 'ruling at a distance' means that it becomes more active – demanding a greater degree of the very authority and legitimacy that the move towards multi-actor governance threatens to undermine. Instead of being concerned solely with its own capacity to 'row', the 'steering' state has to wield authority over, and generate knowledge from and about, a wide range of social institutions in an effort to co-ordinate and regulate a diversity of policing and security practices. Here the 'state as idiot' critique offers some sharp – albeit not, in our view, fatal – insights into the state's capacity to undertake the effective governance of security networks. We turn to these in due course. Let us begin though by recalling and describing some of the key trends and developments.

State-led, police-centric

Consider first those security strategies and practices that one might describe as state-led and police-centric – an array of subnational, national and international practices in which the state retains a privileged place as both provider and regulator. Prominent here are an assortment of strategies that travel under the banner of community policing. As noted in chapter 4, such strategies have acquired global prominence and received much warm official rhetoric in recent decades (Skolnick and Bayley 1988; Brogden and Nijhar 2005), whether in the form of policies aimed at embedding the patrol officer as a dedicated, exemplary, networked and knowledgeable presence in local social life, or, more ambitiously, of attempts to make the police into local civic leaders, spearheading efforts – in consultation with local people – to 'activate the good' within communities (Alderson 1979; Innes 2004). We can cite also the coming to the fore of 'problem-oriented policing' (Goldstein 1990), with its conception of the police not as a force reacting willy-nilly to outbreaks of crime and disorder, but as an institution proactively engaged with others in attempting to forge holistic solutions to deep-seated problems of which crime and disorder are merely symptoms. And we can note the rise and global spread of 'broken-windows' and 'zero-tolerance' policing with their superficially alluring prescription of the police shoring-up majority communal norms by 'cracking down' on incivilities which, left untended, can send communities spiralling towards chronic forms of criminal victimization (Kelling and Coles 1996; cf. Harcourt 2001).

There are, it should be said, important differences of emphasis between these approaches, even if they do not warrant the quasi-theological battles that take place between their respective champions. They have, in addition, given rise to endless – apparently technical, but always also highly political – debates about whether, and under what conditions, each of them 'works' (see Tilley 2003).[3] For present purposes, however, we are less concerned with whether these strategies are instrumentally effective than with what they tell us about trends in security governance, and here we can pinpoint some significant commonalities between them. Uppermost among these is a police-centred and top-down conception of the production of order within communities – the rhetorical claims of community policing notwithstanding. The police are posited in each case as the lynchpin of local security, as the institution best placed to diagnose problems, design solutions and mobilize individuals, organizations and businesses to implement them. The police, in short, are elevated to the status of community leaders orchestrating practices of local ordering (Innes 2004), a position justified by the resources, know-how and capacity for decisive action that they bring to bear on problems of crime control and order maintenance. Such claims, it seems to us, are implicit in each of the aforementioned policing strategies and constitute an overlapping consensus in the conception their respective advocates hold of the relationship between policing and the social.

Yet if these presumptions are present within policing strategies deployed in circumstances where the state possesses the territorial control and sovereign authority necessary to generate knowledge of local communities, they are even more apparent in respect of the

---

[3] We return to some of these issues when discussing the consumerist syndrome in chapter 8.

'export' of policing 'models' to places where such knowledge is almost entirely lacking. The propensity of crime and policing policy to 'travel' has increased markedly under conditions of globalization (Newburn and Sparks 2004; Melossi *et al.* forthcoming). Broadly speaking, this has taken one of the following forms: (i) the regular import/export flow of apparently successful and increasingly 'commonplace' anti-crime strategies (e.g. neighbourhood watch, broken-windows and zero-tolerance policing, crime-reduction partnerships, restorative conferencing) between liberal democratic societies (Wacquant 2003; Jones and Newburn 2004); (ii) the more active efforts of police entrepreneurs (Bratton 1998) or 'transnational police elites' (Marenin forthcoming) to market and sell new or rebranded community or zero-tolerance policing 'models' to cities and states across the world (Ellison forthcoming); (iii) the provision of external assistance such as personnel, equipment and 'know-how' to weak or failing states in dealing with problems of organized crime and insurgency (e.g. Goldsmith *et al.* forthcoming); and (iv) training police forces in 'transitional states' so as to bring them up to the standards of liberal democracies (Bayley 2006) – something that explicitly underpinned the 'twinning arrangements' between EU police forces and their counterparts in former communist states in central-eastern Europe in the lead-up to the latter's accession to full EU membership (N. Walker 2002a) and marks the current missions of the US and British governments in Afghanistan and Iraq. Common to each of these cases, as mentioned in chapter 4, is the promotion of security solutions in simplistic ignorance of local histories, conflicts and priorities, coupled with an implicit 'occidentalist' presumption as to the ' "sameness" of key cultural categories, practices and institutions' (Cain 2000: 71). To this one can often add a missionary determination to bring 'our' guidance and standards to those Rudyard Kipling called 'lesser breeds without the law' – a neo-colonial ambition that demands little or no understanding of 'their' ways of seeing and doing things.[4] There can be few better illustrations of the intimate relationship between idiocy and obduracy.

---

[4] We should note here that the international traffic in security practices is not entirely one way. The remarkable global diffusion of restorative justice ideas and programmes rooted in Aboriginal and Maori dispute-resolution processes offers one of the best counter-examples of crime policy travelling from the periphery to the centre (cf. Blagg 1997). So too do the efforts of Clifford Shearing – discussed further below – to promote to other parts of the world forms of non-state

A cognate series of difficulties underpin the 'very mixed' record (Linden *et al.* forthcoming) of United Nations (CIVPOL) and European Union peacekeeping 'missions' dispatched in recent years to post-conflict societies such as Kosovo, Haiti and East Timor (e.g. J. M. Wilson 2006). Such missions have proliferated since the end of the Cold War. They have also become international and multi-agency in terms of personnel (commonly today comprising the police, military and humanitarian NGOs), as well as assuming broad remits encompassing such activities as law enforcement and patrolling, human rights monitoring, training local forces, organizing the return of displaced persons, overseeing elections and assisting economic reconstruction – in short, governance (United Nations 2000). But these missions have been bedevilled and undermined by a catalogue of recurring problems: multiple sources of authority and accountability; confused, conflicting and shifting mandates; logistical problems in acquiring suitably trained staff and adequate equipment; a lack of law enforcement as well as longer-term institution-building capability, and a dim awareness of, and inability to acquire, the knowledge of local history, culture and conditions that is prerequisite to their effectiveness (Oakley *et al.* 2002; Linden *et al.* forthcoming). All this, of course, is grist to the mill of those who charge such missions with cultural misrecognition and imperialism, as we have seen. But it also attests to the *cognitive* imperialism that so readily accompanies the state's overweening idiocy.

Reconfigurations of state authority

We can point, secondly, to the reconfigurations of state authority that one encounters within a range of contemporary 'partnership' arrangements aimed at delivering public safety – arrangements found today across several jurisdictions. Some of these remain steadfastly top-down and orchestrated by the state. They involve police efforts to extend their capacity through the deployment of a new tier of dedicated patrol or community support officers, as has happened in both the Netherlands and England and Wales in recent years. Or they amount

Footnote 4 *(cont.)*

> security governance first developed in poor communities in South Africa – practices that Shearing claims 'can be adapted and transferred to practical use in many nations of the world, including the established democracies of the West' (Shearing and Kempa 2000: 206; Wood 2006; cf. B. Dixon 2004).

to state-sponsored attempts to encourage individuals, community groups and businesses to participate in 'responsible' anti-crime activity (through, for example, a bewildering array of 'watch' schemes), or to exhort individuals to provide the police with the information they need to tackle crime (as evident in the spread across several jurisdictions of programmes such as *Crimestoppers*). On occasions, these amount to the public police actively striving to reassert the state's capacity to steer, as recent initiatives aimed at creating an 'extended policy family' in England and Wales attest (Home Office 2001; Blair 2002; Johnston 2003). Starting from a recognition that the police have lost their monopoly of patrol provision to a range of alternative (local government and commercial) suppliers, the state police seek here to mobilize their symbolic capital in a bid to tempt consumers (such as local authorities) to purchase 'police community support officers', as well as putting themselves forward as a network regulator, training and accrediting a plurality of 'authority figures linked to the police' (Home Office 2001: 90). The police, on this view, are to be the hub of, rather than a mere node within, 'partnerships for civic renewal' (Home Office 2001: 35).

But alongside initiatives such as these which indicate new linkages between state and market sectors, we can highlight – across several jurisdictions – developments that reposition the police in more radical ways within multi-agency arrangements for governing security, initiatives that point at the same time to a new pervasiveness of security concerns and consciousness across government (Crawford 1997, 2003). The enhanced and in many respects novel role of subnational tiers of government (e.g. local councils in Britain, city mayors in France, regional authorities in parts of Italy) in such matters as employing city guards and neighbourhood wardens, policing and punishing anti-social behaviour, developing urban safety strategies and (in the British case) factoring crime-control considerations into all fields of local government activity is a clear indicator of this (Karn 2007); as is the prominence of the security question within campaigns by civic leaders to market their cities and attract inward investment, and the networking of such local policy elites in bodies such as the 'European Forum for Urban Safety' (Melossi and Selmini 2000; Ocqueteau 2004; van der Vijver and Terpstra 2005). So too is the embryonic development within the EU of a concern to coordinate the control of (especially) juvenile, urban and drug-related crime within and across member states, a concern given institutional form with the formation in 2001 of the European Crime Prevention Network (den Boer and Peters 2005). The multidimensional, networked conception of policework fashioned by the British Crime and Disorder Act 1998 can also be highlighted here. This encompasses: (i) the formation of statutory 'crime-reduction partnerships' according the police a prominent strategic role, in collaboration with municipal authorities and other public agencies such as health authorities and probation, in the local governance of crime; (ii) various measures – notably, 'anti-social behaviour orders' and 'local child curfew schemes' – that require of the police and local government a strategic role in shaping and monitoring their use and the active deployment of their resources to enforce them, often in ways which blur or traverse the boundaries between the institutions and processes of criminal and civil law; and (iii) aspects of the legislation – 'child safety orders', 'youth offending teams', the aforementioned crime-reduction partnerships – which call upon the police either to supply information needed to activate 'welfarist' interventions, or to actively share information with criminal justice and social service agencies. All in all, this amounts to a diffuse and expansive role for the police in the administration of civic governance (Crawford 2003; Newburn 2003).

We can point finally, under this head, to new configurations of security governance in which commercial organizations are the lead or sole actors. The provision of security in shopping malls, leisure and office complexes and other sites of what Shearing and Stenning (1983) call 'mass private property' provides the clearest example of this – settings in which owners establish particularistic forms of social and moral order and enlist private security firms to enforce it on their behalf using property law (Wakefield 2003; Kempa *et al.* 2004). The growth of private residential associations and the formation of 'Business Improvement Districts' (most commonly in the USA) offer analogous cases in point (Alexander 1997). These are best characterized as forms of 'private government', security pursuits from which the state has been displaced and where commercial actors assume the task of both 'steering' and 'rowing' – albeit within a market space constituted by law. But we can also highlight the tendency of market actors, as well as local authorities and groups within civil society, to enlist police capacity – for instance, by purchasing police officers or police time for allotted periods and thereby seeking to redirect public resources (with their attendant symbolic power) towards the pursuit of communal order through the mechanism of contract (Gans 2000; Crawford and Lister 2005). Here, it seems, we encounter security partnerships in which the state continues to 'row', under contractual arrangements in which non-state actors play a greatly enhanced role in 'steering'. They form, as such, but one of the ways in which private policing developments impact on and complicate the regulatory tasks required of the state and the knowledge which it requires for their successful accomplishment, matters to which we now turn.

The production and limits of state knowledge

The two broad developments in security governance highlighted above – those which remain state-led and police-centred, and those which reconfigure state authority in potentially more far-reaching ways – both have a further consequence which is pertinent to the variant of state scepticism we are concerned with in this chapter – namely, they give rise to new forms of knowledge production and deployment. These forms have developed both as tools for doing police-work in the first case, and as a means of trying to regulate the plurality of agencies now involved in efforts to realize security in the second. In respect of the former, an obvious illustration is the current popularity among both the British government and police forces of 'intelligence-led' policing with its focus on generating and analysing information on crime patterns, 'hot-spots' and 'known offenders' in an effort to sharpen law enforcement practice (Maguire 2000). The 'Compstat' crime-analysis programme that figures so dramatically in ideological representations of zero-tolerance policing and its claimed impact on crime in New York City is a further case in point of the same trend (Bratton 1998; cf. Manning 2001; Weisburd *et al.* 2003). Extrapolating from developments such as these, and from their own research on the police in Canada, Ericson and Haggerty (1997) contend that the 'modern' police project of tackling crime and securing territorial order is in fact being transformed by a pervasive concern with information management organized around risk. The police, they argue, have been reconfigured as 'knowledge workers', generating, brokering and disseminating socially authoritative information to other governmental agencies (insurance companies, licensing bodies, credit agencies, local authorities, the media, etc.) in order to assist them in constituting individuals and populations 'in their respective risk categories' (Ericson

1994: 168). On this view, community policing becomes 'communications policing' as the police are embedded at the centre of loosely coupled informational networks whose purpose is to sort and administer the population with a view to suppressing risk.

Such highly circumscribed, pre-formatted information has, moreover, as Ericson and Haggerty intimate, come to play a pronounced role in the state's efforts to govern security. Recent British experiments in applying the techniques of 'new public management' to policing and community safety are instructive in this regard – not least because they are now being taken up elsewhere (McLaughlin and Murji 2001). Under this umbrella, though with antecedents in earlier initiatives aimed at 'policing by objectives' (Butler 1984; Waddington 1986), we have witnessed in the last decade or so an increasingly heavy reliance on audits, consumer surveys and nationally established performance targets as vehicles for proactively disciplining the police and crime-reduction partnerships. These, in turn, form the basis for a performance management regime comprised of routine monitoring, inspection, evaluation and 'Best Value' reviews conducted by a proliferating complex of organizations – Her Majesty's Inspectorate of Constabulary, the Audit Commission, the Association of Chief Police Officers, the Private Security Industry Authority, the Police Standards Unit, the National Policing Improvement Agency, Home Office-funded evaluators – all in the name of ensuring compliance with national standards, weeding out poor performance and spreading what is deemed to be good practice (N. Walker 2000: ch. 4; Jones 2003). Such today is the form taken by the state's rationalist ambition to plan and administer policing.

These trends in security governance have attracted a large policy literature concerned with their instrumental effectiveness in cutting crime and disorder – some of it, in these terms, fiercely critical (e.g. Bullock and Tilley 2003). But they have also been subject to wider forms of critical social analysis, much of which highlights the predilection of the state to think in a top-down fashion about communal order (and accounts for its failures in these terms), or pinpoints the state's incapacity to bring into alignment and hold to democratic account the plurality of institutional actors involved today in the production of security (Crawford 1997; Hughes and Edwards 2002; Herbert 2006). This critique of the state's role in security governance raises concerns that we in large measure share, and which the project of civilizing security must find ways of circumventing. Using the 'state as idiot' perspective as our guide, let us elaborate upon three of them.

The first – spanning both the policy and sociological literatures – addresses the coordination problems found within multi-agency security partnerships. It raises sceptical questions both about the state's impulse to subject the field of policing and security to forms of hierarchical planning and about the difficulties of steering multi-agency arrangements towards meeting their stated purposes. Part of this has to do with the state's cognitive limitations – its idiocy; commonly found impediments to the success of multi-agency partnerships, or community, problem-oriented and intelligence-led policing, are short falls of relevant information (about public anxieties, or local crime patterns, or community priorities), or an incapacity to analyse available data and discern its meanings and implications (Wright 2002: ch. 5; Tilley 2003: 329–34), or recalcitrant actors supplying required information to managers and external bodies in formally compliant, line-toeing 'rituals of verification' (Power 1997). Hayek, of course, would have expected little else. But this remains closely connected to the pronounced tendency of the state to refuse to acknowledge these limitations and to plough on regardless – its obduracy. Steering, as we noted earlier, requires greater knowledge of underlying social dynamics, and a higher quotient of authority and legitimacy, than mere rowing, entailing, as it does, complex relations of trust and cooperation between a multiplicity of actors both within and beyond the state. The serious question that the 'idiot' critique poses, one that finds support in the repeated implementation failures of contemporary policing and crime-prevention programmes (Crawford 1998: chs. 5–6), is whether the state is capable of undertaking, or is best placed to perform, the necessary coordination and regulatory tasks. The suspicion is that an entrenched attachment to linear and hierarchical forms of ordering (Thompson 2003: ch. 2) leaves the state deficient in the kinds of flexibility and nimble-footedness that are needed to bring reflexive coherence to today's interorganizational, multilevel security networks.

A second, closely related, critique focuses on the democratic deficits that attend the pluralization of policing and security provision (Crawford 1997; Loader 2000). There are several strands to this complaint. First, that state-sponsored policing and crime-prevention programmes remain for the most part remote and top-down, answering to their own bureaucratically set priorities. They either act on behalf of the 'community' whose concerns and priorities state security actors presume to know, or practise forms of consultation whose claims to inclusiveness are radically deficient – practices that tend to elicit the demands of, while at the same time helping to constitute, communities of the 'trustworthy' and 'law-abiding'. The state's resultant ignorance is, of course, greatest in respect of excluded, unpopular or 'hard-to-reach' constituencies (Jones and Newburn 2001) – something that becomes an additional factor in forging a security politics which tends to reinforce intolerance towards local minorities. It can be argued, further, that the expansive conception of the police role projected by crime-control programmes such as community and problem-oriented policing not only lacks a theory of police limits (Braithwaite 1992: 17), but entails the police extending their reach as 'expert' local problem-solvers into areas where they can claim 'no more legitimate authority than the non-expert citizen' (de Lint 1997: 260). And one can point, lastly, to an increasingly complex institutional pattern of local security that presents as a closed bureaucratic system, opaque and unresponsive to its wider public environment (Crawford 1997) – something buttressed by centralized and self-corroborating systems of accountability that exhibit slavish devotion to supposedly objective and politically agnostic forms of auditing and statistical performance measurement, while 'disallowing other competing sources of judgement' (J. C. Scott 1998: 93) about local security priorities and the performance of policing institutions. Once more, it would seem, the state manifests itself as the problem, unable to realize security in ways that contribute to, rather than undermine, prospects for democratic governance.

A third charge is that the state, convinced of its own security imperatives and ignorantly certain of its knowledge and objectives, pursues security in ways that give it an ideologically and emotionally charged pervasiveness across political and social life. The practices of what Jonathon Simon (2006) calls 'governing through crime', or what, as we saw in chapter 3, is referred to in the international relations literature as 'securitization' (Buzan *et al.* 1998), have been amply documented in this respect and contain several connected dangers: (i) that the security question – with its accompanying language of urgency, imperative and exception – pervades and colonizes public life in ways that threaten to undermine the purpose, values and efficacy of other social institutions;

(ii) that policing institutions and practices thereby become materially and symbolically 'wide' rather than 'narrow' components of social relations; and (iii) that a felt sense of public insecurity – with its affectively saturated discourses of risk and blame, and attendant lines of affiliation and division – is heightened in ways that make the task of constructing 'open, tolerant and inclusive communities' ever more intractable (Crawford 1997: 274). The state's dearth of knowledge – and lack of cognizance of, and reflexivity about, that dearth – thus makes an independent and distinctive contribution to the process of making security pervasive and to dynamics which gnaw away at, or obstruct the formation of, the social and institutional conditions under which security may be made axiomatic.

This is in many respects a persuasive critique of the state's security ambitions and their deleterious effects. It is also, as noted, one whose concerns we in large measure share – a perspective that raises some thorny regulatory problems that we return to, and consider more fully, in chapters 7 and 8. We must first, however, turn our attention to a variant of the 'state as idiot' stance that transcends the practice of critique. Sure, this perspective has significant 'left-Hayekian' things to say about the state's limitations as a security provider and the radical implications of multi-actor governance. But it also aims to explore – both conceptually and in social practice – the prospects for enhancing security to be found in those forms of local knowledge and capacity building that the state, it is claimed, has a nasty habit of stifling.

Promoting nodal governance

We have in mind here the influential recent work of Clifford Shearing and his co-workers in the 'Security 21' network based at the Australian National University.[5] Unlike many of the state sceptics considered elsewhere in part I, Shearing and others take security seriously as a valued social good (Johnston and Shearing 2003: ch. 1). They refuse, however, to privilege the state – in either their explanatory framework

---

[5] There exists now a large and evolving literature on nodal security governance. An inventory of the most important contributions to date would, in our view, include: Johnston and Shearing (2003); Shearing and Wood (2003a, 2003b); Dupont (2004); Shearing and Johnston (2005); Burris (2006); Johnston (2006); Shearing (2001, 2006); Wood (2006); Wood and Shearing (2006).

or normative register – among the multiplicity of bodies that may con-tribute to its realization, whether as provider or regulator (Johnston 2006: 34). Foremost among the reasons for this is the Hayekian claim that the state lacks the knowledge and capacity to deliver security to diverse local communities and, moreover, that its attempts to acquire such knowledge and capacity evince a strong tendency towards authoritarian outcomes. The state is an entity whose bureaucratic remoteness renders it at best unable to make good on its well-inten-tioned promises, at worst a clumsy, homogenizing force riding roughshod over the possibilities created by locally responsive, bottom-up security institutions embedded within civil society.

According to Johnston and Shearing (2003: 148), the state has become but one 'node' among several now engaged in the governance of security – to the extent that we should no longer grant it conceptual priority under nodal arrangements. Whether as 'auspices' (sponsor) or 'provider' (Bayley and Shearing 2001), the state today collaborates with, competes against, or supports a range of security actors from the private sector or civil society, as we have seen. This, it is contended, has contributed to the chronic security inequalities – or 'governance deficits' – one encounters across the globe today, with poor communi-ties being unable to tap the kinds of policing and security resources that more economically advantaged groups have ready access to. In these respects, Shearing and others subscribe both to the empirical claim that the state has been decentred from its once (more) pivotal place in crime control, and to many of the criticisms that have been levelled at emer-gent forms of multi-actor security governance.[6]

But proponents of nodal governance refuse, in seeking to make good these deficits, to resort to what they term the 'nostalgic, hopeful' path of 'turn[ing] our back on this trend and seek[ing] to reinstate strong state governance' (Shearing and Wood 2003a: 217), not least because the legacies of oppressive state violence form part of the security problem across many of the sites – notably South Africa and Argentina – in which the 'Security 21' team have intervened. Thus, instead of

---

[6] Johnston and Shearing (2003: 35, 148) also contend that the state today has become both the subject and object of regulation (see also C. Scott 2002), a feature of contemporary governance that, they argue, 'problematises the attempt to conceive it as the exclusive locus of public interests' (Johnston and Shearing 2003: 35) and requires us to rethink regulatory practices in networked, non-hierarchical terms. We return to the issues this raises below.

depending on 'familiar and comfortable' 'mental schemata' associated with the state (Dupont *et al.* 2003: 347), and the blanket dismissals of neo-liberalism that such thinking tends to invoke, Shearing and his colleagues urge that we recognize the force of the Hayekian critique of state forms and seek to harness local knowledge and capacity in ways that expand and enhance what they call 'community governance' (Shearing and Wood 2003a: 217).

Bottom-up, non-state-based security programmes are, on this basis, promulgated as alternative solutions to problems that the state's deep-seated idiocy leaves it institutionally incapable of tackling successfully. Remedying 'governance deficits' means creating security markets that poor communities can effectively participate in such that security is identified, promoted and regulated as what Shearing and Wood term a 'common' – rather than 'public' or 'private' – good. In a recent theorization of this strategy, Shearing and Wood (2003a) argue that this entails thinking and acting along the following three lines. The first is acting and thinking in ways that enhance 'community self-direction'. This means communities defining and pursuing their common interests in respect of security, thereby functioning as autonomous security auspices rather than simply administering central plans or striving to meet alien objectives established by other nodes (Shearing and Wood 2003a: 213). The second entails creating and sustaining different forms of 'community capital'. This means not only the social capital (or strong social networks) with which Shearing and Wood argue poor communities in developing societies are replete, but also the economic capital that reinforces it, as well as knowledge and capacities (cultural capital) and recognition (symbolic capital) (see also Dupont 2004). Thirdly, strategies aimed at improving 'community regulation' or 'accountability' should be developed (Shearing and Wood 2003a: 218), whereby local people – in determining, for instance, how to allocate policing budgets – regulate the provision of their own security in ways that 'respond to local needs, reflect local morality and take advantage of local knowledge' (Bayley 2001: 212).

What Shearing and Wood offer here is a theoretical elaboration of the community peace programmes that 'Security 21' has helped to develop and disseminate – notably the Zwelethemba model of local capacity governance (Johnston and Shearing 2003: 151–60; Shearing and Wood 2003a: 218–21; Roche 2002; cf. B. Dixon 2004). This model – which was initiated in South Africa and then 'transplanted' to

Argentina (Wood 2006), but which is currently being promoted elsewhere – aims to enable community members to resolve their disputes
(the criminal justice lexicon of 'offender' and 'victim' is explicitly
eschewed) in ways consistent with justice and human rights (peace-
making) while also aiming to address the sources of local insecurities
(peace-building). Through 'gatherings' of disputants convened by local
peace committees, negotiated resolutions to conflict are sought in ways
that avoid resort to force – though disputants retain the option of going
to the police throughout. In promoting this model, Shearing and others
emphasize the following key elements: actively developing and harnessing the skills of local people as facilitators; collecting and analysing
data on disputes and their sources, and on dispute-resolution processes
and their outcomes, so as to ensure the reflexive monitoring and 'iterative adjustment' of programmes; mobilizing local knowledge and
capacity to solve problems; moving participants away from a past-
oriented punishment mentality towards a focus on reducing future
risks; and a funding allocation system that rewards facilitators and
invests in local communities on the basis of the peace committees'
accordance with good – that is to say, human rights-regarding – procedures and principles (Wood and Font forthcoming). It adds up, its
advocates claim, to a sustained attempt to use a combination of market
incentives and situated practical knowledge to bring security to poor
communities that free markets and historically despotic states have had
a shabby record of neglecting or oppressing.

This clearly amounts to a theory and practice of security that actively
seeks to relegate, or in some settings stand in for, the state as a player
in its local production. This move is Hayekian in that it rests upon the
free market champion's axiomatic epistemological claim that the state
necessarily lacks the knowledge to respond effectively to – in this case
– demands for order. We must, Shearing and Wood (2003b: 415) urge,
'recognize the soundness of many of the values that neo-liberalism and
associated sensibilities of governance advocate. This involves looking
afresh at many Hayekian arguments, particularly the view that governance is best exercised when it relies heavily on local knowledges and
capacities along with the view that markets often provide the best
means of mobilizing these knowledges and capacities.'

But this new approach is distinctly '*left*-Hayekian' in that it seeks to
supplement or supplant the state, not in the name of the sovereign individual and unfettered market forces, but through deliberative local

capacity-building practices informed by the values of equity and human rights. It offers in this sense a provocative challenge to state-centric thinking about security issued in the name of experimental local democracy; one that works through the 'window of security' (Shearing and Wood 2003b: 417) in an effort to forge common interests and collective problem-solving mechanisms within dispossessed communities. It offers, at the same time, a radically decentred account of belonging and political authority, a theory and praxis concerned more with securing 'denizenship' for poor people across a range of communal spaces than with the old social democratic ambition of connecting people as citizens of national political communities (Shearing and Wood 2003b).

In these respects, there are some instructive parallels between Shearing and others' account of 'nodal governance' and the pragmatist-inspired work of Charles Sabel and his collaborators on 'directly-deliberative polyarchy' (e.g. Cohen and Sabel 1997; Gerstenberg and Sabel 2002). Two such parallels are of particular interest. The first is a radically processual concern with democratic experiments in local problem-solving and 'learning by doing' that both sidesteps the question of what motivates people to put and pursue things in common in the first place, and eschews the communitarian language of belonging and solidarity. Solidarity, on this view, is an 'instrumental solidarity' (Thompson 2003: 41), a coming together that develops out of the experience of tackling specific common problems, but which is not, and has no reason to be, any 'thicker' or more enduring than that. This relates, secondly, to the belief that certain emergent governance practices (whether they be South African peace committees, or new techniques of coordination and regulation in the European Union) need to be understood and encouraged using a novel conceptual language not tied to outmoded and state-centred political categories. It is in this experimentalist spirit that the promise of a nodal conception of security governance is both descriptively mapped and energetically pursued (Johnston and Shearing 2003; cf. Loader and Walker 2004; N. Walker 2006b).

Bringing the state back in?

Matters however are more complex than they at first appear. A close reading of the evolving body of work on nodal security governance reveals that the state in fact continues to assume a far from insignificant role in its proponents' preferred conception of security. At least three such roles can be discerned. First, Shearing and Wood concede that, as well as fostering community security institutions beyond the state, one must continue to 'explore regulatory strategies designed to retain state control over non-state providers where their actions affect public interests' (2003a: 217). Second, Shearing and others envisage a role for the state in generating and re/distributing the collective resources that are needed to place local community capacity-building projects on a firmer footing (Johnston and Shearing 2003: 155). Third, radically reformed state police forces are clearly intended to remain as the site of 'last-resort' coercive intervention, acting as 'responsive regulators' (Ayres and Braithwaite 1992) in ways that are sensitive to the ordering mechanisms of local communities (Wood 2004: 39–40; see also Brogden and Shearing 1993).

This is hardly a trifling set of competences. Rather, Shearing and his collaborators detail a key set of continuing regulatory, allocative and coercive roles for the state in a manner which indicates important areas of overlap between the nodal governance perspective and the position we are seeking to develop in this book. Yet in respect of each of the above three roles we find in the work of theorists of nodal governance a markedly undeveloped account – both sociologically and normatively – of how the state may be reconfigured in these ways, and of the relationships that can be expected (or ought) to obtain between the state and the locally based peace-making and peace-building programmes that Shearing and others ultimately seem concerned to privilege and promote. This, it seems to us, invites a series of difficult but unavoidable questions. Let us conclude this chapter by considering each of them in turn.

First, there is the question of what constitutes the 'public interest' and how the 'public interest' gets constituted. This remains deeply underspecified. So too does the related issue of what the purposes and limits of the state might be in acting as (meta) regulator of the security practices of both rich and poor. How are we to discover or construct the kinds of common regulatory norms that may prevent community security practices becoming a 'medium of injustice' (Markell 2003: 158), driven by what James C. Scott (1998) concedes is the 'partisan knowledge' of local actors who possess a passionate stake in particular outcomes? How, moreover, can the state act to ensure that local security practices contribute to, rather than undermine, equity and human rights, or use *its* knowledge and capacities to enable effective social learning to occur between what might otherwise constitute isolated and parochial nodes of local security (Hirst 2000: 19)? And on what basis and on what terms does the state, as opposed to any other putative holistic regulator, get to play such a central role in the refinement and monitoring of what is in the public (as opposed to private or communal) interest?[7]

There is, on these matters, an evident tension between the approving if passing references Shearing and his collaborators make to the state as mediator of the public interest and their overarching concern with facilitating 'community self-direction'. Several related issues arise here. First, faced with a situation of deep security inequities between rich and poor – or what Markell (2003: 181) calls 'a relation of privilege and subordination' – Shearing and others prioritize a strategy that strives to 'include' poor communities by providing them with resources to enhance their own security, rather than seeking to 'dismantle or attenuate the privilege itself' (Markell 2003: 181) – in this case, by calling into question the anti-social security practices of the rich. Indeed, Shearing and others often appear fairly relaxed about the rise of gated communities, privately guarded corporate enclaves and other risk-management security practices deployed by affluent elites (Johnston and Shearing 2003: ch. 5), electing a strategy that leaves

---

[7] It is important to note in these respects that we currently lack a grounded sociological account of the dynamics of the local security practices that Shearing and others advocate, still less any independent assessment of them from someone who is not a member of the 'Security 21' team – an asymmetry of information that leaves external observers having to take their arguably somewhat rosy portraits of them on trust. Evidence from other forms of citizen security elsewhere in South Africa (Tshehla 2002), together with the scepticism of other authors deeply immersed in questions of post-apartheid justice (B. Dixon 2004: 373–6; Dixon and van der Spuy 2004), suggest that we are wise to retain some critical distance from a model of non-state security that is running the risk of appearing non-falsifiable. It is somewhat ironic that at a time when such suspicion is bubbling up in the place of its inception, the Zwelethemba model is being actively canvassed as a security solution in ways that have yet to answer searching questions about how and whether the 'model' can successfully be imported into, say, divided societies or liberal democracies with strong state traditions. We would stress, however, that it is vital not to replace one set of presuppositions and premises with another and opposite set, and that is certainly not our intention. The Zwelethemba model is no more doomed to fail than it is bound to succeed. The issue, as we have said, is one of evidence, and of its systematic collection and evaluation.

these forms of communal security untouched while seeking to extend their loss-prevention logics and security dividends to poor communities. What this forgets is that security nodes are sites for the production of culture as well as order, a means of forging individual and collective identities and of communicating social meaning about matters such as membership and belonging, inclusion and exclusion, risk and blame. In this respect, the security politics of Shearing and others does little to foster civic solidarity and identification *across* the boundaries of local or ethnic 'community' – a point we return to shortly. But it also tends to invoke a fantasy of security as sovereign mastery of one's own destiny, though on Shearing and others' account such 'mastery' is to be exercised by communities rather than – as in Hayekian neo-liberalism – by sovereign individuals. What is entailed in each case, however, is a downplaying of the mutually dependent relationship that exists between the security of the privileged and the insecurity of the subordinated and, more broadly, of any recognition that the public good of security requires forms of political authority that can help nurture and sustain the mutual acknowledgement of this social connectedness and interdependency.[8]

Secondly, the far from trivial – and not unrelated – question of how the state can obtain for itself the authority and legitimacy required to raise and distribute funds to ensure the longer-term prospects of 'bottom-up' local security programmes is glossed over, as is the wider matter of how levels of economic, cultural and symbolic capital inside communities can be enhanced without the resource-allocating and recognition-granting functions provided by the state.[9] At the very least this would appear to require the existence/cultivation of a sense of belonging to a wider political community sufficient to persuade, in this case, South Africans or Argentinians to identify with the plight of their co-citizens and support, for non-instrumental reasons, both a framework of common regulatory cause and acts of solidarity towards them.

[8] Shearing has on occasions in the past recognized this connection. In their oft-quoted paper Shearing and Bayley on 'The Future of Policing' write: 'All policies that have any prospect of mitigating the growing class differences in public safety depend upon the affluent segments of our societies recognizing that security is indivisible' (1996: 603).

[9] It is noteworthy in this respect that the principal funding for these programmes has to date come from foreign governments, the Finnish and Swedish governments in the case of South Africa, and the Canadian International Development Agency with regard to the project in Rosario, Argentina.

The locally oriented, state-sceptical politics of Shearing and others – with its tendency to treat community, democracy and security as unmediated, face-to-face relationships – has little to say either about the necessary virtues of these mediated forms of political community, or about the institutional 'architecture of sympathy' (Sennett 2003: 200) that may give practical effect to them. Nor do Shearing and others appear sufficiently alert to the paradox that the programmes of communal ordering they advocate may (however much they succeed in generating safer, self-governing communities) weaken the very bonds of solidarity towards strangers that are an essential prerequisite of their continued viability and success. As Charles Taylor has pointed out, forms of 'tribal protection and advancement' can – just as much as market-driven atomism – erode the sense of common purpose, the willingness to put and pursue things in common, that comes from, and is reinforced by, a sense of confident membership of a broader political community (1995: 282–5).

Thirdly, in what is otherwise a potentially promising rearticulation of Kinsey *et al.*'s (1986) theory of 'minimal policing', relatively scant attention is given to the question of how – historically violent, deeply partisan – states are to be democratized, constrained and reoriented along the lines suggested, such that they come to respect the integrity and outcomes of local peace-making processes and intervene only when called upon to do so (cf. Dupont *et al.* 2005: 15). In this context, we are led to reintroduce the question that we first posed in chapter 2, one that neo-liberal advocates of the minimal state have not in our view adequately answered, and which contemporary theorists of nodal governance have scarcely begun to address: namely, how can one create the kind of rights-regarding constitutional state that is needed to encourage and facilitate local security practices that are consistent with democratic values such as 'equity and human rights' (Shearing and Wood 2003a: 212)?

In our judgement these various lacunae are common symptoms of the sceptical perspective that we have described and brought under scrutiny in this chapter. It is a stance that – in the case of Shearing and others at least – gestures towards the positive ordering and cultural work that the state performs in the production of security. But it is also animated, as we have shown, by the idea that the state is obtuse, hubristic and for these reasons flawed as a security actor, as well as by a desire to situate the main frame of analysis elsewhere – in the democratic experiments in local peace-making that can make good the state's cognitive shortcomings. There is much of value in both this assessment and this ambition, as we have tried to indicate. Yet, ultimately, this portrayal of the state – as a necessary evil, wanted but not welcome – prevents a full appreciation and exploration of its necessary and virtuous role in giving practical effect to security understood – in sociological terms – as a 'thick' public good. It is to this exploration that we now turn our attention.

PART II

Securing states of security

> Thus far . . . we have no reason to suppose
> that there is any better general solution to
> the problem of security [than the state], and
> little, if any, reason to regard any other
> possible countervailing value as a serious
> rival to security as the dominant continuing
> human need.
>
> (John Dunn, *The Cunning of Unreason*, p. 212)

6 | *The good of security*

T HE cumulative critique of the role of the state in policing laid out in part I cannot easily be gainsaid. The state *can* be and often has been a physical and psychological bully. It *is* prone to meddling, to interfering where it is not wanted. It *does* take sides, and in so doing packs the hardest punch. It undoubtedly *does* seek to set the cultural climate and in some measure is successful, as it is in making life difficult or impossible for those who do not conform to the norms it encourages and defends. Finally, it *will* tend towards stupidity. Not only does it lack the means to answer all the key questions about individual and collective security, it often seems unable or unwilling to recognize this deficiency.

Yet, as our scepticism about state scepticism has sought to make clear, in concentrating on its dangers and limitations, the state sceptics have tended to be inattentive towards the continuing positive contribution of the state. They have paid insufficient regard to the case that the state, or its functional equivalent, remains indispensable to any project concerned with optimizing the human good of security, or, at least, have neglected the full implications of that possibility. To remedy that defect, and move beyond mere scepticism about state scepticism, demands a closer appreciation of the role of the state in the generation of social meaning and in the ordering of social practice pertaining to security. But to achieve that more intimate understanding of the state and its possibilities, and avoid a circular justification of its security function, we must first gain a little distance from it. We must begin in the present chapter by revisiting the concept of security and asking what, if anything, makes security decidedly – perhaps even peculiarly – suited to public provision. Only then will we be in a position to address the task of reconnecting that imperative of public provision to the particular 'public' institutional form of the state.

Security as a 'thick' public good

The best place to begin an examination that seeks to refine our understanding of whether and why security is a candidate for public provision is with the general literature on 'public' or otherwise collective
goods. Such an enquiry, however, cannot proceed without some initial
conceptual ground-clearing. As is obvious from even the most cursory
reconnaissance, the terrain of 'public' goods is an overcrowded and
potentially treacherous one. In the first place, there is the sheer
expanse of terminology available. Goods may be public, collective,
communal, common, shared or social, to take only the most common
terms in currency, and there is both considerable inconsistency and
much overlap in their use. Similarly, the term 'good(s)' has many distinct meanings and many shades within these distinct meanings.
Goods can designate material objects or conditions with some use
value, such as a bridge or a railway network or clean air. Or, as the
plural gives way to the singular, the relevant object of analysis may
become abstract institutions or forms of social organization that are
considered to be good, such as friendship or democracy, or even generally valued features of institutions or forms of social organization,
such as conviviality or solidarity. Finally, and most abstractly of all,
the 'good' can be shorthand for 'conceptions of the good' – for those
general attributes that are claimed to contribute towards or even be
definitive of the common good or the 'good society', such as justice or
equality.[1]

In the second place, and accounting for much of the variation in the
choice and use of terminology, different writers working within different disciplines have very different reasons for entering this conceptual
terrain. Economists, lawyers, sociologists and political theorists are all
regular visitors, but each has their distinctive 'knowledge-constitutive
interests' (Habermas 1974). Economists tend to be primarily concerned with the identification of those goods that cannot adequately be
provided for in the marketplace. Lawyers focus on the question of
whether certain diffuse public benefits may be the subject of fundamental rights, or of justiciable claims more generally. Sociologists
emphasize the functional prerequisites of the survival of the social
system. Political theorists are more concerned with ideal conceptions,

---

[1] This discussion draws upon and develops that of Geuss (2003: 8–9).

with what ought to be viewed as central or conducive to the *bonum commune*.[2]

Rather than a reason for despair however, the richly diverse genealogy of the idea of public good may be helpful to our enquiry. Instead of viewing the different conceptions as concerned with quite different *problématiques* and as theoretically incommensurable, we may understand and represent them as more or less ambitious appreciations of what is involved in something being viewed as a public good. At the thinnest level, which we associate with economists' understanding of public goods, and which tends to be taken as an initial point of reference across the various literatures, the social or public element is entirely *instrumental*. What is at issue here is the indispensability or importance of a social or public element to the very process of producing or otherwise providing the goods in question. Thereafter, all the factors that bear upon their value as goods, including the effects of their enjoyment, the manner in which they are enjoyed, and any other conditions prerequisite to their enjoyment, are to be understood in entirely individual-centred terms. At a thicker level, we may, by contrast, think of public goods as having just that *social* dimension in terms of effects or experience or conditionality that is passed over in the instrumental conception of the economists. Finally, at the thickest level of all – one that is at best only implicitly recognized in the various literatures – we may understood public goods as having a *constitutive* dimension, as being in some measure implicated in the very dynamic through which particular publics become conceived and self-conceived *as* publics.

In what follows, we seek to show how the concept of security repays analysis as a public good at each of these levels and in consideration of the relationship between these three levels. In so doing, we necessarily advance a more ambitious understanding of security as a public good than is common in the literature. We go beyond the familiar instrumental dimension, seeking to place fuller emphasis on the social dimension and to develop the notion of a constitutive dimension as the controlling idea. As we shall see, not only does a layered approach help

---

[2] Some of the most interesting current literature – with an emphasis upon material that tries to talk across disciplines – includes Raz (1986); Waldron (1993, 2004); C. Taylor (1995); Heritier (2002); Mayntz (2002); Murphy and Nagel (2002); Geuss (2003); and Etzioni (2004).

to account for the terms in which we make our case, it is also vital to the substance of that case. As to its terms, it is precisely because of the importance accorded to the constitutive dimension that we retain the language of '*public* goods' to describe security, albeit in a significantly fuller sense than that intended within the economics literature. As to the substance, it is only through the density of the web of connections made between instrumental, social and constitutive conceptions of the idea of security that we are able to do full justice to the argument for the public provision of security, and so establish the platform necessary to address the task of re-establishing the vital nexus between security and the state.

Security as an instrumental good

Under the standard economic definition public goods are those whose consumption is 'non-excludable' and 'non-rival'. To provide for one is to provide for all, and enjoyment by one does not detract from enjoyment by all. Street lighting, clean air and national defence are among the paradigm cases of public goods so conceived, as, crucially, is internal security itself.[3] This definition rests upon recognition of the possibilities and implications of market failure. A public good is a good that, on the one hand, is hard or even impossible to produce for private profit, yet, on the other, if supplied does not exhibit the normal problems of consumption scarcity. The dimension of non-excludability creates a free-rider problem, so removing or reducing the usual incentives for anyone to supply the goods in the marketplace. The dimension of non-rivalness, or jointness of supply, points to the large beneficial externalities of providing the good to any particular group of consumers who register their demand – an added value of untargeted and cost-free supply to which the market by definition is insensitive. Because of these twin concerns, it is typically claimed that public goods, with their economies of scale, require some mechanism of compulsory collective commitment if they

---

[3] According to Olsen (1971: 14), for example, 'the basic or most elementary goods and services provided by government, like defence and police protection, and the system of law and order generally, are such that they go to everyone or practically everyone in the nation. It would obviously not be feasible, if indeed it were possible, to deny the protection provided by the military services, the police, and the courts to those who did not voluntarily pay their share of the costs of government.' See also Murphy and Nagel (2002: 45–8).

are to be adequately provided at the relevant scale or even provided at all, with the state generally considered as the best or at least the default candidate for public provision.

The basic attraction of the economists' approach is twofold. First, by focusing on the fundamental question of whether and how goods get to be produced *at all*, it poses the question of the necessity of public provision in the most stark and straightforward terms. Secondly, the crisp questions it asks seem to promise clear black or white answers. So it may seem self-evident why security, and in particular such security as is capable of being generated or assured by the public police, is viewed by many as one of the pre-eminent public goods (Jones and Newburn 1998: 33). The provision of a secure environment is an accomplishment the benefits of which cannot easily be restricted to a determinate group of users who have paid the appropriate charge. Equally, there is an intuitive appeal in the argument that security is a non-rival good, that the security of some members of the community at best necessarily implies the security of all, and at least should not and need not come at the expense of the security of other members of the community.

Yet, as with many candidate cases, particularly in technologically advanced, highly mobile and informationally sophisticated societies (Hardin 1999: 66), the purity of security's credentials as a public good in the economic sense do not withstand close enquiry. Excludability is only partly a function of the intrinsic nature of a good. It is also in some measure a consequence of variables such as the state of technological development and of other structural conditions including the nature of the built environment and the prevailing regime of property rights. Adjustment to these variables may work either for or against exclusive provision. So technology can generate new non-excludable goods, as with street lighting. New technology, however, can also allow us to target particular audiences, as with the encryption of broadcasting or electronic road tolls, or, more pertinently for present purposes, with restricted codes and communication mechanisms for accessing and alerting specialist security services. The concentration of populations involved in the long-term process of urbanization intensifies mutual dependence in countless ways and makes it difficult to avoid or control 'spill-over' risks in matters such as public health, fire and, of course, security against crime and public disorder. But by the same token urban planning can help to design out crime for particular locales and their

discrete communities, as in the case of the location and layout of buildings and building access to allow blanket coverage by CCTV cameras.
And, as the growth of 'mass private property' in the form of shopping
malls and various other forms of widespread public access to sites of
commercial activity in much of the western world in the last half-
century indicates (Shearing and Stenning 1983), regimes where property rights are individually or collectively assigned tend to be more
amenable to the targeted control of risks and distribution of goods,
including the good of security, than common systems of property
enjoyment and access.

   None of this indicates an ineluctable trend towards the corruption
and erosion of the public good of security. It does, however, suggest a
number of points which, if taken together, underwrite the precarious-
ness of the instrumental argument in favour of the public provision of
security. In the first place, the excludability of the good of security is a
question of circumstance and degree. Not only does technological
innovation and market demand consistently generate new security
commodities – burglar alarms, electronic security hardware and so
forth – which are perfectly assignable, but even those forms of security
provision whose benefits are less easily targeted towards particular
individuals may nevertheless be concentrated on determinate groups.
Benefits might be difficult to restrict, but the task is by no means impossible. Some economic agent or social collectivity may discover the
'enlightened self-interest' required to seek to supply security services
discriminately that might otherwise be left to the indiscriminate provision of the state. As the paradigm case of 'gated communities' reveals,
across many societies active or affluent citizens are increasingly taking
the initiative to 'club' together in order to generate a safe environment
by excluding others from it (Elliot 1989; Blakely and Snyder 1997;
Caldeira 2001; Low 2003).[4]

   In the second place, the fragility and contingency of the argument
from non-excludability both alerts us to and reinforces similar deficiencies in the argument from non-rivalness. As with non-excludability, the
immunity of security from considerations of scarcity and subtractability

---

[4] This possibility is acknowledged within the economic literature on public goods,
   the term 'club goods' being reserved for those which are excludable but which
   remain non-rival within the membership of the predefined club (Jordan 1996;
   for applications to security, see Hope 2000; Crawford 2006).

in consumption is always a matter of circumstance and degree. We saw in our discussion of the uniform and equal quality of aspects of the provision of general order in chapter 4 that sometimes security clearly does possess the attribute of non-rivalness. To protect one member of the community from a terrorist attack is also, and without additional cost, to protect all other members. To apprehend a serial killer as he stalks his prey is also to protect all potential future victims. To restore public order in response to the complaints of some locals is also to provide a tranquil environment for the rest of the neighbourhood. Yet general provision is by no means always a necessary and necessarily cost-free incident of particular provision. Much policing and much security work generally is more discretely targeted – whether incident-specific, victim-specific, offender-specific or otherwise locale-specific – and to that extent it is transformed into a scarce resource with unequal distributive consequences. And while this is true even of the broadest and presumptively non-excludable public scheme of policing and security provision, it is more emphatically the case where exclusionary arrangements are developed. To the extent that civilly generated or commodified security and 'enclavization' creates safer environments for insiders and purchasers (Bayley and Shearing 1996), this is patently not matched among those who lack the economic or social capital needed to transform policing and security into a 'club good'.

What is more, those who can afford to indulge in such exclusionary security practices may achieve protection at the direct expense of the less economically advantaged or socially well-positioned citizens and groups – the 'clubbing' of security existing in almost inverse relation to the distribution of crime risks (Hope 1997). The provision of club goods, in other words, not only sacrifices the 'externality benefits' of non-rivalness by reintroducing targeting and treating resources as zero-sum, but actually introduces new 'externality costs' (Hope 2000). By displacing crime to excluded and less well-protected areas, it contributes to their ghettoization and social marginalization. And the resulting inequality of security distribution and overall disutility may be exacerbated by the harsh treatment of intruders within the boundaries of secured enclaves, or the plight of victims of the 'illegal, violent, retributive, arbitrary and judgmental' manifestations of those forms of 'civil policing' which descend into vigilantism (Johnston 1999: 153). Moreover, any kind of exclusionary private or civil security framework may also ultimately frustrate or curtail the aspirations of insiders. Its strategy is necessarily premised upon the existence of and danger posed by a hostile wider environment, thus providing a constant and potentially debilitating reminder of the self-limiting, costly and contingent quality of the version of security to which it subscribes.[5]

Taken together, these points suggest an inherent instability in the economists' conception of security as a public good. If reduced to a question of how to produce a benefit which might otherwise be treated as a private good in terms of the conditions, manner and significance of its enjoyment, then the status of security as a public good is doubly vulnerable. On the one hand, those qualities that make it particularly amenable to public provision are shown not to be inherent and self-evident, but to be contingent upon a wide complex of variables and of disputable relevance to any particular set of circumstances. On the other hand, at least some of these variables, including the nature and distribution of property rights and the development of a demand for and supply of commodified security, are within the control or sphere of influence of those who would prefer to see either security in general, or at least *their* security, provided other than within a non-exclusive public framework. So there may be a self-fulfilling element in the undermining of security as a public good conceived of in these thin terms.[6] It may become vulnerable to the broader arguments of welfare economists discussed in chapter 2 concerning the presumptive inferiority to an 'exit'-sensitive market system of *any* regime of public provision, with its dependence on 'voice' mechanisms and its susceptibility to capture or unequal influence. It may also become vulnerable to the more narrowly self-regarding calculations of those whose relevant conception of the public goes no further than those with whom they share short-term 'clubbing' interests and capacities, and who are as uninterested in negative externalities as they are oblivious to the longer-term, self-undermining implications of their social myopia.

In summary, a purely production-orientated conception of public goods can neither provide a compelling *normative* argument in favour of the monopoly or dominant provision of security within one privileged or indeed *any* particular site of production, nor can it *in fact*

---

[5] It is in this deep sense that the very concept of *private* security may be considered oxymoronic (Loader 1997b). See also note 12 below.
[6] This self-fulfilling element is at the core of the spiral of fragmentation, one of the pathological syndromes of modern security discussed in chapter 8 below.

guarantee such a framework of production. The institutional potential of the classic public goods approach is undermined by the contingency, fragility and circular presumptiveness of its foundations. In particular, it is undone by its inability to locate the good reasons and the actual motivation to invest exclusively or predominantly in this rather than any other 'public' or 'private' community in anything other than arguments about the functional benefits of aggregate collective provision that presuppose that the good reasons and actual motivation for such an exclusive or predominant mark and measure of collective self-identification already exist.

Security as a social good

If the understanding of security as a public good and the argument in favour of the public provision of security is not to be open to these types of critique and susceptible to these kinds of undermining, an additional dimension is clearly required. If we cannot just argue that a general scheme of public provision trumps all other contenders in its simple capacity to deliver – and in the acceptance by all members of the relevant public of its capacity to deliver – a level of security coverage that could not otherwise be guaranteed, then our argument for public provision must appeal instead to something distinctive in the character of such public provision. We must locate the significance of a public mode of provision by shifting from a quantitative to a qualitative mode of analysis; by looking beyond the bare calculation of whether and how security gets produced for an aggregation of individuals to the question of the value of the good so produced or supplied. Or in Waldron's (1993: 358) terms, we must seek out those ways in which, if at all, security possesses a societal dimension that cannot 'be adequately characterizable in terms of its worth to any or all of the members of that society considered one by one'.

Yet we should note at the outset that there is a reluctance to concede much, if at all, to a more social conception of security, and by no means just from those who view state and social production as no more than a poor substitute in the event of market failure. For example, Charles Taylor, no friend to an individual-centred social ontology, explicitly contrasts the merely 'convergent' (1995: 191) good of security – one that corresponds to the economists' version – with those goods that are in some way intrinsically and irreducibly social. To take but one more example, Joseph Raz, in the course of a notable attempt to justify liberal rights by reference to their promotion of a public culture that serves the common good, nevertheless wants to exclude a category of 'personal rights' that includes personal security from the liberal lexicon – arguing that their primary justification lies instead in their intrinsic value to the right-holder (1986: 255–62).

Why such reluctance? We may speculate that the reasons are as much ideological as intellectual. Ideologically, given the deeply ambivalent position of security in the modern social and political imaginary as both condition of and standing threat to individual freedom (a matter discussed in chapter 2), we should not be surprised to encounter a widespread squeamishness about thinking of security in ways that register the collective rather than the individual dimension of its virtue. Intellectually, it appears insufficiently appreciated – for reasons not unrelated to such squeamishness – that consideration of the social dimension of security raises not one but several questions, each of which suggests quite different answers. In one respect, as we shall see, the recognition of a social dimension to the value of security is quite uncontroversial, but does not decisively advance the case for the public provision of security. In a second respect, such recognition is clearly excluded. In a third respect, the answer is more nuanced but perhaps most crucial, as it points us towards what is the most distinctive social dimension of the good of security, and what in the final analysis is the most promising way of justifying public provision. Let us deal with each of these social aspects of security in turn.

The first and, in principle, least controversial social aspect of security concerns the social effects of the enjoyment of security. As with the economists' definition, we find an instrumental logic at work, but in this case the causal relationship is reversed. We are not here concerned with the social means required to produce the individual good of security, but rather with the subsequent link or links in the causal chain – with how the widespread production of that individual good in turn may have socially valuable consequences. On this view security, and the liberty that is guaranteed by security, provides the platform for the development of the common good – or at least some common goods – however conceived. This common good may itself be viewed in highly individual-centred terms. As we have seen, it is axiomatic even to theories of the *minimal* state that without measures put in place to protect the person and property of individuals through some framework of coercive self-organization, those individuals will be unable to pursue their ends free from interference or the endemic threat of interference. Equally, however, the basic security of person and property may be seen as instrumental to all sorts of other collective goods that are necessary to a more expansive or positive conception of human freedom – one that comprises the well-being or wherewithal to enjoy negative freedom fully. For example, it is impossible to envisage stable and reasonably inclusive and responsive democratic decision-making – for many, an important collective good in itself and one that may also be conducive to other individual and collective goods – without the prior and continuing guarantee of private freedom (Habermas 2001). Equally, the various infrastructural goods which many associate with a more positive conception of freedom, such as widespread availability of health provision, social security and even a common public culture, cannot be conceived of without the baseline of security – of negative freedom – and the stability of democratic politics and public administration which flows from this. Further, to the extent that we might want to treat some collective goods such as solidarity as valuable components of the good life in themselves, quite apart from their instrumental contribution to a more positive conception of individual freedom – a deeply complex and controversial issue between liberals and communitarians to which we shall return – then again the security baseline is indispensable. In sum, however modest or expansive our conception of freedom, and irrespective of whether negative freedom and other individual-centred values are the key entries in our index of the good society or whether and to what extent other collective goods consequential upon security are deemed to have their own instrumental significance or even independent value – all matters of disagreement – security is a constant foundational presence as the most basic instrument to the realization of any particular conception of the common good.

The strength of the consequential approach towards security as a social good is also, however, its weakness. The social dimension, while not as thin as in the production-centred approach of the economists, is still conceived in a somewhat attenuated or detached fashion. The emphasis merely on social effects leaves unexamined the more intimate question of the intrinsic social dimension – if any – of security. Indeed, we are offered little encouragement even to approach that question indirectly, by asking what kind, or quality, of good security has to be in order to provide the effects we associate with the common good. For precisely because there is disagreement about the content of the common good towards which security is deemed instrumental, we might on closer analysis find that different conceptions of that conse-quential common good require or permit rather different understand-ings of the prior security instrument. The overlapping consensus on security as a necessary platform towards any conception of the common good security may, in short, mask considerable disagreement as to the social properties of that platform.[7] And just as the platform hypothesis dramatizes the strength and urgency of our convergent commitment to take security seriously, it again begs the question of *how* we are supposed to take it seriously – and in particular the basis upon which and the form in which a common and broadly acceptable scheme of *public* provision might, if at all, be justified and guaranteed.

If consequentialism offers a suggestive but, in the end, precariously thin way in which to conceive of goods in social terms, at the other extreme we can also discount an inappropriately thick understanding. On this view, a good is social because the very manner in which we enjoy or experience the good in question is irreducibly social. We are talking here about what Taylor (1995: 190) calls 'immediately' common goods – where the good lies in the simple fact 'that we share'. That is to say, the generation of the good for one person and its enjoyment by that person is wholly, directly and reciprocally dependent upon its simulta-neous generation for and enjoyment by certain others (Waldron 1993: 358–9). We can indeed imagine such goods at various levels of abstrac-tion – from our shared enjoyment of a conversation or a party, to spe-cific social institutions such as friendship or comradeship or love, to the most general sentiments of valued sociality such as fraternity or solidar-ity. Security is clearly not a constitutively other-regarding sentiment in

---

[7] As a rough rule of thumb we may assume that highly individual-centred con-ceptions of the common good – those that emphasize the importance of freedom of choice and minimize the value of collective goods – are more likely also to view possible 'social' aspects of the prior instrumental good of security, such as the degree of redistribution of private resources allowed for its comprehensive and equal provision, in minimalist terms, whereas those who hold to a more col-lectivist conception of the good are more likely to countenance collective means to its realization. This is a matter both of consistency and coherence of value commitments at different points within a single theoretical worldview and of instrumental logic – the more socially ambitious the solution sought, the more socially ambitious the means required.

the sense of these other goods. My security and your security are more than simply a product of our relationship. Whatever the forms and degree of mutual dependence of our respective states of security, they are not exclusively mutually *constituted*.

What is more, it is important to note that even if security were appropriately conceived as a social good in the purest and most immediate sense that would be a strong argument *against* rather than for its public provision. What immediate common or public goods have in common, after all, is precisely their insusceptibility to social engineering through public plan and provision, whether this is on account of their intimate texture, their spontaneous motivation, or their necessary grounding in long-standing experience or practice. Any attempt to fabricate such goods in the public domain is doomed at best to produce a poor replica of the real thing – as with the 'organized fun' and false conviviality of many official celebrations – and at worst to provide a sinister perversion of public purpose – as in George Orwell's Ministry of Love. And if the paternalistic – indeed imperialistic – impulse to tell people 'how to' experience associative benefits or to dictate what counts as the authentic way of experiencing such benefits must be resisted even in the case of genuinely immediate goods, then, as we shall shortly have cause to recall, we must treat with even greater suspicion any lurking temptation to stretch the meaning of security in the same constitutively other-regarding direction.

If, however, we move beyond the extremes of consequentialism and immediacy, it is possible to imagine a third and more promising sense in which security may be considered a candidate social good. What we are here concerned with is that part of the social dimension of security that rests neither upon its consequences nor upon the manner of its expression and experience, but upon the fulfilment of certain social preconditions. To begin to unpack this idea, we need to identify two separate but connected senses in which the security of any individual is dependent upon the action and attitudes of others, each of which displays a characteristic that is quite unique to the good of security.

First, and most obviously, there is what we might call the objective or intersubjective dimension of security. When we think of the objective 'security situation' of any individual, we have in mind the relationship between the catalogue of person- and property-securing measures in place to protect that individual, on the one hand, and the propensity of third parties to threaten that individual's security interests notwithstanding the catalogue of protection, on the other. Both aspects of the situational calculus depend crucially upon the actions and attitudes of others. The positive side – the catalogue of protective measures – rests in large part upon the commitment and cooperation of public security providers and others – commercial security agents, neighbours, friends or concerned co-citizens – who are strategically located such that they are able to contribute to an individual's objective security situation, as well as, at a further level of remove, on the preparedness of the citizen-taxpayer to fund the provision of public security.

So far, so familiar. All public goods, including material public goods such as clean air, transport or utilities provision, require a high degree of social coordination and regulation as well as a measure of public funding for their successful provision. It is only when we turn to the negative side of security conceived of objectively – the propensity of third parties to avoid or overcome the security measures in place and threaten or harm our security – that we encounter its first truly distinctive feature. For unlike purely material public goods or even those collective contributions to the common good such as public education or a common artistic heritage whose accomplishment is wholly or partly concerned with the quality of how we live together and so registers in the social or cultural domain, the public good of security has the added dimension that it addresses a root problem that is itself socially generated. Whereas the solution to the 'problem' addressed by public goods is invariably social at least in terms of the means required and perhaps also in terms of the quality of the end desired, in all cases other than security the problem in question is defined simply as the absence of the desirable good. Only in the case of security does the problem describe a pathological state – *in*security rather than merely non-security – whose pedigree itself is entirely social.[8] So security refers not only to the provision of the objective measures of safety put in place in the form of police officers, crime prevention equipment, a safety-aware built environment, etc., at the level of 'problem-solution' but also, and more fundamentally, to those risks and dangers that are inherent in and a product of the social environment.

---

[8] In many other cases, such as education and health, the problem to which the public good responds, respectively ill-health and ignorance, may of course be exacerbated by certain features of the social environment. Yet unlike insecurity, the 'bads' of ill-health and ignorance are not purely a product of social relations.

But, in the second place, even at the level of 'problem-solution', the individual's sense of security does not just depend upon the person- and property-securing measures objectively put in place and sustained by others, but also upon how these objectively constituted measures are subjectively interpreted and experienced by the individual. This double foundation indicates a second peculiarity of security as a social good. On the one hand, whereas many public goods may be accomplished and ascertained in purely objective terms, albeit various positive states of mind may flow from their realization,[9] the socially inflected experience of feeling or not feeling secure is itself internal to and partially constitutive of what we mean by (in)security. On the other hand, whereas immediate public goods refer only to (shared) states of mind, albeit many objective benefits may flow from their realization,[10] security, as we have seen, also and in the first instance depends upon and is constituted through certain objective accomplishments.

How does the second, experiential dimension of security manifest itself, and in what sense or senses is it socially preconditioned? Individuals, in order to feel secure, must be confident that they can pursue their ends without harmful interference or its threat, and so in turn must feel reasonably secure that the conditions for the effective and ongoing realization of their objective security are themselves reasonably secure. That is to say, there is an internal relationship between the experience of security and the existence of stable social expectations. And this means that our current sense of security is always to some extent based upon a prediction about future security. Not only must we feel safe in the here and now, but we also need to be reasonably assured that the conditions guaranteeing our safety will continue for the foreseeable future (Waldron 2004). Such confidence is a function of two sets of factors, each of which has a strong social dimension. In the first place, it depends upon the individual's perception of a complex social 'fact', namely the objective state of and prospects for his or her security, which in turn depends upon the individual's sense not only of the current propensities but also of the long-term commitments and resilient attitudes of official security providers and other

---

[9] For example, the sense of social confidence that one may derive from education.
[10] For example, all kinds of material benefits may be derived from a sense of friendship or, on a wider social canvas, from a sense of solidarity, but we understand these benefits as consequential upon rather than intrinsic to the goods in question.

individuals whose behaviour may be capable of having a bearing upon his or her security. In the second place, it depends upon how and where this impression fits in terms of the individual's personal threshold of manageable fear, of vulnerability to intimations of insecurity. We will have more to say about this type of vulnerability in due course; suffice it to say that it, too, is socially conditioned in the sense that the more citizens possess a sense 'of effortless secure belonging' (Margalit and Raz 1990: 447) to a particular community the less they will be prone to unease about marginal security risks. In sum, then, the overall measure of an individual's sense of security is the extent to which that individual feels free of *anxiety* about the existence, extent and stable reproduction of the objective or intersubjective conditions of his or her security. Clearly, the objective 'security situation' of the individual is a highly significant factor influencing his or her level of anxiety, but, just as clearly, its significance is mediated by a number of other social factors.[11]

We may have begun to identify what is distinctively social about the good of security, but it is by no means yet clear what this implies for public provision. Even if we accept that security is intrinsically socially conditioned or dependent in the ways elaborated, the specification of the optimal conditions for the generation and provision of a low-risk and anxiety-free security environment remains complex and far from uncontroversial. There may be a temptation, having produced the social card and revealed something of the scope and intensity of our

[11] As has been demonstrated by countless studies of the non-linear relationship between people's 'fear of crime' and their antecedent levels of objective risk (see Hale 1996). It should also be clear from the foregoing discussion that we are breaking with the psychological reductionism that one sometimes encounters in the 'fear of crime' debate, a reductionism which says that such fear is rooted in the make-up of 'vulnerable' individuals. To conceptualize security as having a subjective dimension in the manner we have just done is precisely *not* to resort to the common-sense notion that some people are 'resilient' while others are 'fragile', thereby making security a question of individual mindsets. Our point, rather, is that the emotional states which are bound up with (in)security – anxiety, fear, vengeance, hope, pleasure, etc. – are deeply social and that different political arrangements permit or constrain the production and expression of them. Just as we have plenty of historical evidence of social conditions that are more or less likely to licence and foster the so-called 'authoritarian personality' (Adorno *et al.* 1950), so it is possible to imagine and (re)configure states that are more or less likely to supply the material and symbolic resources which enable individuals to be resilient in the face of the risks posed by their environment.

reliance on others for our security, to start the bidding high by claiming that the optimal fulfilment of our sense of freedom from anxiety about security depends upon the equal fulfilment of the sense of freedom from anxiety about security of all others to whom we are socially 'connected' inasmuch as they may affect the conditions of our security. In other words, we may be encouraged to conclude, *pace* the economists, not that the security of each *implies* the security of all, but that the security of each *depends* upon the security of all, and in that way to reassert the priority of a comprehensiveness of coverage that only a system of public provision can ensure. Yet this temptation should be resisted, as such a proposition rests on assumptions that cannot be convincingly sustained.

In the first place, the proposition would hold in conditions of precise equality of vulnerability and of strategic deployment of harm capacity between all individuals in a community. Where each were as able and willing as each of his or her significant others to affect the security of each of his or her significant others (full symmetry of vulnerability), and if this were fully mutually acknowledged (full consciousness of that symmetry), we would be able to conceive of mutual security in terms of a self-reinforcing social equilibrium. But absent a Robinson Crusoe-type scenario, this does not describe the conditions of any actual human society. Secondly, short of these conditions of equality of influence, if we could nevertheless envisage conditions of full mutual empathy and altruism as regards the security concerns of significant others (however widely defined), then again we might be able to sustain the strong mutual dependence thesis. If our anxiety about security could not be assuaged unless and until we were sure of the security of others, *just because* we defined security as a good which was devoid of value unless enjoyed by all and so were unable or unprepared to take comfort in our own security unless and until it was equally guaranteed to these others, then our very moral orientation would be such as to guarantee security as a collective virtue. Again, however, beyond the scale and scope of 'immediate' social units such as families or otherwise tightly knit groups where the affective ties of friendship or loyalty may be particularly strong, this is an implausible assumption to make about actual human societies. Indeed, if made without qualification such a claim would seem to redesignate security as an immediate public good – the good residing in its sharing – in a manner we have already explicitly rejected.

The two scenarios of reciprocal vulnerabilty and altruistic concern do however offer a clue as to how we can begin to flesh out the social dimension of security. Our level of anxiety *is*, after all, affected in at least some measure by our appreciation of the capacity of others, officials and laypersons, to affect our security, and by our appreciation of how our capacity and propensity to affect their security influences their attitude towards our security. So in the day-to-day monitoring of our anxiety about security and evaluation of the conditions of such anxiety, we do take account of the relationship between the threat posed to us by others and the threat posed to them by us, even if there is no equality of mutual influence and even if we understand others' propensity to affect our security as being of a different order than our propensity to affect theirs. Moreover, since, as noted, our (in)security has a reflexive dimension – as anxiety about our security is itself a form of insecurity and as a sense of assurance about our security is itself an augmentation of our security – to the extent that our monitoring of our levels of anxiety preoccupies us and our evaluation of our conditions of security requires sustained vigilance, then this itself is an indication that our existential state of security is suboptimal, that we are too vulnerable to our perceptions of insecurity.[12] It follows that we typically aspire to a situation where our monitoring of our security environment may be a highly tacit and routine affair, an activity which takes place largely at the level of 'practical' rather than 'discursive consciousness' (Giddens 1984); one where we rarely feel it necessary to peep round the veil of our security cover, and our checks when we do so need only be cursory. So, ideally, our level of trust in our security environment should be very high, the reminders of our vulnerability few and routine, neither palpable in our physical environment, intrusive in our daily routines, nor prominent in our discursive consciousness.

As well as reinforcing our appreciation of the importance of the strategic nexus connecting our security to others, this sense of the exacting conditions of optimal security also helps to explain how more altruistic considerations may enter the security equation. We need make no assumptions about altruism being a natural human condition

---

[12] One may, among many illustrative instances of this, cite the case of gated communities and other affluent middle-class enclaves, environments where conditions of objective security tend to coexist with a pervasive sense of subjective insecurity, especially in relation to the conditions and possibility of social life 'beyond the walls' (see, on this, Girling *et al.* 2000: ch. 5).

to conclude that in our techniques for monitoring and reducing anxiety about security, concern for the security of others finds certain prompts, some contexts in which it can come to appear to us as 'natural' – as a necessary virtue. For our strategic monitoring of our own security concerns inevitably makes us aware of the security concerns of others, and our desire to lower the anxiety 'transaction costs' of taking care of our own security anxiety may lead us to conclude that the best guarantee – the most transaction-free insurance policy – of our own security is the equal guarantee of the security of others to whom we are connected and by whom we may be affected. And in this complex and iterative calculation, it becomes easier to appreciate the security of others as a good in its own right. That is to say, the very circumstances of security anxiety are such that we may become educated in the virtues of security altruism and endorse a qualified version of the very proposition whose pretensions to innateness and universalizability we criticized above; namely, that the enjoyment of security by others does indeed have a positive bearing on our enjoyment of our own security in a manner that goes beyond its function as a strategic prerequisite. And though there will be limits to that altruism, in some circumstances the practical coincidence between prudent self-interest and independent concern for the security of others may be sufficiently strong, sustained and self-reinforcing that these limits are not regularly put to the test.

These arguments are far from resurrecting the boldest proposition that might emerge from an analysis of the social prerequisites of security; namely, that the optimal security of each depends upon the security of all. They do, however, suggest a much more conditional proposition along the same lines; namely, that there is a tendency for the quality of security, with its distinctive twin traits of a socially generated problem and a subjectively experienced solution, to be enhanced in the case of any particular individual when the security of those with whom that individual shares a social environment is also reasonably attended to. And while this does not provide a compelling argument in favour of the comprehensiveness of coverage that only a system of public provision can guarantee, it does supply one consideration in its favour.

Security as a constitutive public good

Yet the more important message to be drawn from our analysis of the socially conditional aspect of security, as indeed of the socially consequential aspect of security, is indirect rather than direct: it concerns the way in which this aspect connects to our final *constitutive* dimension of security. What we refer to here is how security as a social or collective good of the sort we have begun to describe in consequential and in conditional terms is implicated in the very process of constituting the 'social' or the 'public'.

Such an approach has to overcome an initial objection, one that would doubt the very validity of a distinction between constitutive and other social dimensions. For is our sense of the 'social' or the 'public' not merely the fluid, context-dependent and diversely manifest outcome of the multifarious situations in which individuals put or find things in common? Clearly our understanding of who 'our' relevant public is and the nature of our social bond is indeed constantly mediated through new experiences, new strategic and affective contexts of coming together. But this does not do justice to the independent and constitutive role of the public in the social imaginary. Our most basic anthropological understanding of human sociability tells us that the symbolic organization of 'publics' and of the 'public domain' is more than a random series of ripples in the stream of social consciousness. Our sense of societal organization and identity, rather, helps to embed and direct the flow of social meaning, and is typically continuous across different situations and progressive over long periods of time. Fundamentally, there are two reasons for this relative stability, and these refer to the capacity of large social groups to meet two sets of purposes. First, there is their instrumental significance for resolving collective action problems: this allows us to achieve under conditions of relatively stable agreement what we cannot do in the absence of these conditions. Secondly, there is their significance for consolidating a social sense of self: this provides an identity whose self-affirming traits, the way it speaks to positive conceptions of self generally such as personal dignity and a sense of personal authenticity (Smith 2001: 25–33), recognize and draw upon the irreducibly social character of our experience.

Now, it is clear that in any actual context of social development these two sets of factors – instrumental and affective – will be closely linked, indeed mutually interdependent. As we suggested earlier in our discussion of the economic conception of a public good, the instrumental reasons for getting or staying together to resolve collective action problems are finally insufficient, for in stressing the functional benefits of such an approach in overcoming the short-term self-interest and informational deficiency of the market model they assume the very collective commitment to put things in common in this rather than any other group that it is their burden to demonstrate. If the missing factor is not, should not and cannot be (or, at least cannot *only* be, certainly in the long term) this or any other variant of strategic action, such as the brute persuasion attendant upon the coercive potential and display of some already powerful group, then the glue can only be supplied from a non-instrumental source, and in particular from an ongoing investment in a sense of social identity and aspiration. This affective dimension, conversely, needs to be grounded in the many particular lessons of social experience, in the varied contexts of practical reason from which the very idea of social identity derives meaning. It must, therefore, be predicated upon a set of actual or projected ends which vindicate the very value of conceiving and pursuing ends *as* common ends and which as such provide ongoing corroboration of our self-understanding as social animals. It demands, in short, some reference to and some grounding in the experience of instrumentally effective collective action. In other words, action presupposes identification which is vindicated by action.

In saying that for communities of purpose to stabilize and to enjoy sustained instrumental success they must also be affective communities, and that affectivity is itself generated through a commitment to common purpose, we are not pointing to some abstract ontological puzzle of first causes, but to countless mutually reinforcing dynamics of cause and effect. And in the operation of these dynamics, it is inevitable that the sense of social identity that is cultivated in the generation of stable communities is itself heavily infused with the content of the instrumental purposes that both ground and are abetted by that sense of social identity – as well as with the practical means and conditions conducive to the pursuit of such instrumental purposes, most notably common language and common territory. The wish for common security is one of these instrumental purposes; indeed, perhaps, for the very reasons we rehearsed in chapter 2 in discussing security's foundational role in the collective project that is the constitution of liberty, *the* most important such instrumental purpose. Accordingly, it is no surprise, as we have already remarked, that the celebration of or yearning for common security against internal and external threats often looms so large in the materials – the mentalities, metaphors and iconography – through which stable communities register and articulate their identities as stable communities, as indeed does the sense of common language and common territory.[13] This, then, is the sense in which we can talk of security, just as we can of language and territory, as a *constitutive* public good – one whose actualization or aspiration is so pivotal to the very purpose of community that at the level of self-identification it helps to construct and sustain our 'we-feeling' – our very felt sense of 'common publicness'.

How does the idea of security as a constitutive public good help with our basic task of justifying the public provision of security? It does so, quite simply, by bringing together external and internal registers of explanation – by showing that the best external account must pay key attention to the process of accounting internal to the social world under investigation. For what the constitutive dimension introduces, crucially, is an idea of reflexivity. It pinpoints how and why social collectivities, given the inextricability of collective purpose and social sense of self and the centrality of the idea of common security in the forging of that inextricable link, come to think of themselves and sustain thinking of themselves as social collectivities, such that they both possess and may further pursue a common sense of and collective commitment to security and to various other collective-commitment-presupposing and identity-vindicating common goods. A vital dimension of that reflexivity, moreover, points to an as yet unconsidered sense of security as an irreducible social good – one that overlaps with but crucially differs from the rejected idea of security as an immediate social good. Security, in this adjusted perspective, is irreducibly social not in the sense that the good lies exclusively in the fact of sharing but in that, alongside its objective and individuated conditions of achievement, it nevertheless provides an example of goods that 'essentially incorporate common understandings of their value' (C. Taylor 1995: 140). *That is to say, our capacity to reach some level of common understanding and recognition*

---

[13] See chapter 4 above, where the historical relationship between policing and state building and state maintenance was discussed. At that point, we simply sought to show that the close dependence of state building and state maintenance on policing and security produced a symbolic dividend or legacy. In taking the analysis a stage further, we now want to stress how that security-signifying symbolic dimension and the affective sense of identity that it helps to articulate should be viewed not just as an effect of political community whose most basic motivation lies in other factors, but as *co-constitutive* of the very idea of political community.

*of the terms of our collective security is itself a contributory factor to
that collective security.*

Common security, then, is simultaneously and recursively, first, a
motivating factor in the formation and sustenance of reflexive publics;
second, a way of social being or common sensibility of such a public;
and, third, a platform of public power from which material provision
for objective security can be made. Not only is each element – reflexive mobilization, collective self-understanding and instrumental capacity – crucial, but their relationship is symbiotic. These different
elements of security, now conceived of as public-constitutive, allow us
to rethink the various social dimensions of security introduced earlier
so as to help vindicate our 'internal account' of the indispensability of
public provision.

First, the very sense of common publicness, the mobilization and sustenance of which owe something to the instrumental and affective
dimensions of the idea of common security, helps generate the commitment necessary for *this* community to provide the stable material
and regulatory wherewithal required for a general scheme of security
provision – something that theorists of the minimal state and those of
nodal governance have both neglected. Regardless of the possible
divergence of our views on the more remote beneficial consequences of
a scheme of common security supplied at different levels and in different forms, provided we have a common sense of who 'we' are and a
constitutive commitment to put things in common, we will be able to
fund and order the mix of steering and rowing mechanisms required to
provide whatever indispensably minimum level of common security we
can agree on.

Secondly, given that, as argued, the objective security situation of the
individual depends not only upon the commitment to public provision,
but also upon the propensity of some to aid or cooperate in the provision
of one's personal security cover and on the disinclination of others to
threaten one's personal security, both the collective self-understanding
associated with the security-mediated constitutive achievement of
relatively stable political community and, again, the instrumental capacity of affective political community have a crucial role to play. On the
one hand, and most directly, to the extent that the sense of common
social identity presupposed by and nurtured within a stable political
community can encourage a sense of confident and committed membership of that community, this can lead to more active support for and

cooperation with official and unofficial security arrangements, or at least to less intense threats towards these arrangements. On the other hand, more indirectly, such a community can use the 'battery of power' (Canovan 1996: 72–5) it derives from its common affective commitment to put things in common to combat socially generated *in*security; to provide through distributive measures the spread of resources and associated forms of social status likely to minimize the mutual resentments, antipathies and indifferences which lead to non-cooperative or hostile and directly security-threatening behaviour. This combination of direct and indirect influences may, in short, help to trigger a 'virtuous circle of crime control' (Audit Commission 1993: 49) – the optimal use and effective supplementation of the scarce resources of security provision, and the minimization of the pressures on these resources, necessary for achieving effective levels of objective security.

Thirdly, and finally, we should note that the relationship between the constitution of political community and the uniquely and irreducibly social condition of security is not just causal, in the complex ways suggested above, but finally also conceptual. Freedom from anxiety about security, as we have argued, is a function not just of one's objective security situation, but also of one's perception of the adequacy of one's security coverage, which is also in some part derived both from one's sense of the long-term stability of the social environment and one's place in it and from one's ongoing general threshold of psychic vulnerability, or manageable fear in the face of one's social environment. These appreciations depend, in turn, upon a more general sense of 'ontological security' – of 'confidence or trust that the natural and social worlds are as they appear to be, including the basic existential parameters of self and social identity' (Giddens 1984: 375). Where this sense of 'ontological security' comes from is of course a deeply complex and multilayered question, but as Giddens himself intimates, one crucial level is that of social identity. A sense of dignity and authenticity, of ease with and acceptance within one's social environment, are crucial to ontological security: and, as we have seen, it is these very aspects of social identity that are implicated in the collective self-understanding attendant upon the accomplishment of political community. In other words, to be a member of a stable political community and to feel oneself confident in that sense of membership is already to raise one's threshold of vulnerability – to possess crucial resources in the management of fear and avoidance of security anxiety.

Towards axiomatic security

Let us, then, conclude our discussion and finish our preparations for the reintroduction of the state by revisiting a theme introduced in chapter 1 and seeking to demonstrate that to conceptualize security as a thick public good along the lines set out in this chapter is, at the same time, to think about and promote it as an *axiomatic* element of lived social relations. In summarizing our argument using this term, we mean to recall and emphasize a number of things. The first is that security is a necessary platform *for* any kind of political society, irrespective of the range of other goods that it chooses to value and pursue. But it is to argue, further, that security is an education *in* society.[14] Security concerns educate, they teach people how to be with each other, they offer a daily tutorial in the rudiments of being social. Thus it is, or so we have argued, that the social dimension of security inheres, first, in the fact that it responds to a root problem – insecurity rather than non-security – whose provenance is inescapably to do with one's relations with others and, second, that security is partly constituted by a subjective feeling of freedom from anxiety and an attendant confidence in one's capacity to manage the dangers posed by one's environment. While the security of each may not depend on the security of all in any foundational sense, the security of each *is* clearly enhanced if the security of all

---

[14] The idea of security as having a value in educating people how to live together owes much to a similar analysis Niklas Luhmann once made of trust (1979: 64). For Luhmann, the practice of 'winning trust' can easily and very plausibly be analysed in strictly instrumental terms. People make themselves seem trustworthy in order to win the confidence of others and increase their influence with these others. Moreover, often this is a two-way or multiple-way process – a drama of mutual display. However, over time, the initial instrumental motivations tend to become habitualized, and strategic interaction is often replaced by or augmented with what is literally a more 'educated' sense of the virtues of trust (both personal and impersonal) – by a greater appreciation of and sympathy with the standpoint of the other and by the development of an affective mutual orientation on the basis of that enhanced appreciation and sympathy. Security can be seen as providing a similar vehicle towards deeper forms of sociality. The whole thrust of our analysis is to suggest that while initial orientations towards mutual security may well be strategic – a question of establishing a 'low platform' of convergent interests – the regular alignment of mutual behaviours in terms of these initial orientations can also have an educational dividend. As with trust, it can sharpen our mutual appreciation of, and mutual sympathy in the face of, vulnerability in a way that is both mutually enlightening and helps generate and sustain relations of mutual affect.

is reasonably attended to. Equally, while security is not a good whose value and benefits lie in the sharing of them with others such that it can be described as a good akin to solidarity or friendship, the condition of security *is not* independent of the common understanding we come to have of it.

To arrive at this conclusion is to defend a conception of security which stands radically opposed to one that holds – or makes – security *pervasive* and, in so doing, to dispute that the broader purpose of political community is reducible to security. Security, it seems to us, becomes a pervasive feature of social and political life precisely when it is absent in its axiomatic sense. Under such conditions, security – or rather insecurity – exists on and across the expansive surface of social consciousness, becomes a recurrent trope of political discourse, and tends to colonize other fields of social practice. Or else – under the guise of a 'securitized' form of ontological security – it is elevated to an unhealthily hegemonic category and comes to mean the unreflexive, parochial and anxious cleaving to a security-driven conception of a risk-free society, such that when its seemingly fixed terms are threatened or called into question, hostility to others, and a heightened concern with security shallowly conceived, are never very far away.

The good of security is not to be found, in short, in a situation in which 'security' is 'shallow' and 'wide' – a precarious, routinely fretted-over effect of the supply and presence of (ever-)increasing numbers of policing and crime-control measures. Nor is the good of security to be found in a situation where it is 'deep' and 'wide' – where it is reified as the overweening end rather than the modest beginning of social policy. Whereas the former 'shallow' and 'wide' conception errs in either ignoring the ontological depths or collapsing them into surface considerations of physical security, the latter 'deep' and 'wide' variant errs in the opposite direction of treating physical (in)security as but the symptom and consequence of ontological (in)security. The key, instead, is to think of the surfaces and depths of security as in a relationship of recursive mutual causality – with neither reducible to the other. The pursuit of security, in other words, is best thought of as 'deep' and 'narrow', sensitive to the fact that the physical dimension both responds to and reinforces the ontological dimension, but resistant to any project that would mortgage the entire field of social policy to the dogmatic pursuit of that ontological dimension. The lodestar of that 'deep' and 'narrow' conception should be the accomplishment of a stable condition grounded in the tacit confidence individuals have that their diverse and common legitimate expectations and their diverse and common loyalties as members of a political community are acknowledged in ways that afford them the material and symbolic resources required to manage, and feel relatively at ease with, the threats that are or may be present in their environment. It is security understood and configured not as a form of perpetual *striving*, but as a state of well *being* – a state in which we are able to live – and live together – securely with risk.

7 | *The necessary virtue of the state*

W E have in the previous chapter described and defended the merits of security conceived of as a thick public good and suggested that the practical realization of such a conception requires that security in some significant measure be publicly provided. In staking out that position we argued for the indispensability of the social in the generation and sustenance of individual security, and for the indispensability of some constitutive idea of 'publicness' and of political community to the full flowering of the social – conditions required even if we want the provision of individual security to be tailored to ends whose value may be calculated in strictly individual terms. But an additional level of argument has to be negotiated before we can allocate the state a primary role in the provision of security so conceived. In particular, we must face two further challenges and address two further series of questions. First, why and with reference to what particular tasks or functions should any particular public entity be allocated a pre-eminent or primary role, or – as we prefer for reasons we explain in due course – *take priority* in the matter of security provision? And if we conclude that some such entity should indeed be allocated such a role and if we decide what form such priority ought to take, why need the entity in question be the state rather than some other species of political community? Secondly, even if we can make a persuasive *prima facie* case for the priority of the state, we still have to deal with and overcome its propensity towards meddling, favouritism, monoculturalism and stupidity. In this, and the following chapter, we set out to address these two series of questions in turn.

The agenda of the present chapter, then, is to identify what has to be done in order effectively to pursue the more equitable and solidarity-enhancing conception of the good of security that we set out in chapter 6, and to demonstrate why and how the state is best placed to take the lead in this endeavour. The two limbs of our argument are intimately related. If the public good of security is to be practically fostered and sustained, there is a certain amount of cultural and ordering work that must necessarily and routinely be accomplished. If, in addition, we understand these tasks to be in various ways mutually dependent and mutually reinforcing, it follows that we should locate some species of political community which can take responsibility for the performance and coordination of all of these functions, and to that extent assume a position of priority. We need not, of course, call that entity the state. But, whatever our squeamishness about labels, we would be bound to accept the indispensability of a form of political community that is distinctive inasmuch as it, and it alone, is capable of combining and coordinating the various requisite ordering and cultural tasks.

In a nutshell, the answers we suggest to these two questions are as follows: first, such is the importance and degree of interconnectedness of the core cultural and ordering work that it is indeed necessary that some single entity take priority in the provision of security as a public good; and secondly, that given both its track-record and its continuing scope to perform the tasks necessary to such provision, the state alone, or its functional equivalent, is capable of exhibiting the 'necessary virtue'. If we are interested in civilizing security, we have no choice, accordingly, but to accept that necessity, in so doing seeking to recover and extend what is indeed virtuous about the state tradition while finding ways to eradicate or minimize its vices. This, we suggest by way of conclusion to the present chapter, translates into what we shall call an *anchored pluralism*. In chapter 8, we then examine more closely how the state's vices manifest themselves in contemporary security politics and practices, before seeking to develop the idea of anchored pluralism in terms of the institutional principles and design that can tip that always precarious balance between the state's virtue and its vices in favour of the former.

The priority of the state

Let us recall the rudimentary terms of our puzzle. What needs to happen if collective security understood in the terms outlined in the last chapter is to be realized, and who needs to do it? Our answer to the first element of this puzzle is that there exists a range of tasks or functions the fulfilment of which meets certain key conditions of security production: namely, identification, resource mobilization and allocation, deliberation, regulation and commitment. We will have more to say about what each of these tasks amounts to and just why each is vital shortly. Before that, however, we should say something about how the tasks hang together and how this informs our answer to the second element of the puzzle.

Three closely connected points are worth highlighting. In the first place, these tasks or functions form an *aggregate* whole in the sense that they are each indispensable to the public good of security. These tasks, secondly, are not only separately prerequisite to the optimal production of security as a public good, but are also mutually implicated and so must also be considered an *integral* whole. That is to say, the successful accomplishment of one is to no avail without the successful performance of the others – the parts of the jigsaw are meaningless or essentially incomplete unless and until constituted as a whole. Accordingly, the tasks have to be performed in harness with one another and any attempt to parcel one or other of them up and hive them off to different agencies is likely to prejudice this. Finally, the integrity of the various tasks rests most fundamentally on a basic relationship of mutual *dependence* and mutual *support*; for, as already noted, these various tasks possess wide-ranging cultural and ordering dimensions that exist in relations of mutual synergy. That is to say, they entail the crafting of stable social identities which both supply the motivational force behind any infrastructure of order and help nurture a social environment in which civility is relatively high and security risks are relatively low (cultural work), as well as providing the ordering infrastructure itself – the rules, resources and administrative capacity – necessary to the sustained production of collective security (ordering work).

Each of these three points indicates a reason for which the state or its functional equivalent is required to perform a distinctive and prior role. First, there is a question of responsibility. If the five tasks are indeed indispensable, then unless some entity takes responsibility for all of these tasks, there is simply no guarantee that each and all will be effectively performed, or even performed at all. Secondly, there is a question of coordination. If the tasks are mutually implicated, some entity must be aware of and must be able to monitor and shape these mutual implications. Thirdly, and underpinning the first two justifications, there is a basic question of capacity. The various tasks are indispensable and mutually implicated on account of the fact that the functions they serve are mutually dependent and supportive, but just because these relations of dependence and support do indeed hold in such intimate ways and across such a wide canvas, they cannot simply be reassigned or transferred from one responsible and coordinating centre to another. The range of cultural tasks of the state and the synergy between the cultural and the ordering tasks of the state are deeply embedded in particular forms of social organization, and indeed, as we saw in chapter 2, deeply coded in certain social imaginaries, and we simply cannot discount that massive legacy when thinking through our security arrangements – particularly given the enduring 'centring' imperatives of responsibility and coordination.

It is important, however, to be clear about what is and what is not being postulated here. What precisely does the triple imperative of responsibility, coordination and capacity entail in terms of the distinctiveness and priority of the state role? On the one hand, we should not claim too much for the state. It is no part of our argument that the state should perform a monopoly role in the provision of security conceived of as a thick public good. Indeed, this disclaimer applies to two different variants of the monopoly idea – to both strong and weak versions. In the first place, palpably nothing in the claim to priority requires that the state be the exclusive source of active security provision. Pointedly, the five vital functions we enumerated all concern how to secure the social and political preconditions of security, so to speak, and do not include the basic 'rowing' function of the security practitioners itself. It follows that the actual providers of policing and security services certainly need not be 'state operatives' – a concept whose legal translation and operationalization in different national settings in any case indicates diverse and by no means necessarily cumulative criteria of relevance, and so defies reduction to any single threshold test.[1] In the

---

[1] Legally relevant factors which may indicate different answers include: (i) identity of formal employer and source of remuneration; (ii) source of detailed performance control and sanctions, including dismissal; (iii) repository of legal liability in case of wrongful conduct; and (iv) locus of political accountability and answerability for operational choices. Not only do different legal systems stress different factors or combinations of these factors as relevant to the formal legal status of police officers, but even within a particular system the answers to different questions may tend in different directions. For example, within the British system, traditionally viewed in terms of a balance between constabulary independence and local government control, a more detailed consideration of these various questions suggests different answers or a combination of answers

second place, priority does not require that the state be solely responsible even for these 'steering' functions where its contribution and coordination is indispensable. That the state must take a key role in identification, mobilization and allocation, deliberation, regulation and commitment, and also in the coordination of these tasks, does not mean that it need monopolize all or indeed any of them, as we shall see. What is more, in searching for an appropriate vocabulary short of monopoly, it is precisely because the state is typically one actor amongst many others in a shifting assemblage of security provision that we prefer a relational term such as 'priority' to one with more absolutist connotations such as 'pre-eminence', or with a more rigidly hierarchical sense such as 'primacy'. Crucially, as our discussion of anchored pluralism should make clear, such ascendancy as the state possesses is always articulated and affirmed in and through its dynamic relationship with a plurality of other actors, without any requirement that the state need at all times and in all respects be the most prominent actor or even the loudest or most influential voice in security production.

On the other hand, however, we should not claim too little for the state. Clearly, the state does not take priority if it is treated as just one of many equal partners with other subnational and transnational public and private bodies. Nor is it enough to view the state as no more than *primus inter pares*, if that implies, as it does in at least some versions of the increasingly influential network or nodal model of security governance which we addressed in part I, an entity whose priority is merely circumstantial and so empirically contingent.[2] The joint imperatives of responsibility, coordination and capacity argue against either

Footnote 1 (*cont.*)

    including not just local government and the police themselves, but also, and increasingly, central government (in particular, in the novel form of the Serious Organized Crime Agency, which from 2006 has taken over and integrated the functions of the erstwhile National Crime Squad and National Criminal Intelligence Service) and various other politically independent central institutions such as the Inspectorate of Constabulary and the National Policing Improvement Agency. See, for example, N. Walker (2000).

[2] See, in particular, chapter 5 above. We present this proposition in a carefully qualified form for a number of reasons. In the first place, the nodal governance literature is a large and burgeoning one (e.g. Shearing 2001, 2006; Johnston and Shearing 2003; Shearing and Wood 2003a, 2003b; Dupont 2004; Cherney 2005; Johnston 2006; Wood and Shearing 2006) and we simply cannot and should not assume that all who speak within that literature do so with the same voice. Secondly, it is also a dynamic literature, one still in a state of theoretical

the likelihood or the acceptability of any realignment of functions which would have the effect of denying the continuing precedence of one particular centre of security governance. What is required in our model of state priority, then, is something rather more than fortuitous ascendancy, even if less than fixed pre-eminence or constant primacy. What remains distinctive to the state's role in the tasks of identification, mobilization and allocation, deliberation, regulation and commitment is that *its* exercise of each must *in the last analysis* take precedence over the exercise of a similar role at any other public or private site.

At this point, however, abstract definition and purely conceptual distinctions and differences reach the limit of their utility. We cannot illuminate further the meaning of priority, nor the importance of the coordinating role of the state in linking the functions in which it has such priority, without considering each of these functions separately – a task to which we now turn.

Securing the preconditions of security: five tasks of the state

While it is no part of our purpose to suggest that the cultural and ordering dimensions of the state security role are neatly divided up between the five tasks – quite the contrary – we can nevertheless draw a rough distinction between those tasks where the cultural dimension is more obviously to the fore and those where the ordering dimension

flux – as for example in the increasing preference in some quarters for an emphasis upon the fluidity of the nodes and of their originary power to mobilize knowledge and capacity, rather than upon the strength and resilience of the network which connects the nodes and provides a grid for the heterarchical transmission and coordination of power and influence (e.g. Burris 2004; Shearing 2006). Thirdly, it is a literature with which we have engaged on previous occasions (Loader and Walker 2001, 2004, 2006) and to which we have received constructive responses that seek to emphasize and develop the degree of common cause underpinning our respective approaches (e.g. Johnston and Shearing 2003; Shearing and Wood 2003a; Johnston 2006; Shearing 2006). With regard to such a richly diverse, fast-moving and theoretically open literature it is therefore difficult and probably invidious to draw definitive conclusions. In particular, although in principle nodal theory is often at pains to deny 'conceptual priority to any particular locus of power' (Johnston 2006: 34) including the state, in practice it has often not been slow to acknowledge either the continuing – and perhaps increasing – strength of the state 'node' (e.g. Shearing and Wood 2003a: 208) or the location of that strength in frameworks of authority and in regulatory and resource capacities of enduring viability and importance.

is more obviously to the fore. We will begin, therefore, with the three 'cultural' tasks of identification, mobilization and allocation, and deliberation – paying particular attention to the core 'cultural' task of identification – before moving on to the two 'ordering' tasks of regulation and commitment.

Identification

In chapter 6 we discussed the ways in which political community is constituted through a mix of the instrumental and the affective – the individual and the social – and how central security has been as a medium for these mutually supportive processes of constructive imagining and of imaginative construction. What we are concerned with here is the latter dimension – with the state's actual and potential role in the imaginative construction of identity and in the constructive contribution that work of imagining makes to collective security. In arguing that the state's identification work is indispensable, and takes precedence over other forms of political identification in securing the preconditions of collective security, our argument proceeds in several stages.

In the first place, there is of course a significant empirical legacy. Historically, it is the state – and typically the *nation* state – that has at least sometimes and in some places stepped forward as the form of political community equipped to perform the various kinds of public-constitutive affective tasks outlined in the previous chapter. We must recognize that nation states have thereby been strongly implicated in the development of a sense of belonging, dignity and authenticity in the form of national membership. In so doing, they have often also been engaged in crafting social identities which provide both the motivational impetus necessary to establish and maintain an ordering infrastructure for security and the sense of empathetic familiarity prerequisite to a social environment in which civility is relatively high, security risks relatively low, and the ordering infrastructure thus reasonably sufficient for its task. We must, equally, allow that the identity-construction work of the nation state, quite apart from this complex of instrumental benefits, has also sometimes and in some places been importantly continuous with the very sense of social rootedness and secure belonging that makes the self-management of unease and anxiety a manageable task. And in accepting that the state can succeed, and in some cases and to varying degrees has succeeded, in performing these tasks, we must also remind ourselves that it is at the level of the nation state rather than any other candidate form of political community that notions of security – just because of their deep inscription in the kind of purpose and practices for which political communities are formed and through which they are sustained – provide an important part of the vernacular of collective identity formation (Walden 1982; Emsley 2000), reformation (Glaeser 2000) and maintenance (Loader and Mulcahy 2003: ch. 2).

In the second place, the fact that the state has frequently demonstrated that it *can* do this kind of security-enabling identification work points us precisely in the direction of the capacity-based justification of its indispensability and priority standing. The capacity argument, we may recall, concerns the remarkable and self-reinforcing ability of states to accomplish a wide range of complementary cultural and ordering tasks in various areas including – in the complex ways set out above – security work. Yet a capacity-based argument can never offer a full explanation. The very fact that at other times and in other places the state has *not* found or has *not* effectively exploited the capacity to develop a wide-ranging instrumental facility and an inclusive sense of affective community in a mutually supportive fashion, but has either simply failed or has allowed undue rein to its meddling, partisan, imperialistic or obdurate tendencies, suggests as much. And underlying that empirical qualification, the capacity argument also reveals a theoretical gap. There are two related elements to this. First, and most obviously, just because it is about potential rather than achievement, the capacity-based argument begs the question of what is necessary in order to turn potential into achievement. Secondly, *au fond* the capacity-based argument is a functional one, and as such it suffers from the basic limitation of all functional explanations. It can show, through its demonstration of beneficent outcomes, why it might have been a good reason to adopt – and, even more so, why it would have made sense to many to maintain once adopted – a particular set of arrangements or course of action in certain circumstances. But it cannot by reference to these same outcomes offer a full explanation of why a particular set of arrangements or course of action was *in fact* adopted or maintained – or not, as the case may be – in any particular circumstances.[3]

---

[3] Within the literature on nationalism, functionalist thinking has played an influential role – sometimes explicitly so and sometimes only implicitly – especially within those schools of thought which link nationalism exclusively or

This, then, forces us to move our argument to a third stage. If the
state is not a functional machine, if, as is palpably if inconveniently the
case, it cannot be guaranteed to develop its role in social and political
identification in a particular manner just because of the beneficial consequences for collective security that might ensue, then how can we
nevertheless insist upon the indispensability and necessary priority of
its role as an identifier of political community? To answer this, we have
to go back to the actual circumstances under which modern statehood
emerged, and so to the discussion we developed at length in chapter 2.
As we saw there, it is the very shift in the social and political imaginary
away from a predetermined order of social and political relations and
towards the individual as the basic unit of moral worth that reveals the
dual foundational motivation of the modern state. It accounts for why
the modern state was concerned to provide a framework for instrumentally beneficial mutual relations amongst formally free and equal
individuals. Yet it also explains why the modern state was concerned
with the facilitation and recognition of a sense of active and purposive
political community, and indeed offers both positive and negative
reasons for this. Positively, the new sense of universal and equal moral
agency made it possible for the first time to found a sense of belonging
and of primary associative ties on the basis of collective authorship and
its secular potential or accomplishment. Negatively, with the fading of
older notions of natural or transcendental hierarchy, the possibility of
an alternative grounding for large-scale affective community in any
case began to recede.

But there remains the fundamental problem of the reconciliation of
these individual and collective dimensions. If these are not adequately
reconciled – and, to repeat, we cannot just assume the serendipitous
development of a functional feedback mechanism as the ignition or
motor of that reconciliation – then as a framework for collective action
and affect the modern state courts the opposite dangers of being too
'thin' and under-motivated or too 'thick' and culturally imperialist.
That there is indeed widespread acknowledgement of this problem can
be seen from the most cursory examination of the terms in which
modern statehood has tended to be conceptualized, and, in particular,

Footnote 3 (*cont.*)
  predominantly to the development of the social and economic conditions
  of 'modernity' and 'modernization'. For a useful overview, see Lawrence (2005:
  ch. 4).

in the development of various tense couplings. Witness, for example, the uneasy marriage of nationalism and citizenship (Cox 1987), of the particular and the universal, of affinity and proximity (Waldron 2003b), of common fate and common membership, or even of *idem* and *ipse* – of *identi*fication as a recognition of prior sameness and of identi*fication* as a reflexive process for developing and refining a sense of collective selfhood (van Roermund 2003). We also see the same dynamic at work in certain neologistic constructions that bring together divergent themes in intendedly productive but also question-begging – some would even say oxymoronic – ways, whether we are talking about 'constitutional patriotism' or 'abstract solidarity' or 'contextual universalism', or even that seemingly bland modern favourite, 'civic nationalism' itself (Fine 1999). The examples could be multiplied, but the immediate point is simply to record that these kinds of conceptual juxtapositions and innovations tend to illuminate and perplex in equal measure. They illuminate in that they go immediately to what is at stake and what is unresolved in the development trajectory of the modern state. They perplex in that the 'nested oppositions' through which they frame the world do not easily permit them to go *beyond* the antinomies that they identify.

There is, thus, a well-known narrative which unfolds in many and colourfully diverse theoretical languages around the ambivalent meaning and ambiguous development of the nation state. On the one hand, the conjunction of nation and state hints at the alchemy of abstract solidarity. Under the sign of citizenship in particular, the nation state has helped cultivate the notion of a community of strangers bonded only by a democracy-enabling impersonal sense of interlocking circumstance or common predicament grounded in shared possession of a territory rather than, as in the case of pre-modern constellations, by interpersonal connection and allegiance or through common fidelity to some transcendental order (Habermas 1996; Brunkhorst 2005). On the other hand, some deeper sense of common purpose has frequently been invoked to inspire, invited to homologate, or urged to corroborate a common commitment founded on the accident of geographical proximity. Nation*alism*, as an ideology which links territory to common history, language and culture, has provided a powerful and protean candidate for this task (see, for example, Yack 2003). Yet nationalism carries with it the enduring danger of reification – partly a legacy of pre-modern collectivism and partly a tendency within any process whereby social meaning is imputed to a collective. It risks being naturalized as a self-corroborating story of collectively motivated but individually predestined belonging and exclusion, one that comes with strict criteria of exclusion and diversity-denying standards of inclusion. And, of course, what is true of the cultural dimension of the nation state generally is emphatically true of its constitutive preoccupation with security. As a contributing ingredient of national identity construction, the idea of common security, as we have seen, is also delicately balanced between instrumental and affective poles. And depending on how this balance is struck, the discourse of security can either underpin an impersonal and difference-accommodating solidarity or unduly thicken cultural community, and so be either broadly inclusive and accommodating or narrowly exclusive and divisive (see chapter 4).

Whatever conceptual language we use to convey its origins and abiding legacy, then, the identification function of the state is a double-edged sword, and ineluctably so. It is at the root of the cultural work of the state, and therefore crucial not only to the internal relationship between belonging and security but also to the common mobilization effort required for an ordering infrastructure to address problems of insecurity. Yet it can also be the catalyst for many of the state's pathologies, in particular its intemperate meddling and its cultural imperialism. In the final analysis, if we are to overcome rather than dramatize this, we have to go beyond grand abstractions and accentuated opposites. Rather, and this is the fourth and final move in our argument, in order to resolve the ambivalence of the nation state's identification function in a civilizing rather than a tribalizing direction, it is crucial that we look in closer detail at the novelty of the sense of the political imaginary it frames. In so doing, we may come to see its *priority* as a site of political identity as an intrinsic part of the solution rather than as a question begged or as an aggravating part of the problem.

Let us again take up and pursue the thread of chapter 2 in order to make this point. As we noted there, the modern state is not just a new and experimental recipe for politics, with 'abstract solidarity' or some other 'x' factor as its key (and elusive) ingredient, but a new dish entirely. For the modern state is the harbinger of the very idea of politics conceived of as a comprehensively unified, separate and specialized public domain that in its operative logic is distinct from the society over which it rules, and so no longer as an untidy and overlapping series of decisional spheres in each of which collective action concerns and special interests are deeply intertwined. The new specialized system of generic politics possesses the dual attributes of immanence and self-limitation. On the one hand, it purports to be self-legitimating, in that what justifies the continuing claim to autonomous authority of the generic political domain and what fuels the impersonal solidarity that may lend it the requisite sociological support is nothing more or less than, first, the procedural promise of the operation of the generic political domain itself as one in which all matters of common concern beyond intimate face-to-face contexts of community can be treated in common without fear or favour of special interests, and, secondly, the substantive promise or bounty of these public goods, such as security, that are both defined and enabled – and, moreover, enabled at a suitably 'economic' scale – through the operation of that generic political domain. On the other hand, and as the flipside of this, alongside the idea of a generic political and public sphere, there emerges the corresponding and complementary idea of a generic sphere of purely private action and negative freedom that lies beyond either the specialist sphere of generic politics or the now redundant special mixed regimes of public and private right and obligation based upon prior forms of privilege or advantage (Habermas 2001; Loughlin 2003: ch. 3; Grimm 2005; N. Walker 2006c). And as we have repeatedly noted, however difficult it may be to define its precise boundaries, such a private sphere – the zone of forbearance or non-interference with the integrity of individual choice and action on the part of public or any other authority – also makes a crucial contribution to security as a public good.

These twin attributes – a generic politics dedicated to the identification and delivery of public goods and the protection of a private sphere from excessive meddling – both require the priority of the state as a site of political identity over other sites to be internalized. For in each case the guarantee – of generic scope and of protection of a private sphere – relies upon the legitimacy of the state's claim to political community prevailing over other more local or specialist claims to legitimate authority and the sense of political identity that underscores these. That is to say, the distinctive potential of the state as a site of political identity and community, and the source of its peculiarly encompassing contribution to the generation and protection of public goods amongst adjacent and closely interconnected populations, and so of the plausibility of its continuing claim to authority before the 'people' that comprises these populations, lies, in an ultimately circular and self-justifying manner, in its priority in the last instance over other levels of political community being acknowledged. It follows, of course, that for the state to do the cultural work necessary to identify and pursue the best sense of its collective purpose in the pursuit of public goods and the protection of private freedoms, it should be able to play with as full a deck of cards as possible. It should, that is, be able to rely upon the equivalent priority of its other functional attributes – to be discussed below – in support of and in coordination with its basic nurturing of a sense of common politics and political identity.

Mobilization and allocation of collective resources

Charles Tilly (1985) has famously characterized state-making at various points through the pre-modern and modern ages as a form of 'organized crime'. On his provocatively one-sided view, the state may be conceived of as the 'quintessential protection racket'. But, as with Nozick's (1974) 'dominant protective *association*', which under the 'invisible hand mechanism' gradually evolves into the 'ultra-minimal' and then finally the 'minimal state', it is one that gradually acquires the power to define itself otherwise. Beyond the arresting metaphors, Tilly points us towards something fundamental here. One of the central features of state activity and one of the key indices of state capacity is the extraction of resources – or what states themselves call the 'taxing' of population. This work of extraction has often been historically justified by and stimulated by war-making and external security (see also Mann 1986: 486; Herbst 2003), although extraction clearly also serves the closely related purpose of internal security. However we precisely understand the dynamic of extraction, there is no doubt that when harnessed to the imperatives of security it can operate as a self-reinforcing dynamic. The costs of war stimulate the demand for resources, while the costs of servicing the expanded territory that is the spoils of successful war demand yet more resources; expanded territory also provides an extended population from which to extract these resources. Equally, in a non-expansionary scenario, the consolidation of internal security can strengthen the tax base, and in turn further reinforce the state's wherewithal to enforce internal security. And, of course, it takes only a slight change of perspective to see the business of resource extraction and the development of administrative capacity in response to intensified resource extraction as being about ends rather than means – as concerning the vested and proactive interests of state elites. At this point, furthermore, the argument from resources feeds easily into our discussion of the dangers both of partisanship (see chapter 3) and of cultural imperialism (see chapter 4) in the state's pursuit of internal security.

While these considerations serve as a salutary warning against too idealistic a reading, we must acknowledge that resource mobilization and (re)allocation are nevertheless crucial tools in any endeavour to craft security as a public good.[4] They provide key mechanisms for channelling whatever sense of affective identification and associative obligation exists within a population towards two complementary sets of ends. They enable the securing and servicing of the ordering infrastructure, whether or not directly provided by state functionaries. And, through the raising and deploying of resources for other purposes – education, housing provision, social security, healthcare, etc. – they also serve to alleviate those forms of relative deprivation and social exclusion whose alienating effects may act both as a stimulant to crime and as an aggravator of security anxiety. In so doing, they help to reduce the forms of ontological insecurity that can give rise to a heightened focus on security shallowly conceived.

But none of these arguments necessarily implies the priority of the state in matters of resource mobilization. Indeed, that brand of scepticism which sees the incessant call for 'more resources' to be both narrowly self-serving for the state bureaucracy as well as more broadly self-defeating in its tendency to tackle the symptoms rather than the causes of insecurity would be understandably suspicious of any attempt to place too much emphasis on this aspect of state

---

[4] Whether the distribution of resources in the forms of public expenditure of tax revenue is aptly conceived of as a *re*distribution or *re*allocation of the private wealth or income of those presented with the highest tax bills is itself a moot point. Some would argue (e.g. Murphy and Nagel 2002) that the state's overall control of the regulatory environment, including its property laws and labour laws, means that our notions of pre-tax wealth and income are themselves artifices – no less dependent on the particularity and partiality of public policy than the tax regime itself. To the extent that this argument is persuasive it alerts us to the myriad other ways in which the state is involved in matters of distributive justice as well as helping shift the burden of proof from those who would otherwise have to justify any progressive taxation before the charge that it is a form of expropriation.

functioning.[5] Nevertheless, for at least three reasons, it remains important to affirm the prerogative of the state to command the level of resources it deems necessary and to allocate in the manner it deems appropriate to the direct and indirect service of security, and to ensure that the capacity of any other potential resource provider does not interfere with or prejudice that prerogative.[6] These concern, in turn, the depth, the flexibility and the 'security' of state resources.

The argument from depth is based on the premise that the call for additional security resources is more likely to be a function of scarcity than of plenty. As the evidence of failed or failing states indicates, or indeed of any state where the tax base of public expenditure is put under unusual pressure, the political claim for security spending tends to become more strident the more depleted the overall level of public resources, the sharper the competition between the demands of different services, and the less matters of ontological security are being attended to.[7] What is more, as security rhetoric is typically most seductive where the choices can be presented as starkest and most urgent, such claims are often successful in their own myopic terms, as it was with Margaret Thatcher's 1979 election promise to 'spend more on law and order as we economize elsewhere'. Yet as the largest territorial level of government charged with basic matters of internal security in particular and public service provision in general, the central state – at least in principle and notwithstanding these sharp exceptions – retains the widest and deepest tax pool from which to draw. It follows that it typically remains easier for the state than for any other public or market provider to immunize itself against the problem of scarce

---

[5] See, in particular, the discussion of the authoritarian syndrome in chapter 8 below.

[6] While other levels of government can (and, especially in federal systems, frequently do) possess independent resource-raising capacity in matters of security and in other matters indirectly relevant to security, this should not be at such a level or involve such decisional autonomy that it effectively undermines or threatens to undermine the capacity of the central state to shape the overall level and distribution of tax revenue. Equally, private spending on security should not be allowed to such a level and across such a range of activities that it encourages or permits an effective opt-out on the part of physically or metaphorically 'gated' communities from state provision and its financing, and so from the consideration of the complex trans-neighbourhood externalities associated with state provision.

[7] For example, in the neo-liberal governments elected by many western states in the 1980s, including the Thatcher government in the UK. See, for example, Reiner (1980), Gamble (1988).

resources and the excessive or disproportionate claims on behalf of shallow security concerns which may flow from that.

The argument from flexibility follows a similar logic. A government genuinely concerned with deploying resources most effectively in pursuit of increased security will want to find an optimal balance between direct and indirect forms of spending, between spending on policing and protective services and guaranteeing those types of wider social provision that can prevent (in)security becoming pervasive. It will want, in other words, to engage in 'joined-up' thinking about and 'joined-up' funding of the right mix of policies. This is easier to achieve against a backdrop of a wide tax base and a multifunctional remit. Where the tax base is narrower and the functional remit more restricted, tax demands may become more closely linked to specific programmes and services in electoral politics in a manner which again threatens to pit different sectoral needs against each other and to present overstylized choices. Once more, a shallow and wide conception of security – and of its appropriate funding – may be the most likely outcome of this dynamic.

Finally, there is an argument that stresses the assured quality of state funding. As we stressed in the previous chapter, security as a public good is strongly future oriented. The promise that security will be well served – and so adequately financed – tomorrow as well as today is part and parcel of what makes us feel secure today. The state, with its broad and deeply embedded tax base, is in a better position than other putative providers – whether commercial or communal – to issue that promissory note, and to guarantee funding when other security providers prove fleeting or unreliable.

Deliberation

By deliberation we mean the various ways in which the state encourages decisions to be made in the field of security provision on the basis of careful consideration of arguments and evidence and through the development of good reasons. Deliberation in politics, including security politics, serves a variety of different functions, five of which we will briefly consider in due course. Before we do so, however, we should acknowledge that if, by separate or cumulative reference to these functions, we can demonstrate that the state effectively promotes deliberation, by necessary inference we will also have demonstrated that the state should assume priority in the last analysis over other deliberative forums. This is so for the simple reason that deliberation as we have defined it is internally related to decision, and since the priority of decision at the state level has already been argued for in the case of allocative decisions and will in due course be argued for in the case of regulatory decisions, no additional justification is required for the deliberation process itself.

The first four functions of deliberation can be roughly divided into those that serve the 'input' requirement of a democratic polity and those that help meet its 'output' requirements (Scharpf 1999). The two major input requirements concern representation of and responsiveness to diverse interests and the dignitarian virtue of participation respectively. As regards representation and responsiveness, deliberation implies a basic commitment to recognize and include representatives of the broadest range of constituencies within the wide political community of the state in the range of decision-making over the balance of preferences in security policy. As regards the direct value of participation, there is clearly some trade-off between opportunity and gravity of input. Not all who want to can necessarily be involved in the most consequential forums of central deliberation. However, this can be compensated for through mechanisms of institutional design – both in the form of 'top-down' delegated or secondary spheres of local decision-making and through 'bottom-up' channels of consultation.

The two major output functions of deliberation concern its encouragement of compliance and its epistemic quality respectively. Each has a special resonance in security politics. Clearly, as the resilience of the 'policing by consent' label demonstrates, policing remains highly compliance-dependent. As we saw in the previous chapter, a unique feature of security as a public good is that the problem which it seeks to treat – insecurity – is itself socially generated. What is more, the dispersed nature of insecurity-generating activity means that the police remain heavily dependent upon public support for basic operational information conducive to the detection and repression of such activity (Kinsey *et al.* 1986; Tyler 2004). To the extent that deliberative involvement in policy-making may encourage a more supportive and understanding attitude towards the problems and predicaments of security professionals, therefore, there is a high premium on encouraging such involvement on the part of those affected by and capable of making a difference to the implementation of security policy.

Professionalism is a more central theme as regards the other output-centred deliberative function. Here what we are concerned with is the way in which deliberation and the power of the better argument can improve the intrinsic quality of security decision-making. Unlike the other functions of deliberation, the advantages of state-centredness, such as they are, have less to do with the relationship of decision-making to the wide state-level 'demos' and more to do with knowledge and coordination gains associated with the pooling of expertise and information. As we will discuss in due course, strong claims are often made about the importance of professional discretion and the superiority of professional decision-making in matters of security policy, where knowledge may be, or may be asserted to be, arcane or experience-dependent and confidentiality at a premium.[8] And while such claims may be countered by the argument that a broader base of decision-making consultation can bring a wider and more detached cross-section of views and considerations to the table, there is no doubt that the epistemic argument is in some tension with the more directly democratic justification of the other deliberative arguments. What is more, this reflects a broader trend in deliberative theory and deliberative politics. Partly in response to the increased vulnerability of the supporting framework of representative politics, including the secular decline of mass political parties, contemporary thinking about deliberation has undoubtedly accorded greater priority to the epistemic and problem-solving dimension (e.g. Dorf and Sabel 1998; Estlund 1999). So much so, indeed, that some writers have begun to talk about the emergence of a depoliticized form of democracy (Pettit 2004) or about 'democracy without the demos' (Mair 2005).

Yet if we consider a fifth and final case in favour of deliberation, the value of widespread public involvement at the level of the wide political identity of the state is reasserted. Building significantly on the compliance argument, this line of enquiry concerns the extent to which, as discussed in chapter 6, not just the 'implementability' but the very standing of security as thick public good between different groups with presumptively different immediate security concerns depends upon its being a matter of common understanding between them. For insofar as we can find a common resolution of our understanding of security requirements and priorities – insofar as we can thereby articulate

---

[8] See the discussion of the paternalism syndrome in chapter 8 below.

meaningfully what security means *to us* – then in that measure we have already developed the very 'we-feeling' which is itself a basic ingredient of security. Here, unlike the four other arguments from deliberation, questions of 'input' and 'output' legitimacy – of process and outcome – merge. Here, moreover, the idea of an inclusive framework of deliberation over security at the level of the anonymous but deeply interconnected political community of the state finds its clearest and most distinctive vindication.

Regulation

That the state should assume priority in the overall system of normative order associated with security is on reflection perhaps the least controversial aspect of state ascendancy to assert in principle, if the most complex to develop in practice. On first impressions, however, even the in-principle assertion of state priority might seem to rest on distinctly shaky ground. There is a huge literature – *literatures* in fact – which seek to question the old Westphalian view of the state as the fount of all regulatory authority. Whether we look at work on the concept of governance (e.g. Kjaer 2004), or in regulation studies (e.g. Parker and Braithwaite 2003; Jordana and Levi-Faur 2004) or in legal pluralism (e.g. de Sousa Santos 1995), we see a formidable range of challenges to a command-and-control model of state regulatory authority. Such critical perspectives, which often owe much to the kinds of scepticism about the centralization of social intelligence portrayed in chapter 5, hold that the idea of the state as the only legitimate regulator in and for society, if ever it was a reasonable claim, is now no more than a quaint anachronism. Moreover, even a rather more subtle variant of the Westphalian idea that allows the existence of regulators other than the state, but which holds that whatever legitimacy attaches to these other regulators is merely a delegated legitimacy – still owed to and dependent upon the imprimatur of the state – is also increasingly treated as outmoded and inappropriate. Rather, it is claimed, we have to take seriously the myriad forms of ordering we find in society – private, hybrid, substate, suprastate as well as state – in their own terms, without assuming any monopoly of recognition or authorization on the part of the state (N. Walker forthcoming b).

What is more, there is no sense in this new literature that policing in particular and security in general are or should be considered as an exception to the trend towards the 'post-regulatory state' (C. Scott

2004). Quite the opposite in fact. As a harbinger of the contemporary turn towards nodal policing, an influential thesis has gradually taken hold over the last decade or so to the effect that state policing is undergoing a post-Peelian 'third wave' (Shearing 1996) – one where not only is the direct 'rowing' of the Peelian phase in decline but even the broader 'steering' functions inherited from the pre-Peelian phase are under threat (e.g. Johnston 1992; Bayley 1994; O'Malley and Palmer 1996; Loader 2000; N. Walker 2000: ch. 10). And in the work of such scholars (e.g. Grabosky 1995; Johnston and Shearing 2003; Parker and Braithwaite 2003), we see a significant cross-fertilization between the particularity of security ordering and regulation in general, with students of security sometimes even taking the lead in innovatory forms of post-state regulatory thinking.[9]

Crucially, however, just as we have argued that the state retains a key role in coordinating its various indispensable functions, so too, and as a necessary incident of that very task of functional coordination, it must retain a key role in harnessing the various systems of normative order that are developing in a post-Peelian age. It is indeed perfectly possible, as many scholars of the new wave assert, to allow that forms of security regulation other than the state – whether in local or sub-federal government, or at transnational or supranational sites, or in forms of private orderings – possess a legitimacy which is prior to and by no means eclipsed by the state's authorization. At the same time, we may continue to insist that some authority-in-the-last-instance is required to ensure both that these systems are in mutual harmony, and that they neither frustrate those aspects of the state's conception of security as a public good that conform to widely agreed standards of distributive justice or are otherwise the fruit of broad deliberative input and consensus, nor threaten such side-constraints as are in place to ensure the universal protection of a sphere of private autonomy.

In other words, we can and must divorce pedigree from priority. We can happily acknowledge that there are many pedigree lines – many forms of original authority in matters of security as elsewhere – within any social formation. That does not mean, however, that we should

---

[9] Apart, again, from the work of Les Johnston, Clifford Shearing and their various collaborators on nodal policing, we can think of other interesting 'bridging' analyses such as the growing body of work by criminologists on restorative justice and on the innovative regulatory model of the Truth Commission. See, for example, McEvoy and Newburn (2003) and Roche (2003).

leave the mutual coherence of these forms of authority unattended. Neither does it mean that in some respects – in particular in terms of its breadth of democratic input and its power over resources – the state does not possess a stronger pedigree and should not prevail in the final instance. Against this, the crucial feature of the claim of priority that saves it from the charge that in giving precedence to the state it allows it a potentially unbounded 'power to decide the extent of its power' is simply that it concerns the priority of a *normative* order. The state may not be bound by any other site of authority over the extent and use of its security power (with the possible exception of the supranational authority of the European Union, discussed in chapter 9), but it is hedged in by the discipline of the operative norms themselves, and by the broader framework of constitutional law within which these rules are generated and by which they are checked. These ensure both, formally, a level of generality, predictability and accountability in pursuit of these rules and, substantively, whatever degree of respect for the plurality of security centres and diversity of security concerns may be reflected in the content of these rules. The devil, of course, remains in the detail of the institutional design, a point to which we will return in our discussion of anchored pluralism below.

Commitment

We argued in chapter 1 that perhaps the most potent image feeding state scepticism, and certainly one that helps fuel each of the featured variants of scepticism, is that of the state as bully. Underlying this image is a simple – perhaps overly simple – connection. On the one hand, we have the famous Weberian understanding of the state as the monopolist of the legitimate use of force. On the other hand, we have policing, a practice understood as the key societal 'mechanism for the distribution of non-negotiable coercive force' (Bittner 1970: 46). The fear is that if we put the two together then the police and other similarly endowed central security services simply become tools of the state, the vehicle of its violence; and since when force meets other forms of power or authority – of resources, of reason, of culture and affect – force tends to prevail, the idea that such force be 'legitimate' may become redundant, no more than an empty boast.

The danger, borne out many times in the history of the modern state, that state officials may exploit the police to undermine rather than promote the security of those they are charged to protect – the deepest paradox of police power – arises out of just this connection. Yet we need not succumb to fatalism in the face of this paradox. Instead, two sets of answers are called for. The first is a prudential answer. It simply reiterates the importance of the other functions of the state considered above in securing the preconditions of security as a public good, including, minimally and most immediately, the prevention of a 'police state'. As we have seen, the police can be shaped and civilized against this possibility by political culture, by resource decisions, by deliberative processes and deliberated decisions, and by the general authority of rules. The second response is more difficult but equally necessary. It stresses that while the dangers of state excess can indeed be addressed with some confidence through the proper deployment of the state's other security functions, the idea of the state bedrock of the 'legitimate use of force' as referring to something other than everyday police capacity remains a viable one, and one that is valuable precisely in terms of its indication of an independent mechanism to underpin the proper and effective use of that everyday police capacity. What is more, it is a mechanism which needs itself to be separately acknowledged within the litany of the state's priority functions. This we set out to do under the heading of 'commitment'.

What do we mean by commitment as an indispensable and priority function of the state and how precisely does it connect with the legitimate use of force? Drawing in very broad terms on the insights of institutional economics, we may think of the state as an institution or as a cluster of institutions involved in ensuring 'credible commitments' (e.g. North 1993). Furthermore, we may understand the capacity to ensure the credibility of commitments as applying both to the actions of the state itself and, in a close reciprocal dynamic, to the actions of others – institutions and individuals – with whom the state stands in a relationship. For the likelihood that these other actors will honour their commitments to the state will, in some measure at least, depend upon the degree of confidence and trust they have that the state can and will keep its own promises as registered in the array of positive and negative incentives at its disposal, whether through the constancy of its rule following, the effectiveness of its rule enforcement, or the continuing guarantee of its capacity to raise and deploy resources.

Of course, like all forms of power, this is most effective when it operates in latent mode, based on 'the rule of anticipated reactions' (Friedrich 1963: 199) rather than upon repeated shows of strength.

Nevertheless, it remains the case that the state's ultimate and overriding capacity to deploy force does help to secure the credibility of its commitments to tax, to apply rules, and to enforce sanctions and so to underpin the credibility of the commitments of others to comply with the rules and directives of the state, which in turn further reinforces the credibility of the commitments the state can make, and so on. In this regard, crucially, there is nothing special about policing and security. The meta-level coercive potential operates in the area of policing in exactly the same way as it operates in respect of other public goods under state influence, such as education or health, which unlike policing are *not* also coercive at the point of delivery. In all cases, the ordering and resourcing infrastructure needs some kind of coercive underpinning in the final instance for reasons which bear upon effectiveness and reliability of delivery in general without influencing the detailed enforceability of any particular operation. What the state's priority role in ensuring its commitments provides, in short, is just that guarantee of the security of its security (or health, education, etc.) ordering and resourcing powers that allows people to invest in them and their civilizing qualities with a degree of confidence in their effectiveness.

On anchored pluralism

Could not, however, the state sceptics respond to our invocation of the necessity and indeed necessary priority of the state in these various interconnected functions with a necessity clause of their own? The flipside of the historical record of instrumental and cultural work is another historical record which traces the propensity of the state to meddle, to reflect and enact the bias of the most powerful, to mobilize and celebrate an intolerant idea of cultural uniformity, and to decide without sufficient knowledge or foresight. Equally, the flipside of the state's continuing potential to perform this ordering and cultural work effectively towards the production of security as a thick public good is the danger that it will merely consolidate or reinforce its pathologies. Perhaps, moreover, the two are intimately connected and the vices are the unavoidable downside of the virtue; and that any attempt to mobilize the positive face of state policing is fated, in the long run at least, to stimulate and mobilize the vices. The only answer to that concern, and the note on which we will finish this chapter, is to focus in more detail on the deliberative and regulatory elements within the state's functional catalogue and argue for two things: first, as much openness to concerned interests in the production of security and the reduction of insecurity as possible, and as many checks as can be incorporated against undue meddling, bias, uninformed decision-making and cultural imperialism in the ordering and cultural work of the state; and secondly, as much recognition as possible of the ordering and cultural work of other sites of collective security as is consistent with the elements of state priority set out above.

This argument is elaborated at length in the second half of the next chapter. Suffice it for now, by way of conclusion, to say that it translates into what we would call an *anchored pluralism*. The state, in the senses set out above, should remain the anchor of collective security provision, but there should be as much pluralism as possible both, internally, in terms of the constitutional inclusiveness, representativeness and minority and individual protection mechanisms of the democratic and administrative processes through which the aspiration of collective security is reflected upon and pursued and, externally, in terms of the recognition of the appropriate place of other sites of cultural and regulatory production above, below and otherwise beyond the state. In this second and external dimension – the prospects of the flourishing of which are of course intimately associated with and dependent upon the openness of the first or internal dimension – the role of the state in the ordering field should be as a meta-regulator and in the cultural field as a wide boundary of social and security identity within which other sorts of social and security identities may be nested and encouraged.[10]

In both cases, the aim of the state is both positive and negative. Positively, it is to ensure the widest possible community consistent with the minimum affective ties necessary to deliver the regulatory and cultural infrastructure of a single security space, with all the risk-reducing and fear-abating benefits that such a common security environment can bring. Negatively, it is to ensure two forms of limitation. First, there is the auto-limitation of a private domain protected by rights from those forms of intervention by security authorities in general – including most urgently the state itself as the most powerful and wide-ranging security

---

[10] It remains an open question of course, in the light of the development of transnational forms of security practice, whether it must or should be the *widest* boundary of social and security identity. This point is addressed in chapter 9.

authority – that in the name of security threaten in fact to undermine security. In the final analysis, any system of multilevel governance (Marks *et al.* 1996), including our model of anchored pluralism, must be alive to those issues of justice and fairness apt to be resolved not by parcelling out authority and separating powers, but by specifying areas out of bounds to any form of collective power. Secondly, there is a form of external limitation. The state must ensure that other ordering and cultural sites, for all that they can contribute in more knowledgeable, responsive and intimate ways to the production of more localized or more practice-specific security spaces, do so in a way which does not frustrate the attainment of a more inclusive regulation of security and security of regulation, either through regulatory norms which contradict the wider regulatory field or through forms of parochial solidarity which may be inconsistent with membership of the wider security community, or indeed, with the equal security of their own members.

The challenge remains one of finding the requisite commitment and institutional imagination to strike the optimal balance. It is a challenge, in our view, that can only be effectively addressed by abandoning *a priori* scepticism towards the state and by reasserting its necessary virtue and the qualified priority that this implies.

8 | *The democratic governance of security*

I N the previous chapter we outlined what we characterized as the necessary virtue of the state in delivering the public good of security and argued that, in environments in which a multiplicity of actors are engaged in its production or the promise thereof, this virtue is best harnessed through the idea and practice of an anchored pluralism. This entails, we further suggested, seeking to maximize the degree of pluralism within the anchor of state institutions whilst facilitating as much pluralism of delivery outside the state as is consistent with the latter's necessary priority. Having reached this point, two tasks now lie before us. We must first address the question of why, if these virtues are so compellingly virtuous, they appear to remain so thinly, or barely, or even non-existently, evident within so many settings of contemporary security practice. We need, in other words, to consider how and why it is that the state's vices – its propensity to meddle, to be partisan, to impose cultural orthodoxy, and to be idiotic and stubborn – more often shape the politics of security than what we take to be its virtues – a fact about the present that allows state sceptics to lay claim to the mantle of sober, illusion-free, worldliness. Our first task then is to revisit these vices, which were presented in an intellectually stylized form in part I, with a view to grasping how they in fact manifest themselves within the pathologies of modern security practice and with what effects.

Our second, more constructive, purpose is to examine how the vicious circles that these pathological syndromes give rise to, or tend towards, might be broken, or at least loosened, in ways that can foster and sustain a practice of security that is better placed to harness the virtue of the state tradition while seeking to suppress or minimize its vices. Our starting point here is Philip Pettit's (2001a: ch. 7) recent application to democratic theory of the idea of 'false positives' and 'false negatives'. These notions, we argue, can fruitfully be developed as 'hinge' concepts that permit us, on the one hand, to glance backwards in a bid to sharpen our critique of the pathologies we have identified and, on the other, to project forwards with a view to thinking through the kind of institutional matrix required to give practical effect to the idea of anchored pluralism and, with it, the prospect of trying to embed, in what remains an inhospitable climate, the conditions under which security may become an axiomatic, rather than pervasive, element of our social imaginary and political institutions.

Four pathologies of modern security

In the settings in which security problems are today framed and responded to, the virtues of the state tradition are at best unevenly manifest, at worst absent or in retreat. While states do today promise frameworks of conviviality independent of prior affinity, raise and allocate resources, facilitate public deliberation about crime and policing, as well as authorizing, regulating and underscoring the commitment of the full range of security practitioners, these virtues are rarely combined in ways that conduce to the solidaristic and egalitarian security practice we are seeking in this book to defend. Instead, we are witness today to practices and discourses of security seeking which are much more likely to embody and enact the state's problematic capabilities. We devoted considerable space in part I to describing these, though we did so there as a means of illustrating certain prevalent tendencies within state theory. Our focus now is on various pathological syndromes that we think are manifest within modern security practice and on the ways in which these syndromes hail and reproduce the state's vices. We address ourselves, in turn, to four such pathologies which we call paternalism, consumerism, authoritarianism and fragmentation. In describing these syndromes and their effects we are not claiming that they exhaust the terrain of modern security, or seeking to understand the full range of ways in which they are interconnected, or mutually reinforcing, or else in tension. Nor are we aiming to establish sociologically their recent trajectories and current salience – matters that will vary from jurisdiction to jurisdiction and consideration of which would take us far beyond our purposes in this book. We merely wish to claim that these syndromes can be found within, and continue to structure, the practices of modern policing and security in ways that variously help to give security its pervasive, uncivil forms and which stand as obstacles to realizing the benefits of security as a thick public good. Let us consider, in each case, how this is so.

Paternalism

This syndrome elevates professional expertise and authority – of government officials, police officers, intelligence agencies, the operatives of the criminal justice and penal system – to pride of place in determining the contours of security practice. It is the view which says that police and cognate security agencies possess the education, training, experience, skills, knowledge and habitus needed to 'know how to act', to be able to judge the causes, scale and likely impact of security threats and to manage public demands for order accordingly – with the requisite good sense and prudence – for the benefit of all. It is thus a position which privileges not popular sovereignty – whether in the form of unmediated (or, rather, *mass* mediated) public demands or the will of elected political actors – but that of detached, relatively autonomous and apparently impartial bureaucratic expertise.

There can be little doubt – as we have known from Max Weber onwards – that the story of modern security is in large part the story of the formation and rise to ascendancy of bureaucratic, expert, professional institutions for knowing about, and deploying the resources to deal with, crime and other risks to public order and security. There can also be little doubt that police, criminal justice and penal bureaucracies, and their attendant forms of expertise, remain significant elements of the present security constellation. But it is also the case that the extent of such ascendancy, and the scale and impact of the challenges to professional paternalism, has varied and continues to vary across national boundaries. There are, of course, many authoritarian societies across the world where police and security agencies do not possess the kinds of autonomy from political regimes that can enable one to speak accurately of them possessing professional security bureaucracies operating with their own logic of practice. Conversely, one can refer to a state tradition in continental western Europe – in societies such as France and Germany notably – where relatively autonomous, professional public bureaucracies have long had, and retain today, a firm hand on the levers of power within police, criminal justice and penal systems, and operate at some remove from the claims of political and popular will (Whitman 2003). Though much less developed in the USA, with its history of subjecting policing and prosecutorial officials to electoral judgement, and in England and Wales, with its ideology of state-sceptical localism, the claims of professional paternalism have nonetheless found strong footholds in both locations – not least during the reign from the late 1890s to the 1970s of a liberal, elitist penal welfare state and its commitment to the expert capacities of, *inter alia*, probation, psychiatry and criminology (Garland 2001; Loader 2006a). In the policing field, one can reference here the hegemonic status enjoyed by 'professional policing' in the USA, and the close to canonical status assumed by the doctrine of 'constabulary independence' in England and Wales during much of the last century – both notions which claimed that policing was best determined by police expertise insulated from political pressures and accountable to law and law alone (N. Walker 2000: chs. 2–4). The related notion that street-level policing is an opaque craft, acquired only by practice and known only to those that practise it, one that depends on the exercise of an officer's situated commonsense judgement, stands as an exemplar of the same basic idea (Muir 1977).

In recent decades, this syndrome has, in these settings at any rate, been called into dispute – victim to some significant sociocultural developments and their neo-liberal articulation. Perhaps the most telling of these has been a transformation of public sensibilities towards social and political authority, trends that have taken the form of declining levels of deference towards and trust in governmental authorities, on the one hand ('you do not know best'), and a simultaneous heightening of expectations towards those authorities, on the other ('we demand you do this'). This has been coupled with a dramatic growth in the period since 1945 of both levels of crime and public anxieties towards crime and disorder, and an attendant saturation of social relations and public life by crime talk and imagery. These, in turn, have served – across the Anglo-Saxon world especially – as ingredients for neo-liberal governments who have attacked and attempted to rein in professional autonomy in the police and criminal justice system; rulers who – faced with what they hold to be a febrile, emotionalized climate of fear – have sought to speak for and give voice to the claims of 'ordinary people' against those of remote, liberal-minded professional expertise. The ever-present popularity, and seemingly permanent reinvention and relaunching, of community policing can easily be interpreted within this framework – as an effort to get 'professional' police authority to listen and attend to the communities they serve. More broadly in the penal field, the turn against elite paternalism can be registered in such developments as the ideological assaults on the rehabilitative ideal, the advent of minimum mandatory sentences (or 'Three Strikes'), the reappearance of antique punishments such as boot camps and chain gangs, and zero-tolerance policing (see, generally, J. Young 1999; Garland 2001; Simon 2006).

One thus finds today that professional paternalism – in the many jurisdictions in which it has become subject to active dispute – is defended from several different quarters. Some liberal commentators – horrified by what they think are the harsh outcomes of more responsive, 'democratic' forms of policing and punishment – have sought to shore up or reinstate the practices and values of expert professional actors insulated from public and political pressures (Zimring and Johnson 2006). Professional elitism is, in this case, mobilized as a bulwark against majoritarian tyranny. Others have sought to counter such 'populism' by investing in technocratic crime prevention and control strategies that create and empower new cadres of security professionals and put to use a broader range of expertise and professional authority – in, for example, situational prevention, urban planning, programme evaluation, community safety, risk assessment and cognitive behavioural therapy (e.g. Smith and Tilley 2005).

But, in the post-9/11 environment, this security syndrome is also promoted by those who claim that the scale of the current threat demands that we empower and (once again) trust the police and intelligence agencies and give renewed primacy to their knowledge and expertise – a rhetoric that is routinely deployed in defence of the numerous anti-terrorism measures states have enacted since 2001. One has witnessed in this climate a certain clawing back by the state of pluralized security authority in favour of a reassertion of the importance of 'old' state security agencies (the police, intelligence services, military), as well as the formation of 'new' ones such as the Department of Homeland Security in the USA and the Serious and Organized Crime Agency in the UK. Beyond this, we may also cite the ways in which the development of policing and security capacity in the international and transnational arena has taken shape largely in the form of new collaborations between, and networks of, policing and intelligence professionals – often in forms far removed from public concern and oversight (Sheptycki 2000; Goldsmith and Sheptycki forthcoming).

We are concerned then with a syndrome that is perhaps rather less secure than it once was, but a powerful presence nonetheless, a situation in which public bureaucracies and their logics and practices remain significant security players. Whether it remains hegemonic, contested, in defensive retreat, or an aspiration, there is little doubt that professional paternalism persists as a significant template for thinking and acting in the security field – an available and for many deeply resonant security heuristic. We must, thus, pay due care to its pathological dimensions – to the ways in which giving primacy to security professionals and their 'expertise' is bound up with the vices of the state tradition. Here, we should remind ourselves of how acting paternalistically in the security interests of others may nonetheless be to meddle illegitimately and without proper cause with individual rights and interests. We should note that professional security interests may not necessarily equate with the public good but act, rather, as a mask for the pursuit of factional interests. We should remain alive to the propensity of police actors to seek to impose cultural uniformity whether in the name of formal bureaucratic equality or professionally constituted security imperatives. And we should beware, perhaps above all, of the difficulty that professional elites encounter in generating the information about their environment needed to guard against the above three vices, and thereby act efficiently and effectively towards goals that have been reflexively deliberated upon by all affected interests rather than imposed by elites from above.

It may well be, for reasons we elaborate upon below, that professional expertise and bureaucratic authority have a necessary and legitimate part to play within an institutional matrix oriented to realizing security as a public good. It is also relatively easy to think of security settings, such as post-conflict situations, or societies which lack mature and functioning state institutions, where creating such expertise and authority stands among the most pressing political tasks. But it remains dangerous, and injurious to a democratic and equitable security practice, to leave professional paternalism unchecked, or permit it too much room for manoeuvre. For by seeking to act in the interests of citizens who cannot thereby be treated as full partners in dialogue, paternalism lacks an adequate brake upon its pathological propensity to become opaque and self-corroborating, and to prove and renew its own security worldview and that worldview's attendant priorities and expansionary dominion in ways that may not necessarily coincide with the values, concerns or interests of those whom it purports to serve.

Consumerism

We have opted to term the second security syndrome we wish to consider consumerism. In so doing, we have in mind what Phillip Bobbitt (2002: ch. 10) describes approvingly as the 'market-state', and Margaret Canovan (1996: 80) rather less so as the 'service station state'. These terms signify the advent of a state that does not disappear or withdraw entirely from the task of securing goods for its citizens (albeit that it promises much less) but, instead, redefines and articulates its constitutive task as delivering, or facilitating the delivery by others, of certain basic services to individuals now understood as consumers with preferences the state must elicit and satisfy. It is not so much the replacement of the state *by* the market (at least in fields, such as security, where markets are prone to failure), as the insertion of market logics and disciplines *within* the state itself. In the field of policing and security, this syndrome finds expression in the idea that the state's task is to take steps to discover people's preferences and then seek to meet demands for order – for particular styles and levels of policing, or for certain forms or quantities of punishment – in the terms in which they present themselves. This, of course, represents an inversion of the claims of professional paternalism. It is now the consumer, not the government official or police officer, who 'knows best'. Ours, the state says, is no longer to reason why.

Given the way in which this syndrome is bound up with a critique of professional authority, it is best illustrated with reference to examples flagged in the previous discussion. In the policing field, consumerism has in recent decades increasingly come to underpin the promotion of 'ambient policing' (Loader 2006b). By this we mean the family of policing strategies that share a critique of professional law enforcement and which appeal to, and claim to be able to quench, the demands for order that consumers of policing services make. Some of these – 'quality of life', 'broken-windows', or 'zero-tolerance' policing – draw inspiration and guidance from Wilson and Kelling's (1982) influential, if controversial, account of the connection between policing and neighbourhood disorder (Kelling and Coles 1996; cf. Harcourt 2001). Others – 'community', or 'multi-agency', or 'problem-oriented' policing – proffer a critique of police reacting willy-nilly to calls from the public, proposing instead that they 'join up' with other agencies in search of holistic solutions to social problems of which crime and disorder are symptoms

(Goldstein 1990; cf. Herbert 2006). Their latest incarnation in Britain – 'reassurance' or 'neighbourhood' policing – aims to redress what is alleged to have become the insecurity-generating remoteness of police authority from everyday life (Innes 2004). There are, to be sure, some significant 'internal' differences between these approaches, as we noted in chapter 5. But they can usefully be corralled together under the umbrella of ambient policing in so far as they share an express or implied commitment to raising overall numbers of policing operatives present in the local environment (whether employed by the police, the local state or the private sector), coupled with a conception of the policing purpose that is expansive, proactive and visible. By supplying police resources in a bid to meet public demand, ambient police strategies seek to reduce the legitimacy-sapping distance between police and the policed and satisfy the 'needs and expectations' of the former's today more demanding, less brand-loyal customers (Innes 2004).

But one also encounters something closely akin to this consumerist logic in play across the field of crime control and penality – at least in respect of those sectors of it where the state still aspires to being the principal or monopoly provider. In recent years a whole raft of crime-control and penal measures – especially in the USA and UK – have come to be justified using what Canovan (2005: 77–8) calls 'politicians' populism'. This involves a claim by elected rulers that they are speaking for ordinary people – or, more to the point, the 'median voter' – acting in the name of their experiences and concerns and giving effect to their practical wisdom. In respect of the resort to mass imprisonment, minimum mandatory sentences, anti-social behaviour orders, community notification statutes and cognate controls on sex offenders, crackdowns on asylum seekers, new powers against terrorism and the like, it is now routinely proclaimed that such 'tough' action is required to satisfy the security concerns and demands of the public. A range of alternative measures – cutting the prison population, increasing community penalties, taking economic and social measures to tackle crime and disorder – are, conversely, ruled out or never even reach the agenda of practical politics because they require the hard work of 'selling' an unfamiliar brand to apparently punitive and hence hostile consumers.[1]

---

[1] It is important to acknowledge that what Anthony Bottoms (1995) called 'populist-punitiveness' is neither the only discernable penal trend, nor the only possible interpretation of current trends – as Bottoms himself was quick to recognize (see, also, Matthews 2005). As many analysts have pointed out, these

When one couples together the policing and penal dimensions of this syndrome one is tempted, with Baudrillard (1983: 36–7), to draw the conclusion that the state has 'faked its own death'. Not only has it traded 'rowing' for 'steering', 'providing' for 'enabling', and 'judging' for 'umpiring' (Osborne and Gaebler 1992; Bobbitt 2002: 235), but it has even in those domains where it still aspires to be a pre-eminent actor lost confidence in the possibility of mobilizing its own resources and authority for any social purpose beyond that of meeting the demands of emboldened, contingently loyal consumers whom it stands in fear of disappointing and driving away. It is, on this view, simply no part of the task of political authority to challenge, to elicit reasons, to put another view, to enter dialogue, or in any sense seek to temper or restrain the security demands its citizens legitimately make of it.

There is some evidence – and still more ideological affirmation (Bobbitt 2002; Günther 2005) – suggesting that, while this syndrome may not yet be hegemonic, the tide of history is moving decisively in its favour; that in late modern societies this is the only form in which the liberal democratic state can reconnect with what are today more expectant, choice-conscious consumer-citizens. Part of our broader purpose is to stand firm against the 'end of history' (Fukuyama 1992) move which announces the inevitable triumph of the market-state and to suggest, instead, that it remains possible to imagine and give institutional effect to another viable and legitimate role for the state in the production of citizen security. But first we must pinpoint what exactly is pathological about the consumerist prospectus and the practices that it licenses. Here, four points can usefully be made.

First, consumerism tends too readily to presume that public demands for order are entirely benign. This is an improbable depiction. That many individuals today are or feel insecure and make demands for greater policing resources can hardly be disputed. But these

'populist' penal measures form but one strand of a 'volatile and contradictory' field that includes, *inter alia*, the application of managerialist strictures and risk-based, actuarial thinking to policing and punishment (O'Malley 1999; Garland 2001; Harcourt 2006). However, it is at least possible to interpret such 'counter' trends, and the new forms of professional knowledge and organization that they give rise to, not as alternative security syndromes of the kind that may warrant separate treatment here, but as techniques for enabling government to bend the will of, say, police or probation officers to the express preferences of their customers. On this reading, managerialism and actuarialism are *for* consumerist populism.

demands seldom take shape merely as measured calls for action based upon cool, sober calculations of risk. Rather, public sensibilities towards, and demands for, order are often laced with emotions (anger, resentment, fear, anticipated pleasure, etc.); situated in narratives about the trajectory of one's personal biography, or the past, present and possible futures of one's local or national community (Girling *et al.* 2000); and not infrequently motivated by parochial desires for injustice, xenophobic antipathy towards others, or unattainable fantasies of absolute security (Markell 2003). When, in other words, people speak of crime and disorder, and make claims for this or that level of security provision, they are always also giving voice to a series of fears about, and hopes for, the political community in which they live, and to the insecurities that flow from their sense of place within it. They may do so, moreover, in ways that are by no means consistent with the idea that security is a good available, by reason of their membership alone, to all members of that community.

Second, this syndrome assumes that consumer preferences for particular styles and levels of policing can and ought to be met. This is an implausible aim. Such demands lay claim to resources that are finite, and which have to be funded and prioritized. They may articulate competing visions of what policing objectives and styles should be. They are often pressed by middle-class constituencies replete with economic and social capital in ways that risk distributing policing resources in inverse relation to crime risks (Hope *et al.* 2001). And they make claims that are not easily sated in the terms in which they are presented – claims that all too easily result in a vicious, self-propelling circle whereby lay demands and the security measures put in place in a bid to meet them are both endlessly ratcheted up. Yet at the same time, demands for state policing express forms of solidarity towards strangers and an implicit attachment to the idea of public provision. They indicate, in turn, a prior commitment to putting security in common and pursuing it through democratic institutions and practices – a commitment to the exercise of 'voice' rather than 'exit' (Hirschman 1970). All this, rather than pointing in the direction of implicitly endorsing, and uncritically seeking to satisfy, demands for policing in the name of consumer-responsiveness, suggests that such demands are best recognized by being brought within institutional arrangements that subject them, and their supporting identities, narratives and resource claims, to the scrutiny of democratic dialogue.

Third, consumerism evinces little express concern for the interests of the routinely policed, those once graphically referred to as 'police property' (J. Lee 1981) who either lack the economic and cultural clout needed to make their claims as consumers tell, or whose cumulative experience of policing leads them to the conclusion that it is futile and foolhardy to bother to press those claims. This syndrome tends, in other words, to efface questions to do with public consent to, and the regulation of, police power, and devote insufficient thought to what we have labelled the central paradox of state policing; namely, that as a monopolist of coercive resources the police stand simultaneously as a guarantor of, and threat to, citizen security. This is especially pronounced, and not especially surprising, in official discourse – as, for example, in the British government's rhetorical talk of 'the law-abiding citizen' driving police reform (Home Office 2004: 43). But one finds the same omissions – and, implicitly, the same majority constituencies being mobilized and appealed to – in academic defences of community and related forms of ambient policing, where it is complacently assumed that all social groups find policing interventions benign, welcome and reassuring, and where a silence about police disorder has long been strikingly common (Harcourt 2001: 138–9). In their efforts to remodel the state along market lines, and to subject it to competitive pressures, proponents of the new consumerism have tended to neglect the vices that flow from the state's capacity to act as a – meddling, or partisan, or intolerant, or idiotic – bully. In so doing, they have proceeded as if some perennial questions to do with constraining and regulating police power, and some still vexed problems pertaining to how disadvantaged groups are policed, have somehow been settled, or ceased to matter.

Fourth, consumerism radically misconstrues the contribution that policing agencies most fundamentally make to citizen security in a democracy. The police relation to security is, on this view, shallow but wide – to recall one of our framing formulations. It is 'shallow' in so far as that contribution is limited to a claim to be able to protect person, property and neighbourhoods from the threat of crime and disorder. Policing in this sense is oriented to answering the questions 'How safe am I in the here and now?' and 'How well ordered is my immediate environment?' (Innes 2004), rather than towards any more encompassing notion of the good of security of the kind we described in chapter 6. It is 'wide' because, conceived as such, the policing contribution to public security lies principally in the visible display and activation of police authority across the broad range of local social relations that may carry or threaten 'disorderly' consequences. Security, on this view, depends on the unmediated presence of uniformed officers. The greater their numbers, the more visible, familiar and active they are, the more secure individuals will be or, as importantly, feel. The problem here is that, by seeking to deliver security through the police-centred strategy of supplying a high-visibility policing package in an unthinking bid to satisfy individual preferences, consumerism risks making security not an axiomatic but a pervasive feature of social relations and political life.

Authoritarianism

Security, as the above discussion reminds us, may be said to be 'pervasive' when it becomes the prevailing discourse for understanding social problems, the lens through which they are defined, examined and acted upon. It is pervasive when it begins, in these ways, to acquire a certain colonizing force, or 'everywhereness', when its claims and values (to take 'tough' policing and punishment-centred measures to protect 'us' from 'them') prevail in areas of public life and policy (housing, or education, or urban planning) where they have no proper business. When security becomes pervasive it generally coincides with a sense of impatience and urgency; with calls for the unhindered, speedy hand, and visible display, of executive authority; with deepening levels of intolerance towards minority groups and practices; with evident frustration at, and calls for the curtailment of, basic rights and liberties. When security practices and discourse take this form, one can usually be sure that individuals are, in fact, feeling insecure. The practices of pervasive security also generally do little to confront the conditions generating that insecurity, and much that serves to fuel and deepen it. A vicious – insecurity-sustaining – circle is thereby joined.

Authoritarianism – the third security syndrome we want to address critically – constitutes one form that such insecurity-perpetuating spirals may take. This spiral runs – ideal-typically – something like this. Individuals who live under conditions of pervasive in/security tend to make demands for what they judge to be 'hard' anti-crime measures (more police, more police powers, crackdowns on this offence or those suspects, stiffer sentencing, harsher penal regimes and so on) in ways that display impatience with informed democratic deliberation, seek to suspend or curtail basic rights, foster hostility towards minorities and outsiders, and risk melding their interests and identities with those of the state whose 'protective' power they seek to mobilize and shelter under. This process, once initiated, tends to be vicious and circular because once such demands are met in the terms in which they are presented it becomes difficult to create the political and cultural conditions wherein the pace of such measures can be slowed, or a change or reversal of direction effected – thereby setting in train a potentially endless 'ratcheting-up' in police numbers, or incarceration rates, or restrictions of basic liberties. And if such actions are perceived to have 'failed', or are ideologically depicted in those terms – because crime rates go up, or a child is abducted, or a group of youths run amok, or another terrorist outrage occurs – this overwhelmingly prompts calls for still 'tougher' measures, only this time with a heavier dosage. A democracy- and liberty-eroding spiral is thus entered in ways it becomes hard to escape. A form of security politics gets entrenched that does much to put at risk democratic principles and basic rights, while doing little to make citizens either any safer or any more secure. As the 'war on terror' is reminding us once again, anxious citizens make bad democrats (cf. Neumann 1957; Rorty 2004).

Authoritarianism – with its constitutive tendency to reach for, invest in and defer to footloose executive power – can flow out of either the paternalist or consumerist syndromes we have discussed so far. It is, in this sense, a pathology of the pathological. In the former case, it surfaces when government, or police, or other security actors determine – from the 'top-down' – that the threats of crime, or disorder, or violence are such as to require the grip of strong rule, and the curtailment of dissent or restraint, in order that government can deal effectively, as it deems fit, with the internal or external foes that confront society – rule which frequently demands that its subjects stand either 'for us' or 'against us'. In the latter, one encounters – typically weak – governments taking up, articulating and acting upon whatever revealed preferences they are faced with – in this case the 'passion for authoritarianism' (Gilroy 2004) that can bubble up 'from below' in the face of what are, or are perceived to be, serious and pressing problems of crime and violence, and which take the form of calls for the firm hand of state power to act swiftly and decisively against them. In the settings of security politics, these top-down and bottom-up tendencies tend to be locked in a firm, mutually reinforcing, embrace, such that it is hard to isolate a year zero in which it becomes possible to spot the chicken and the egg. Authoritarian spirals tend, in other words, to involve elements of relatively untutored lay anxiety, fantasy and cries for action and the mobilization, utilization and reinforcement of public sensibilities by political, professional and media actors for specific political ends.

The practical effects of authoritarian spirals are in any case sufficiently similar as to render such an exercise in hermeneutic recovery unnecessary. They conduce – whether from 'top-down' or 'bottom-up' – to outcomes that manifest and magnify the vices of the state tradition while often depicting these vices as virtues. Authoritarianism, in short, calls forth an over-investment in, and over-identification with, the coercive capabilities of the state. Its product is thus typically a state that is overweening, excessively powerful and subject to insufficient legal constraint, few mechanisms for rectifying mistakes, and limited sites of countervailing power. This, in turn, gives rise to a security politics that promises and pursues security at the expense of other valued social goods (liberty, rights, democratic practices) and, ultimately, of security itself – at least in the axiomatic form whose benefits we have sought to elucidate. If the state does indeed have a propensity to meddle with individual rights and interests, to champion sectarian causes, to flatten the cultural landscape, and to proceed without the knowledge required to accomplish its purposes, then the political and cultural dynamics of authoritarian rule merely compound these tendencies. Individual rights tend to count for little in political systems that valorize the pursuit of security by strong executives; authoritarian governments – for all their rhetorical homage to the 'national' interest – tend in practice to shore up specific rather than general order (Marenin 1982); pluralism is generally believed to be, and is depicted by official actors as being, a dangerous luxury that society permits at its peril; and by keeping individuals in a state of what Kant called 'perpetual infancy', and marginalizing or suppressing the institutions, practices and habits that sustain conversations about how to live democratically with risk, authoritarian states generally cut themselves adrift from the sources of information that are in fact prerequisite to their effectiveness.

As a pathology of the pathological, moreover, authoritarianism tends to be the medium and outcome of the 'thicker' variants of pervasive security, or securitization, to which we have referred in earlier discussion – those that are both 'wide' in their claimed ambit of policy relevance and 'deep' in their attempts to harness that wide jurisdiction to a highly prescriptive formula of ontological security. But even in its deep and wide incarnations, authoritarianism can be as much a matter of drift as design, and as likely to be coded as a project of social conservation as one of transformation. For in the security politics of democratic societies, authoritarian politics seldom travels under its own name or announces its arrival in the corridors of power. This, though, is all the more reason to stay on guard against the authoritarian sensibilities that such societies continue to harbour and the dangers that its superficially seductive programmes can unleash.

Fragmentation

The fourth security syndrome we want to consider – fragmentation – is a close cousin of consumerism. Though 'third way' proponents of the latter – notably, in recent years, Bill Clinton and Tony Blair – have conceived of the consumerist reconfiguration of the state as a means to stave off the former, it is at least arguable that by endorsing the market's self-image, and traducing the ethos of the public domain (cf. Marquand 2004), consumerism may in fact ferment further fragmentation of, in the present case, policing and security. Having interpellated individuals as consumers of public provision, there is still less standing in the way of them acting as such and turning their backs on what the state has to offer (Loader 1999).[2]

To speak of fragmentation is to refer to the residualization of the state as a security actor (whether as provider or regulator of provision), as individuals, communities, organizations and corporations define and find ways of managing or seeking to eliminate their own security risks – most pertinently by purchasing tailored protective services and hardware in the marketplace. The market for such goods has today – as we illustrated at various points in part I – become booming business. In situations of armed conflict, and post-conflict peacekeeping and reconstruction, the 'market for force' and a range of ancillary police and

[2] This is not, it should be said, the view of neo-liberal writers like Bobbitt (2002: 237) who seem to accept that the market-state will in future evolve hand in hand with 'devolution and privatization'. Bobbitt cites with approval Martin van Creveld's prediction that 'the day-to-day burden of defending society from low-intensity conflict will be transferred to the booming security business'.

military services is presently mushrooming and in rude health (Avant 2005). In societies where states lack the capacity or will to protect their citizens – from South Africa, to Brazil, to Russia – affluent constituencies routinely turn to hired (often armed) security or seek refuge in fortified enclaves (Caldeira 2000), while people in poor neighbourhoods are left to their own meagre resources to protect themselves in the absence of – or indeed from – the state. And there is now plenty of evidence demonstrating the extent and scale of the private security industry in western democracies as states struggle to meet the demands that citizens, neighbourhoods or corporations have for protection of their person and property (Jones and Newburn 2006). These are the contexts in which the application of market logics – even where intended to quell the commodification of security – may simply add fuel to the flames.

These propensities of the present also contain within them the potential to assume a vicious spiralling quality – in this as in respect of other basic goods (such as education and healthcare) where state and market provision coexist, compete or are in conflict. The logic in the security field runs something like this. Individuals or social groups who feel insecure or unprotected by the state tend increasingly to search for alternative security solutions, either by organizing local forms of autonomous communal ordering (in corporate or residential enclaves, or through citizen patrolling) or by turning to the market in order to purchase desired levels or types of security personnel and hardware (patrols, static guards, alarms, surveillance systems, etc.). The more widespread these practices become the less willing such individuals and groups are to support, fund and engage in dialogue about general forms of policing and security provision. This results in social fragmentation in so far as it erodes people's sense of being participants in an ongoing collective project whose members are committed to putting and pursuing security in common, which, in turn, undermines the 'architecture of sympathy' (Sennett 2003: 200) through which this shared purpose takes practical shape. The security, and forms of political freedom, associated with the sense of belonging to, and identification with, a political community is thereby placed in jeopardy, and with it the collective capacity to forge and realize common purposes, including security purposes (C. Taylor 1995: ch. 7). Society fractures into a world of markets and tribes.

The problems – or pathology – here arise not so much from the state's overweening presence and the attendant manifestation of its vices, as from the relative weakness or absence of state authority and the consequent impotence of the political actor best placed to foster and give effect to the sense of collective purpose associated with the realization of security as a public good. This results, on the one hand, from the formation of individual subjects who come to think of themselves as sovereign consumers utilizing their resources as they see fit in pursuit of security and, on the other, from the development of new security communities – along, for example, class, or ethnic, or territorial, or interest-based lines – who seek to organize or purchase protective services in order to meet their self-defined, particularistic needs in ways that function exclusively for the benefit of members of that 'club' (Hope 2000; Crawford 2006). Two problematic outcomes, in particular, surface when one or other of these variants of fragmentation takes hold.

First, as consumers or communities pursue, or organize themselves around, their own conception of what it means, and what it takes, to be secure, security itself again tends to become pervasive. It is a constitutive feature of markets that consumers are not called upon to justify the preferences they utilize their purchasing power to satisfy. They are thus free – or as free as their resources permit – to operate as 'sovereign' actors seeking to assuage their security anxieties as they see fit, as well as to deal with disappointment, or a perceived increase in risk, or actual instances of victimization, by returning to the market in search of enhanced levels of protection. Similar problems arise in respect of particularistic communities organizing, or pooling resources to purchase, their own security requirements – as we argued in chapter 5 in discussion of Shearing and others' promotion of the Zwelethemba model of local capacity building. But the problems of restraining 'appetites' for security, and of enabling others to influence the way in which it is framed and pursued, are compounded in this case by concerns about how minority voices within communal groupings are regarded and by the tendency to disregard the security interests of those defined as outside the ambit of communal sympathy and protection. In other words, the more security provision fragments, and the weaker public regulatory authority becomes, the more likely it is that security becomes an expression of the 'desire for sovereign agency' (Markell 2003: 22), a condition pursued with little or no acknowledgement of the mutual uncertainty, vulnerability and dependency that flows inescapably from 'the activity of living and interacting with other people' (Markell 2003: 7).

Fragmented security leads, secondly and relatedly, to an accumulating loss of the memory and experience of living in a democratic political community (Lindseth forthcoming). The more security is sought by shoppers in a marketplace, or within the bounds of particularistic enclaves, the less routine will be people's experience of having to tolerate, be civil towards, and 'rub along' with, strangers with whom they coexist and share public space as members of that polity; and the less likely they are to acquire, retain or sharpen the 'habits of democratic citizenship' (Sandel 1996: 332) that flow from the practice of having to think about one's security 'preferences', and the resource claims that they entail, in relation to those of other members of the society with whom one dwells and in dialogue with them. The more the security situation of different groups – of, say, ethnic communities, or socio-economic classes, or the young and old – grows apart and comes to be thought about and acted upon in isolation, the less likely such groups are to experience or understand their fates as shared and the less motivated they will be to make affective and material investments in 'public things' – including collective security (Keenan 2003: 148). This – applied to the field of security – is precisely the vicious circle of public disinvestment of which writers such as Charles Taylor (1991) and Michael Sandel (1996) warn – one in which the *effect* of such disinvestment becomes the *cause* of further democratic impoverishment (Keenan 2003: 146–51). The question that lies before us, and the task that confronts anyone committed to a more democratic and egalitarian practice of security, is how to transform this – and the other vicious spirals that attend the pathologies of modern security – into a virtuous circle. It is to this task that we now turn.

Turning vicious into virtuous circles

We wish now to strike a generally more constructive note and to begin the process of redeeming, by addressing matters of institutional principle and design, the idea of security as a thick public good we elucidated in chapter 6. We want, in particular, to think through the kind of institutional matrix within which it becomes possible to suppress, or at least minimize, the state's vices whilst at the same time harnessing the virtues of the state tradition with a view to making security less pervasive but more axiomatic. How, in other words, can we begin to unsettle, or even break, the vicious circles of modern security practice in ways that enable that always precarious balance between the vices and virtues of the modern state to be tipped in favour of the latter?

Our point of departure for this exercise is Philip Pettit's (2001a: ch. 7) recent application to democratic theory, and our understanding of republican political freedom, of the idea of 'false negatives' and 'false positives'.[3] Pettit is concerned, as we are, with trying to specify forms of political authority, or state power, that can promote non-dominating social relations, and hence individual freedom, by 'tracking' and taking account of the 'common avowable interests', and only such interests, of all parties affected by its decisions and practices. He describes this, in an early formulation of the argument, as the 'all-and-only formula' (Pettit 1997: 292). For Pettit, interests are 'avowable' when they 'are conscious or can be brought to consciousness without great effort', as opposed to being imputed by government bodies; and they are 'common' if they are the product of 'co-operatively admissible' considerations rather than those which are self-interested or parochial (Pettit 2001a: 156). Discovering such interests, he argues, requires institutional processes that seek to eliminate 'false negatives' (the legitimate but unheard or unreasonably disregarded claims of citizens) by searching for, identifying and including in democratic deliberation every relevant candidate for determining how, in the present case, security resources can be distributed and brought to account in ways consistent with it being a thick public good. It requires, further, the removal of 'false positives' by rigorously scrutinizing and disallowing claims – which may be pressed insistently, or with great noise and passion, by well-organized constituencies – that cannot reasonably be encompassed in any negotiated conception of common interest (Pettit 2001a: 156–60).

---

[3] Pettit's mobilization of these notions forms part of his wider intellectual effort to revive and defend a neo-Roman theory of republican freedom and government, other elements of which we will have cause to draw upon in the arguments that follow (see, especially, Pettit 1997). The contrast between Pettit's *neo-Roman* republicanism, with its concern to create institutional forms that preserve individual freedom understood as non-domination, and *neo-Athenian* republicanism, with its view of participation in public life as intrinsic to human flourishing, is important here and is usefully discussed in Maynor (2003: ch. 1). Pettit has himself, of course, both singularly and in collaboration with John Braithwaite, applied republican political theory to criminal justice and punishment, if not to questions of security more generally (Braithwaite and Pettit 1990; Pettit 2001b).

This, in our view, is a powerful and valuable idea. We want, as such, to develop the notions of false negatives and false positives as *hinge* concepts that enable us, on the one hand, to pivot 'backwards' with a view to taking further and sharpening the critique we have offered of the pathological syndromes of modern security practice and, on the other, to lean 'forwards' with a view to prescribing the elements of an institutional matrix within which to develop a deliberative and democratic practice of security. This short section thus itself functions as a 'hinge' between the critical and constructive components of this chapter.

How then do the syndromes discussed hitherto fare when measured against the republican criteria of ensuring that 'common avowable' security interests are not systematically overlooked or disregarded (the problem of false negatives) and identifying and holding to account sectional or partisan security claims (the problem of false positives)? *Paternalism* fails to recognize and cannot deal with the issue of false negatives because it imputes, rather than actively tracking, the interests and ideas of those whom security professionals claim to act in the service of. It similarly leaves open the possibility that professional priorities may be biased, partial and incestuously self-reproductive, and therefore themselves false positives. *Consumerism* can, in principle, handle the problem of false negatives provided that the mechanisms it uses to elicit consumer preferences are sufficiently inclusive – though in practice it often faces difficulties in encompassing the concerns of constituencies whose alienation makes them reluctant to press their claims as consumers, those the British government took for a time to calling 'hard-to-reach groups' (Jones and Newburn 2001). But consumerism does far less well with the issue of false positives because, as mentioned, it lacks mechanisms for scrutinizing, and judging the merits of, the preferences that any consultative or participatory process may generate. *Authoritarianism* fails to address the question of false negatives, either because it simply assumes the will of the executive and those who endorse it to be the only legitimate security consideration, or because it holds that the process of seeking alternative views will destabilize strong government or put at risk vital security imperatives. By similarly treating the question of false positives as a non-problem, this syndrome can provide no check against the possibility that governments are resolutely but blindly pursuing partisan concerns or shoring-up factional interests. *Fragmentation*, finally, fails to eliminate false negatives because it generates and responds to the claims, and only the claims, of those with economic capital to spend in security markets or the social capital necessary to develop their own autonomous protective capacity; at the same time, it possesses no means of identifying and removing false positives because it operates to privilege the interests and claims of those with 'the loudest voices and the largest pockets' (Shearing and Johnston 2003: 144).

The prevailing syndromes of modern security practice do not, it seems, perform well when put through the 'road-test' set by Pettit's republican theory. The democratic credentials of each of them are, for the major part, found wanting in ways that further expose their shortcomings and strengthen the case for a security practice which can transcend them. With this in mind, our aim now is to 'turn' these ideas to constructive effect. We want, in particular, to revisit the concept of anchored pluralism introduced in conclusion to the previous chapter with a view to putting some institutional flesh on the skeleton notion we sketched there. In so doing, we hope to be able to indicate how the necessary virtues of the state may be harnessed and given practical effect in ways that offer all citizens the assurance – and sense of security – that flows from having their ideas and interests routinely tracked and considered by the institutions of a democratic political community of which their membership is fully acknowledged and to which they experience a feeling of confident belonging.

The practice of civilizing security

How, then, can we configure, or more accurately reconfigure, the political authority of the state in order that it may effectively expedite the meta-regulatory, or anchoring, role whose necessity and value we argued for in chapter 7? What kind of institutional matrix is likely to permit such a preponderant political authority to be able to exercise sufficient vertical oversight and control over the plurality of agents and agencies who today promise or deliver security, whilst at the same time ensuring that the state anchor remains, in both its delivering and regulatory dimensions, subject to adequate democratic contestation and public and legal scrutiny? Can we, in other words, give effect to the necessary priority of the state in a fashion that enables it – in Pettit's (2001a: 173) words – to 'protect its people from domination without itself becoming a dominating instrumentality'?

Our task in this section is to address this question and suggest an affirmative answer to it. In so doing, we are not seeking to offer a ready-made – still less utopian – blueprint for institutional design that can somehow be packaged, exported and transplanted into whatever national setting one might wish to embed it in. We have no option, in seeking to civilize security and to release its civilizing potential, other than to begin with actually existing institutional practices of state and civil society, with all their attendant vices, and to act through and upon them. One cannot, in other words, create a civilized security politics *ex nihilo*; one has to work, instead, with the institutional materials at hand along the lines suggested by the metaphor of 'rebuilding the ship at sea' (Elster *et al*. 1998; Shapiro 2003: 54). Conversely, however, we are not in the business of trying to specify in fine-grained detail – with the 'i's' dotted and 't's' crossed – the precise shape and *modus operandi* of the institutions of democratic security practice, or to work through the implications of our argument for contemporary debates in policing and security policy in their diverse national settings (cf. Patten 1999).

We are seeking, in short, to chart a course between, on the one hand, being unduly and conservatively hemmed in by the constraints that extant political realities impose upon our capacity to think imaginatively beyond the present and, on the other, writing what can rapidly be dismissed as a letter to Santa Claus. Our purpose is to set out the elements of an institutional matrix that seems capable of mobilizing and allocating the policing and other collective resources that security requires; democratically governing the demands, appetites, expectations, resentments and conflicts that attend contemporary struggles in the security field; and subjecting to scrutiny and account the coercive power that individual and collective security sometimes inescapably entails in ways that contribute towards a practical realization of the idea that security is a thick public good. We shall call these elements – whose beneficial effects are optimized only when they are combined together – the four Rs of civilizing security practice: resources, recognition, rights and reasons. Our task in what remains of this chapter is to describe each of them – and their purpose, value and relation to each other – in turn.

Resources

The question of resources speaks to the role that the state is uniquely able to play in mobilizing and distributing the collective funds that are indispensable to the realization of security. We set out in chapter 7 the reasons why the state, or some functionally equivalent form of political authority, is pivotal to solving problems of resource mobilization. We are concerned here with how, building upon that foundation, it can be tasked with directly allocating policing and security resources, and also with indirectly intervening in the pattern of resource allocation relevant to security both through its broader work of income redistribution and social service provision, and through its regulation and monitoring of the allocative power of non-state security actors – in all cases guided by the pursuit of the public good of security. We alluded earlier, in our critique of consumerism, to the necessarily finite nature of the policing and cognate capabilities that can be drawn upon and put to use in the pursuit of security. It follows from this that the practice of security must entail the determination of priorities as between, say, competing styles of policing, or between policing and other preventative or protective measures, or in deciding between making interventions in the realm of policing and crime control, or public policy more broadly. It follows further that security politics, like politics proper, involves the exercise of choice in deciding which demands for order, from which constituencies, are to be responded to and how. Acknowledging the abiding presence of these constraints, and the politics of prioritization and resource allocation that comes with them, is indeed a vital part of the constitution of a civilizing security practice – not least because insisting upon their acknowledgement is to place a check on those lay sensibilities, or social movements, or political programmes which yearn for total security in ways that wish them away or strive to override them.

In this respect, the role of the state as anchor within a pluralistic security environment is threefold. There is, first of all, a necessary and legitimate role for the actors and agencies of the state in insisting upon and explaining the limits imposed by resource constraints in the security field, and thereby seeking to 're-direct' (Loader forthcoming b) often emotionally charged demands for order towards a reflexive deliberation on how security for all can best be furthered and on the consequences of the competing paths that may be followed. To iterate and reiterate the language of constraint and restraint is to offer a reminder – in contexts where those who seek more protection, and the non-state actors who promise to provide it, have little incentive to do so – of the competing values and social purposes that are at issue and which can be undermined when societies move to protect their members. It requires, further, that the state highlights and publicizes the value trade-offs that competing courses of action may entail; thinks reflexively about the balance between the direct and indirect resources that can best contribute towards public security; and acts as a broker and disseminator of what is reliably known about the likely effects and effectiveness of alternative preventative or protective measures. In each of these respects, one needs to create institutional processes that can embed and grapple with the consequences of resource constraint, such that demands for order are not greeted by fantastical promises to quench them in the terms in which they appear. These demands must, instead, be brought into arenas of public conversation and contestation with a view to 'satisfying' them in ways that are less unmediated and superficially responsive, but which are ultimately more conducive to the realization of common security. We flesh out further below what this entails in our discussion on the complementary importance of 'recognition' and 'reasons'.

The state's second legitimate and vital task is to allocate the resources it has mobilized, and which it deploys directly or indirectly in pursuit of security objectives, in a manner that contributes to, rather than detracts from, the production of a civilizing security practice. This, as mentioned, requires mechanisms of resource distribution that aim to ensure that policing and security resources track the common interests and ideas, and only those interests and ideas, of all citizens affected by its allocation decisions. The task here is to find ways of guarding against the state allocating resources, and intervening in social life in pursuit of security goals, in ways that depend upon the unchecked professional calculations of its actors, or serve the factional interests of only some of those with a legitimate stake in its actions, or else reproduce the inequalities of access to security generated elsewhere, notably through the market. In the practical contexts of contemporary security, this underscores the importance of forms of political authority that are capable of registering and addressing the inverse relationship that so often obtains between levels of crime risk and people's ability to access policing or other preventative or protective resources. It signals equally the value of institutions that are able to think and act holistically within a pluralized and fragmented security landscape and thereby bring some reflexive coherence to it. This means, in particular, the state taking cognizance of the deep inequities in security provision generated by and through commercial security practices, and by the discrepancies in economic and social capital that afford individuals and groups such differential access to security capacity, and acting to deploy collective resources in order to bolster those constituencies who repeatedly lose, or do not even get to play, the market game. This can, of course, take the form of compensatory adjustments in resource allocation within the public police service. More broadly, it can also involve ensuring that the funding of wider forms of social provision is sufficient to prevent undue demands being made for state security resources shallowly and reactively conceived. More particularly, it can lead to the state using its tax revenue to support non-state policing and security initiatives in locations that suffer from security deficits.[4]

The third role required of the state in this regard is to exercise the regulatory capabilities that it alone can bring to bear within contemporary security constellations – its power to fund, to contract, to license, to set conditions for entry to markets, to monitor, to forbid – in ways that seek to accomplish the more equitable forms of provision that are conducive to security becoming and remaining a public good. Broadly this means trying to tame the worst inequalities that current patterns of security allocation give rise to. More particularly, it means putting in place regulatory frameworks that structure the plurality of agents and agencies who today promise security in ways that ensure that their particularistic or profit-oriented calculations are politically 'fenced-in' behind arrangements oriented to fostering and sustaining a more solidaristic security practice. There are several mechanisms that one can envisage and develop along these lines – not least in terms of setting stringent, socially oriented conditions for licensing security companies; laying down threshold conditions that such firms, or forms of communal security provision, must meet in order to operate; and establishing attendant forms of inspection, monitoring and accounting. But the task in each case remains essentially the same: to deploy the special capacities of public political authority in ways that anchor the sites of dispersed power that have today been unleashed under conditions conducive to pervasive security so as instead to bring market and communal practices of policing and protection within the ambit of an institutional architecture oriented to keeping alive and give effect to

---

[4] Some of the ways in which this may be done are discussed in chapter 5.

a security practice that acknowledges the security interests and aspirations of each and all. Such an approach, then, certainly does not deny the possibility of 'value-added' security in local or functional non-state settings. Rather, it insists that the test and standard of non-state provision should be precisely that; namely, that the new forms of security provided for in or by particular constituencies, including those who view themselves as political *communities* in their own right, should indeed not detract from or neutralize the value of security as a thick public good in the broader political community framed by the state.

Recognition

Recognition registers the vital importance of a state that governs security by fostering routine democratic deliberation among all those affected by its decisions about security problems – about how and whether demands for order can be met, how the state should allocate its limited resources, or how it is to wield its regulatory capacities. The task here is to devise and sustain mechanisms of public conversation and contestation in respect of security problems and how to apprehend them, mechanisms whose guiding orientation is that of inclusion. The value of recognition lies, in short, in recognizing the value of institutional arrangements which make it 'possible for the significantly different voices in the society to express themselves in a way that others have to hear and honour' (Pettit 1997: 131).

The benefits of recognition are essentially twofold and have broadly to do with legitimacy and effectiveness – with both inputs and outputs. In the first place, recognition is indispensable to addressing the problem of false negatives; that is, to preventing state and non-state security actors operating in ways that prematurely and illegitimately disregard the interests and ideas of those who can reasonably claim a stake in the outcome of their decisions. Processes of inclusive public deliberation which track these interests and ideas thus form a vital bulwark against domination, a check against the possibility of state actors proceeding on the basis of their own self-defined and self-corroborating worldviews, or in defence of whatever sectional interests have succeeded in catching or capturing the state's attention. These processes enable all the recipients of state action and inaction – and especially those disadvantaged constituencies whose voices are often unheard or systematically dismissed – to see their claims and concerns reflected in the means by which decisions are arrived at, such that they can understand themselves as being in part their author as well as their addressee (Habermas 1996). The principle of recognition is, in this sense, key to creating within and around the state a public sphere which can sustain an informed dialogue about problems of insecurity and how they are framed and responded to, one capable of ensuring that all voices with a stake in that problem are elicited and considered. Its purpose is to stimulate more informed conversation about security in order that the interests and identities of different constituencies are not only reciprocally acknowledged, listened to and accorded due respect, but also disputed, relativized and unfixed in ways that facilitate possibilities of mutual understanding and learning – a prospect we elucidate further under the heading of 'reasons' below. The institutions of a public sphere may also, more specifically, foster watchful observers and critical scrutinizers of state practices as well as being a conduit through which the state can engage in dialogue about what it means to think about and seek to realize security as a public good.

Recognition is beneficial, secondly, in seeking to reduce or minimize the tendencies of the state towards idiocy; that is, in countering the difficulties that it routinely encounters in obtaining the social information required to accomplish its purposes, including its security purposes. This problem of cognitive deficits is not peculiar to states, but is a feature of the relationship between all organizations and their environments. It is thus not easily rectified, still less wished away. Democratic processes based on the principle of recognition are nonetheless important here not only to grounding the democratic credentials of public institutions, but also to improving the knowledge base upon which decisions are based, and hence their likely quality. Eliciting and listening to the views of the widest range of affected individuals, social groups, non-governmental organizations, professional associations and other voices in civil society is itself to recognize that the state has no monopoly on wisdom. It is also to tap into, and put to use, the practical knowledge whose benefits pragmatist democrats from James C. Scott to Charles Sabel to Clifford Shearing quite properly insist upon. In either respect, the aim is to generate allocative and regulatory practices that are informed by, and take notice of, the experience of those who are going to be affected by them, and to seek to make good through public conversation the respective information deficits that bedevil not only public authority, but all agents and agencies that promise or seek to deliver security. In so doing, one is striving through practices of democratic conversation and contestation to inject into practices of security a permanent and dynamic reversibility – the capacity to experiment, to learn from experience, to rectify mistakes. One is further seeking, through such mechanisms, to break the well-documented vicious circle which sees remote and information-poor policing institutions being required to act coercively in ways that erode still further their legitimacy and effectiveness (Kinsey *et al.* 1986) and to foster, instead, the kind of virtuous circles within which legitimacy and effectiveness become, and are seen as being, mutually reinforcing (Audit Commission 1993; Tyler 2004).

There are an array of mechanisms that can be deployed or developed to give effect to the principle of recognition and its benefits, some of which one finds more or less embedded in actually existing democracies, others that take shape for now in the writings of democratic theorists or the demands of social movements (Shapiro 2003). These include using electoral processes – and the forms of publicity and exposure which equitably funded and properly regulated elections release – for constituting broadly targeted 'policing' rather than narrowly focused 'police' boards or commissions (Patten 1999; Loader 2000; N. Walker 2000: chs. 6 and 10). To this one might add mechanisms – both face-to-face and virtual – for public consultation and participation; procedures that guarantee the representation of disadvantaged groups; practices of deliberative polling and proposals for deliberation days; citizens' panels and juries, notice-and-comment procedures and many more.[5] One may further pinpoint the importance of ensuring that these mechanisms search for and identify the interests of affected parties in ways that 'respect an individual's or a group's method of communication' (Maynor 2003: 84; see also I. M. Young 2000: ch. 2). And one must be alive today to the possibility that the constituency of the affected may no longer be neatly coterminous with the boundaries of local or even national political communities (Benhabib 2004) – the implications of which we explore more fully in the final chapter.

---

[5] There is an extensive theoretical and 'applied' literature on deliberative democracy upon which one can draw in this context. Notable theoretical contributions include, *inter alia*, Habermas (1996); Bohman and Rehg (1997); Dryzek (2000) and Gutmann and Thompson (2004). More practice-oriented interventions can be found in Fishkin (1991) and Ackerman and Fishkin (2002).

These suggestions of course raise deep, perhaps intractable, issues of democratic theory and many tricky questions of institutional design. They also confront some acute practical problems with respect to how to develop or extend them within the settings of mass-mediated, consumerist, post-ideological societies plagued by citizen apathy towards politics, or embed them in societies that lack mature democratic institutions and cultures. For now, however, it is less important to embark on a journey into these terrains than it is to insist upon the value of recognition as a regulative ideal and on the corresponding importance it affords to the formation of institutional arrangements that offer citizens what Nancy Fraser (2003: 36) calls 'parity of participation'. This does not entail that the interests and identities that one seeks to track through such processes need be uncritically endorsed or authenticated (McBride 2005), for reasons we elucidate under the heading of 'reasons' below. Fostering processes of inclusive democratic conversation and contestation is the key here. It matters, most immediately, in respect of trying to generate forms of public authority in the field of policing and security that are legitimate and effective in the ways we have described. But it is also important to point out, recalling the discussion in chapters 6 and 7, that processes of recognition associated with politically constituted authority are themselves an important ingredient of security. Inclusive democratic processes for governing security implicitly and expressly signal to *all* citizens that they will not be left to suffer in silence, that their anxieties and demands for a secure existence will be actively elicited and listened to, that their claims and concerns as full and equal members of a political community will be tracked and weighed. In so doing, such processes supply forms of assurance that contribute to making security axiomatic in ways that are prior to, and relatively independent of, the policing and security outcomes they generate, but which lead us to suppose that those outcomes must not themselves undermine that reassurance (Loader 2006b). Recognition offers, in short, a guarantee of confident membership that enables citizens to raise their thresholds for managing anxiety and be better able to live securely with risk.

Rights

Let us, thirdly, consider the value and significance of rights. In so doing, we want to articulate a conception of rights not as a counterpoint to the claims of security against which the latter must be 'balanced', but as a vital ingredient of a civilizing security practice (Waldron 2003a; Loader forthcoming a). We want, further, to temper the inflated hopes and ambitions that are sometimes associated with the idea of rights – such that rights become the organizing principle of contemporary progressive politics, or the closest that western secular culture comes to having an article of faith – whilst at the same time recognizing their place within any plausible conception of the good society (Ignatieff 2001). Our aim, in short, is to situate rights *within* our four-pronged heuristic for reconfiguring security, and thereby to emphasize their contribution *to* the practice of civilizing security – a theoretical move that leads one to highlight three indispensable elements.

A regime of rights seeks, first of all, to place a check on the coercive capacities of the state. By guaranteeing all members of a political community certain basic political and civil freedoms – to free expression, political association, a free press, privacy, family life, a fair trial, against cruel and degrading punishment and so forth – legally enforceable human rights prevent the state from acting as an arbitrary dominating force, and stop it from meddling illegitimately with the basic entitlements of citizens. They further require that these constraints upon state power are given practical force through the creation of plural mechanisms of enforcement and redress, ranging from an independent judiciary, to ombudsmen, to specialist agencies tasked with monitoring and exposing rights abuses and generally facilitating a human rights culture (Patten 1999). Rights, in this classic 'first-generation' sense, do provide a particular check against those political and social forces who seek to make security pervasive – pursuing it with impatience towards, and disregard for, the limits that rights necessarily place on the unbridled pursuit of public protection. This accounts, at least in part, for the depiction of an opposition between security and rights that has become commonplace within political and legal discussion of these issues (cf. Goold and Lazarus forthcoming). In so far as this routine depiction has a rational kernel, it inheres in the counter-majoritarianism that is the hallmark of rights regimes – in particular, the protections they offer unpopular minorities whose interests the state can easily be tempted to move against in the name of security.[6]

---

[6] It is for this reason, as we intimated in chapter 1, that the idea of a right to security has to be approached with great caution. If, as we find in some of the classic

In the above respects rights protect individuals *against* the state's tendencies to meddle, to enact bias, or to quash cultural difference. But in settings wherein a range of non-state actors – private security firms, forms of communal self-policing, transnational security bureaucracies – also promise to deliver security, rights assume a second, additional, importance. We have argued that these modes of non-state security can, in the absence of adequate regulation, act in ways that disregard the interests of non-customers or evince intolerance towards minorities within local neighbourhoods or other particularistic communities within civil – or uncivil – society. Human rights protections are vital here as a means of trying to harness the practical benefits of pluralized security whilst protecting the basic interests of those who are rendered vulnerable by the untrammelled operation of market or communal policing. Rights in these settings are not bulwarks against the state. They demand, rather, that the state put in place legal and regulatory regimes, and their attendant remedies, that are able to protect individuals from the effects of fugitive commercial power or the enactment of local tyranny. Such legal guarantees of one's basic rights offer, in either case, a significant part of the social benefit that flows from successfully anchoring pluralized security in the institutions of the state.

Rights are necessary, thirdly, as a precondition of, and as a constraint upon, the practice of recognition. They operate in the former instance as guarantees of private freedom of the kind that enables citizens to feel able to participate with confidence in democratic political processes. As Stephen Holmes (1995: 31) nicely puts it: 'Citizens will not throng

post-war international rights charters, security is treated merely as a constituent or reinforcing aspect of the individual's right to liberty against the encroachment of the state, then this is an innocent usage, and indeed serves to emphasize that in one important respect the normative ground covered by security and liberty is identical. However, the more expansive version of the right to security that seeks to impose a positive duty on the state to free the citizen from all forms of violence – a version often mobilized today in public and media discourse, and which has been enshrined, for example, in the South African Constitution (Lazarus forthcoming) – is incompatible with the conception of security, and its relation to rights, that is being advanced here. The right to security in this more expansive sense is dangerous, precisely because, by placing the entitlement and duties associated with the combating of violence on the same normative and deontological level as the basic right to liberty, it neutralizes the counter-majoritarian, populism-trumping, state-constraining properties that give the liberty right and other basic rights their value and force.

voluntarily to the public square if their homes can be ravaged at will by the police.' There exists, in other words, a conceptual symbiosis between, and a historical co-originality of, basic rights and democratic principle. Political autonomy always presupposes private autonomy and vice versa (Habermas 2001a). In the latter regard, rights place parameters around the substantive outcomes that can flow from democratic processes based on a principle of non-exclusion. They prevent these processes arriving at decisions that conflict with the fundamental entitlements of those who are affected by them and thereby stop democratic fora undermining at the level of substance what recognition seeks to accomplish in terms of process. Rights here offer a further counter-majoritarian check – this time against the potentially illiberal effects of a democratized security practice. They shield minorities from politically constituted majorities in ways that embed within the institutional matrix of security governance the idea that security needs to be pursued in a manner that remains consistent with other goods and values that democratic political communities cherish and seek to uphold (Zedner forthcoming). Rights also, finally, provide a more general symbol and reminder of the type of affective community which the modern democratic state at its best aspires to be and which itself speaks to and promotes a security-generative sense of inclusive, confident belonging – a community where, as we noted in the previous chapter, the open-ended egalitarian potential of a generic public political sphere goes hand in hand with the inviolability of a generic private sphere.

Thinking about the value of rights in these ways, within the framework of a solidaristic and egalitarian practice of security, brings to the fore several things. First and foremost, it challenges the idea that rights exist in deep tension with the pursuit of security. In so doing, it calls into dispute the terms of trade that serve, curiously, as common ground between the 'security' and the 'liberty' lobbies – as we noted in chapter 1. Conceived of in the terms described above, rights become not only or mainly a matter of protecting the individual from the power of the overweening state – as liberals so often contend. Nor are they an indulgent, security-threatening burden upon the capacity of the state to protect its citizens – forcing the state, as police officers, politicians and pundits are sometimes wont to put it, to work 'with one arm tied behind its back'. They are, rather, a significant prerequisite to the practice of civilizing security. Rights, in short, are *for* security.

Reasons

Reasons – or, more accurately, the idea of public reason – signal the importance of bringing sustained social contestation to the practice of security. Public reason bears in this respect a close relationship to recognition, which it supplements in significant ways. Recognition, as we have seen, is concerned with searching for and identifying the claims of all constituencies affected by allocative and regulatory decisions in the field of policing and security. It is, as such, geared to addressing the problem of false negatives, to ensuring that the ideas and interests of all citizens are tracked and considered in public dialogue and state decision-making. But recognition, if it operates in isolation, evinces several lacunae. While resolving the problem of false negatives it has no means of addressing satisfactorily that of false positives; in fact, practices of recognition can if they function well bring forth a paralysing surfeit of claims which the principle of recognition offers no way of discriminating between. Recognition lacks, further, any means of resolving a potential and worrisome paradox of public deliberation in the security field; namely, that the more citizens interest themselves in, and talk about, security problems (*qua* security problems) the more threats they will unearth, the more anxieties they will feel, and the more police officers they will demand to tackle or assuage them. Recognition, in short, has a tendency to re-enact the pathologies of consumerism, as well as the problems associated with certain variants of interest-group pluralism or multiculturalism (Pettit 1997: 205). By continuing to treat naked preferences, or group identities and demands, as fixed ingredients and raw materials of political life, recognition risks translating into the field of security a 'politics of identity mired in social resentment' (McBride 2005: 504).

Rights, as we have seen, go some way towards checking the illiberal outcomes that the principle of recognition may licence. But if rights too are treated in isolation, then the solution they offer errs too much in the opposite direction. For rights offer only a negative, defensive reaction to the problem of promiscuous demand, leaving individual preferences and social identities unquestioned and in place. The idea of public reason also in part has this negative quality, weeding out outcomes that cannot satisfy common-interest considerations. But it seeks, in addition, to give more constructive, purposive shape to public deliberation about policing and security. The exchange of reasons sets out to give practical effect to the fact that public conversation has as its resilient 'watchword' that venerable maxim of natural justice – 'always listen to the other side' (Skinner 1996: 15). But this brings with it a refusal to accept that giving a proper hearing to all affected parties within processes for allocating and regulating policing capacities means that 'we consider every possible demand for recognition as morally legitimate or acceptable' (Honneth 2003: 71). The practice of civilizing security cannot and should not mean that. The principle of public reason thus adds to the institutional matrix for governing security the expectation that the demands raised in fora of public deliberation are to be called into question, rigorously scrutinized, and defended and revised, in a process aimed at identifying which security claims can reasonably be said to be oriented to considerations of the common interest, rather than being motivated by unbridled emotion, or the pursuit of self or parochial interests. Public reason aims, in short, to address the problem of false positives that is at least in part generated by efforts to guard against false negatives. It seeks to expose and disallow those demands for order or public resources which are inconsistent with, or a danger to, the idea of security as a public good, and thereby respond to lay demands and allocate resources in ways that sustain the forms of democratic common life that supply their participants with a sense of shared identity and secure belonging.

There exist several different strands of writing on the idea of public reason that one may mobilize and draw upon in this context, not all of which are equally conducive to the above-mentioned purposes. One of these – taking its cue from Rawls (1999) – tends to make the stipulations of public reason too exacting, such that the test of reason becomes overly determining of substantive outcomes – whether by keeping certain hotly contentious items from the agenda of public debate in the name of social cohesion or good governance, or by establishing decision-making protocols that narrowly circumscribe what a rational outcome can look like. The danger here is that the demands of public reason become so heavy that they strip citizens of the motivation to engage in deliberative processes of resource distribution and problem-solving in the first place. The converse danger – one we associate with proponents of agonistic variants of radical democracy (Laclau and Mouffe 1985; Mouffe 2000) – is that the demands of reason are rendered too permissive. In an effort to avoid being overly prescriptive of the outcomes of democratic processes, or of the kinds of claims and arguments that can legitimately be put within them, the idea of reason is limited, on this view, to whatever the participants decide they want it to be: the aim is to initiate processes of inclusive, presumptively conflictual, public dialogue and let their participants make of, and do with, them what they will. The risk here, in our view, is that the idea of public reason stops doing any real work at all, offering neither 'rules of the game' whose at least partial insulation from the game itself may find a principled basis of justification, nor sufficiently robust mechanisms for ensuring the proper scrutiny of irrational, illiberal, sectarian or other false positives. One is left, in effect, with little that has not already been supplied by the principle of recognition.

We want in the present context – taking our lead from the constructivist universalism of Jürgen Habermas (e.g. 1996) – to develop and deploy a third approach to the value of public, or communicative, reason. This holds that something akin to Pettit's (2001a: 156) notion of 'common avowable interests' can serve as a regulative ideal for practices of public conversation and contestation around questions of security, but that the substantive content of such interests, and the reasons that are held to be admissible and inadmissible within institutional processes guided by the search for them, and even the elementary ground rules for allocating reason-generative voice within these institutional processes (Tully 2002), will be formed and reformed by and within the process of reflexive discussion and justification. In the context of the institutional matrix for the democratic governance of security whose elements we are elucidating here, this conception of public reason has both a negative and a positive component.

In the former respect, its purpose is to unfix, and open up to negotiation, the claims and identities that are brought into forms of public dialogue about security. The aim is to fashion deliberative institutions which refuse to treat unreasoned expressions of preference, or emotionally laced demands for order, or the claim of this or that group for particular levels of policing provision or social protection, as immutable facts of political life – demands that have uncritically to be responded to in the form in which they present themselves. This is true, in the first place, of the claims of economically and socially disadvantaged groups which, say, policing or security authorities may be required to make special and methodologically imaginative efforts to elicit and take account of. Having been thus recognized, the claims of these groups must themselves be subject to democratic scrutiny and any pleas for special or additional minority protection justified on common-interest grounds. Such scrutiny must also be extended to the security preferences of those who 'hold mainstream or prevailing conceptions of the good' (Maynor 2003: 87) – groups whose capacity to organize for more than their 'fair' share of the public cake, or access market resources, often mean that their demands are met in ways that elude the democratic gaze – a fact that some radical commentators tend to gloss over (Johnston and Shearing 2003). And one must seek ways of redirecting towards forms of reflexive public deliberation the emotionally saturated claims that so often structure the contemporary politics of security and the fundamentalist yearning for absolute protection that anxious, insecure citizens can easily be moved, or made, to feel.

In the latter, more constructive, respect, the principle of public reason demands not that these various constituencies refrain from initially pressing their claims as passionately as they can in the manner they deem appropriate, but that affected parties are encouraged to apprehend their particular and particularistic security identities and concerns in relation to those of others, and in terms of the insecurity burdens which they may place upon them. This requires, in turn, that in conversations about how to frame security problems, and deploy resources to address them, these groups listen to and seek to understand the claims of other affected parties, and of public security professionals and bureaucracies. By so doing, participants are likely to experience an unforced but insistent democratic pressure to, if necessary, revise and reformulate their demands using criteria that are considered 'cooperatively admissible' within the settings of public deliberation within which they are being considered and weighed (Pettit 2001a: 156) – fora of decision-making that foreground not the collective will, or popular consent, but the practice of discursive reason (Pettit 2004).

There is, of course, no guarantee that such processes will result in negotiated agreement, and that public authorities established to allocate and regulate security resources will be able to dispense entirely with methods of bargaining, or compromise, or aggregative decision-making. But such practices of inclusive and reflexive public reasoning and justification at least maximize the prospect of political communities thinking about security, and acting upon security problems, in ways that foster greater acknowledgement of the mutual vulnerabilities and social connectedness that exist among their members, and generate outcomes that broadly sustain the forms of democratic common life, and its attendant sense of publicness, that are indispensable to the secure belonging of all citizens in ethnically and socially pluralistic societies. The task, as such, is not to pretend that all claims can be acceded, that all can or will be winners. It is, rather, to engage citizens in public reasoning about security in ways that enable them to see that the political freedom of each and all is more likely to be guaranteed through their participation with others in forms of common deliberation (the specific outcomes of which they may not always concur with) than by pursuing their own safety as individual 'sovereign consumers' in the marketplace, or clubbing together within particularistic communities, or falling for the seductive security promises of strong, superficially responsive rulers. And in facing that challenge, we should be aware that the security dividend of a public reason of which citizens may be persuadable is only in part the generation of a separate 'how to' knowledge product. It is also, as we argued in the previous chapter, a dividend which is intrinsic to the very process of seeking common cause, since a publicly reasoned conception of security is one whose pursuit and provisional resolution already gives us more reason to feel secure in our membership of the public in question.

There is clearly more that can be said about each of these elements of a civilizing security practice and about how one might seek, institutionally, to embed them. But we hope to have done sufficient to demonstrate how the state – conditioned in the ways we have described by the four Rs of resources, recognition, rights and reasons – can democratically govern security in a manner that nurtures and sustains the forms of abstract solidarity and trust between strangers that is the hallmark of security as an axiomatic element of quotidian social and political relations. Any political community, it seems to us, that wishes to civilize security and release its civilizing potential will need to find some way of giving practical effect to these four Rs, even if the institutional means by which this is accomplished will necessarily be shaped by the history, culture and social trajectory of a given society, and therefore differ from one national context to another.

Axiomatic security, security understood as a thick public good, security that is consistent with the republican ideal of non-domination, is 'not maximised in a society in which each person cowers behind the

heaviest, highest walls that they can build or that the state can provide'
(Pettit 1997: 266). In such a society, for reasons we have amply documented in this book, security, or rather insecurity, in fact becomes a
pervasive, self-fulfilling and ultimately liberty- and democracy-eroding
phenomenon. Axiomatic security – the capacity to live together
securely and confidently with risk – flows, rather, from the seemingly
paradoxical situation in which individuals are prepared to acknowledge their mutual vulnerability to the intimates and strangers that they
dwell with and amongst, and willing and able to trust both the co-
citizens upon whom their security depends and the social institutions
that give practical effect to their membership of a democratic political
community.

Viewed in this light, the overriding purpose of regulatory arrangements that aim to give effect to more axiomatic forms of security is not
to be the servant of partisan or parochial interests, or to satisfy without
scrutiny appetites for order that may be motivated by desires for injustice, or xenophobic fears of the alien and unknown, or fantasies of
absolute or sovereign security (Markell 2003). Their purpose, instead,
is to subject those anxieties and desires to the power of reflection. It is
to make plastic the apparently fixed interests and social identities that
sustain them. It is to stimulate acknowledgement of the constitutive
vulnerability of life lived inescapably among others, of the dignity of
our interdependence, and of the virtues, but also the risky, unsettling
unpredictability, of the activity of seeking to address and resolve conflict politically (Warren 1996; Keenan 2003: ch. 4; Markell 2003:
177–89). It is in all these ways to subject demands for order to democratic governance. This mode of regulatory politics must, in so doing,
appeal to and mobilize those motivational feelings of identification
with, and belonging to, a common political community that presently
exist among members of such communities, and seek to deepen and
extend the expressions of solidarity with strangers, and commitments
to the security and political freedom of *all* citizens, that are an immanent part of people's sense of allegiance to an ongoing collective
project. If we take this as our lodestar, we can better orient ourselves
towards fashioning – along the lines sketched in the second half of this
chapter – the forms of minimal, rights-regarding policing practices that
can, materially and symbolically, underpin the confident assurance
individuals draw from being recognized as part of the 'common public
culture' of a democratic polity (Miller 1995).

In arriving at this conclusion, one that has sought to specify and defend the security-enhancing value of democratic political communities, we encounter one further, and far from insignificant, hurdle; one that may lead readers to conclude, once again, that we are struggling vainly to hold back the tide of current social and political development. For, under conditions of globalization, and in the face of the burgeoning transnational security practices that we have described at several points throughout the book, one can no longer confidently assume that the nation state can or should remain as the widest boundary of security identity, or that it is the most plausible conduit for the articulation and promotion of common security, whether within or beyond its borders. It is to these doubts, and the challenge which they appear to present to the case we have made for civilizing security, that we turn in the next, concluding, chapter.

9 | *Security as a global public good*

W E began this book by trying to distance ourselves from some of the more immediate manifestations of the security debate and some of the more exotic articulations of security practice. In particular we sought to stand back from the post-9/11 debate on terror, just as we declined the Herculean – even Sisyphean – challenge of a comprehensive mapping of the real world of security provision in all its ever-increasing diversity and intensity. We provided what we claimed were good prudential reasons for these choices. We did not want our thinking about such a highly charged concept as security to be distorted by our taking as a point of departure perhaps its most ideologically sensitive location, that of contemporary international – indeed post-national – terrorism. Equally, we did not want to become bogged down in a level of detail that would threaten our efforts to provide a sharp overview of what is at stake – politically, culturally and institutionally – in the security debate.

Yet, even if, as we maintain, these arguments are persuasive in their own terms, is there not a danger of their carrying one unfortunate and, for us, highly significant side effect? For, the critic might suggest, perhaps it is just *too* convenient for an argument that seeks to rehabilitate the state's prior role in security that its proponents situate themselves at some remove from the very events and very trends which point most insistently *away* from the state as the symbolic and instrumental centre of security work. In the fraught days since 9/11, our newly terrorized political culture has produced a fresh range of rhetoric, regulation and routines that regularly transcends national borders (see, e.g., Chalmers 2004; Günther 2005). As constitutive elements of the 'war on terror' launched in response to 9/11, we have witnessed, alongside the unilateral assertion of US security interests and the strengthening of state security institutions, an extension of cross-border surveillance activity and information sharing, an enhanced role for opaque networks of police and intelligence chiefs in Europe, and the deployment of soldiers, police officers and contracted security guards in post-war 'peacekeeping' efforts on the streets of Afghanistan and Iraq (den Boer and Monar 2002; Lyon 2003; Sands 2005). What is more, in many other ways that owe little or nothing to the terrorist threat, transnational policing has over a longer time-frame become an expanding, diverse and complex field of activity, and so an increasingly important dimension of any detailed security map. In the face of criminal organizations and networks who operate across many states, and whose *modus operandi* involves illicitly trafficking people, drugs, information, nuclear materials or stolen goods across national borders, long-standing international police institutions such as Interpol have been joined, and arguably superseded in importance, by the internationalization of US policing and by the development of new forms of police networking and cross-border cooperation within the European Union – notably in the shape of Europol and, more recently, Eurojust (Nadelman 1993; Anderson *et al.* 1995; Deflem 2003; N. Walker 2003). The problem of weak or failing states engaged in armed conflict for the control of territory, or harbouring criminal or terrorist groups, has prompted overt and covert police/military interventions by outside states, as well as intermittent UN or EU peacekeeping missions and the harm-alleviating efforts of transnational NGOs (Caygill 2001; Goldsmith 2003; Linden *et al.* forthcoming). They have, in addition, provided new opportunities in the burgeoning industry of global private security for transnational security and military firms to promote and sell protective services either to weak states, or to multinational corporations seeking to do business in those states (Johnston 2000; Muthien and Taylor 2002; Singer 2003; Avant 2005; Leander 2006; Abrahamsen and Williams 2006).

These developments traverse symbolic as well as territorial boundaries. As we noted in chapter 1, they signal that a bundle of once clear distinctions – between external and internal security; policing and soldiering; war and crime; state combatants exercising legitimate force and unarmed civilian non-combatants – is fast breaking down (Kaldor 1999; Bigo 2000a; Andreas and Price 2001). They also indicate that states acting alone, or solely within their own borders, are no longer a sufficient means of producing security *within* those borders, still less some more expansive notion of regional or global security. We inhabit a world of multilevel, multicentred security governance, in which states are joined, criss-crossed and contested by an array of transnational organizations and actors – whether in regional and global governmental bodies, commercial security outfits, or the rapidly expanding range of non-governmental organizations and social movements that compose transnational civil society. It is a world in which policing has, however haltingly and unevenly, been both stretched across the frontiers of states and charged with combating what are often overlapping problems of global organized crime and political violence.

The purpose of this final chapter is to address the critical challenge posed by these developments. It acknowledges that there has indeed been and continues to be a shift towards transnational sites and networks of security provision, but insists that this need not diminish the scope, still less undermine the normative framework, for civilizing security that we have formulated thus far. In stressing the priority of the state as a key site for the provision of security as a 'thick' public good, we might seem to be implying either that security beyond the state must in consequence be a 'thin' and anaemic affair, or, alternatively, that the price of transnational thickening might be the loss of the trademark thickness of the state level. As we shall argue, however, we need not look at thick, or axiomatic, security in such zero-sum terms. Rather, the very considerations which underpin our argument at the state level are such that, with the necessary sociological and institutional imagination, we can contemplate at least some degree of complementary thickening in wider sites of political community and in the global arena.

We must stress, however, that unlike the argument at the nation-state level, the transnational argument remains predominantly aspirational rather than grounded in concrete – if only selectively realized – cultural and ordering configurations. As matters stand, the development in transnational policing and security practice is matched neither by a palpable shift in attitudes towards the proper location of security communities nor by systems of regulation that adequately track these developments. The state, as the traditional community of democratic attachment, remains the principal – if by no means any longer the sole – institutional locus of efforts to subject security practices to forms of democratic steering, public scrutiny and human rights protection. This asymmetrical pattern of development can, in turn, encourage opaque, self-corroborating and fugitive sites of public and private power that, in failing to nurture and provide institutional expression for broader public identification with the relevant security projects, simultaneously possess deficits of legitimacy and effectiveness. In asking the question about the thickening of security as a transnational public good, therefore, we must be ever mindful that the very symbiosis of cultural and ordering activity which is the key to the state's special role underscores the difficulty of building a similar dynamic beyond the state. Just as the presence of an affective attachment and a regulatory infrastructure can be mutually reinforcing, so their absence or relative weakness can be mutually debilitating.

Our argument proceeds as follows. Taking as our point of departure recent work on the topic of 'global public goods' conducted under the auspices of the United Nations Development Programme (Kaul *et al.* 1999c; 2003c), we begin by identifying the issues that arise in seeking to reconceptualize and deliver policing and security – with their constitutive links to sovereign statehood – as global public goods. We then briefly review five competing models of transnational security in this light, examining the capacity of each to address and offer an adequate resolution of the problems we identify. Having thus specified the merits and deficiencies of each model, we conclude by sketching the outline of our own thicker account of security as a global public good – one that is sociologically tenable as well as normatively robust.

In search of the transnational public interest

In a recent statement of cosmopolitan intent, David Held has argued that:

The provision of public goods can no longer be equated with state-provided goods alone. Diverse state and non-state actors shape and contribute to their provision – and they need to if some of the most profound challenges of globalization are to be met. Moreover, some core public goods have to be provided regionally and globally if they are to be provided at all. (Held 2004: 16)

How – in the field of policing and security – can we best make sense of this project? How might policing be delivered and regulated in these terms? Can we identify – at the level of normative principle and institutional articulation – a common public interest in the diverse, multisite, multi-actor field of transnational policing? It is a formidable enough task, as we have seen in the previous chapter, to seek to mobilize the four Rs of civilizing security practice – resources, recognition, rights and reasons – within the more familiar terrain of state policing, and to do so in a sufficiently generous and integrated fashion as to avoid the various and often linked pathologies of paternalism, consumerism, authoritarianism and fragmentation. But these difficulties are compounded in a transnational context. Paternalism is encouraged by the introduction of another layer of private and public authority – a further tier of professional bureaucracy even more remote from the concerns of national *demoi* and even more self-confident in the primacy of its security knowledge and imperatives (see, e.g., Bigo 2000b; Deflem 2003). Consumerist mindsets and methods are stimulated by a focus on crimes of an economic or otherwise esoteric nature (e.g. art fraud, currency counterfeiting) that are of primary interest to specialist corners of the security market. Authoritarian tendencies may encounter an environment made more receptive by the emphasis upon another set of crimes of which most citizens have only mediated knowledge and which, they are consistently informed through the relevant political and professional intermediaries, represent threats that are both existential and increasingly urgent (e.g. terrorism, nuclear theft). And fragmentation is encouraged by the *ad hocracy* that attends a set of developments which are diversely demand-driven and which lack a prior sense of political community with which they can connect and an established governance framework to which they are required to adhere (Sheptycki 2002, forthcoming; Johnston 2006). How might we steer a prudent course through these dangers?

A useful starting point here, and one that connects closely with the broader analytical theme of the book, is the collaborative project conducted under the umbrella of the United Nations Development Programme (UNDP) on 'global public goods' (Kaul *et al.* 1999c; 2003c).[1] This project begins with a standard economic definition of public goods as those whose consumption is 'non-excludable' and 'non-rival'. We have criticized the deficiencies of such a thin definition at length in chapter 6, and we will address the drawbacks of this limited perspective for our understanding of transnational security in due course. However, the very thinness of the initial definition is also helpful in highlighting the formidable obstacles that a purely state-centred logic and architecture places before the realization of global transnational goods. Because of the externality and free-riding problems associated

---

[1] This is also an important point of reference for Held (2004: ch. 6).

with the (market) provision of economically defined public goods, they typically require some mechanism of compulsory collective action if they are to be adequately provided or even provided at all, with the state generally considered as the most appropriate such mechanism. While global public goods share all the elements of domestic public goods, according to Kaul *et al.* (1999a) they possess the added criteria that their benefits – or, in the case of 'public bads', costs – 'extend across countries and regions, across rich and poor population groups, and even across generations' (Kaul *et al.* 2003a: 3). A pollution-free environment and financial stability are cited as examples here, as, importantly, are peace and security.[2]

Let us try to tease out some of the more detailed implications of this analysis. The gradual shift in the level of optimal provision of public goods to the global level raises opportunities and dangers which are different not only in s*cale* but also in *kind* from those which pertain where the major and most appropriate site of provision of public goods is the state level. The differences in scale are self-evident. The prize of the successful institutionalization of a mechanism of compulsory collective provision becomes the inclusive and cost-efficient supply of a good at a broader transnational or global level, while the penalty of failure is exclusion, cost-inefficiency and perhaps, in a context where the scope for negative externalities is greatly increased, an unravelling of domestic solutions to problems of collective action, such that some (and perhaps all) states become net losers in the endeavour to secure the benefits of the relevant goods to their respective populations.

In order fully to appreciate these possibilities, however, we must turn to the differences in kind in the structure of public goods provision as we move from the national to the global. In the classic economic analysis, the alternative and perhaps competing unit of supply of the good in question is either, on the one hand, the market agent supplying the private individual or group of private individuals, or, on the other, the 'club'. In the latter case, a self-defining and so exclusionary group come

---

[2] In the course of their analysis Kaul *et al.* make a valuable distinction between 'final' global public goods, which are outcomes (such as a pollution-free environment) rather than goods in the standard sense, and what they term 'intermediate' global public goods (such as international regimes) which contribute to the production of these outcomes (Kaul *et al.* 1999b: 13). We might, in this vein, describe security as a final global public good and transnational policing as an intermediate good that can, under the right conditions, contribute to its production.

together to provide for their own consumption at least some of the benefits associated with non-rivalness; namely, cost-efficient provision of a good whose common supply is no detriment to individual enjoyment. As we move to a context of high transnational interdependence, however, not only do the number of market agents or clubs who are candidate suppliers of the same or overlapping goods exponentially increase, but *other states* also become relevant as alternative and perhaps competing suppliers of the same or overlapping goods.

The introduction of other states into the equation changes the picture dramatically, for a number of reasons. First, these other states are typically authoritatively constituted in such a way that their role in the solution or creation of collective action problems is, broadly speaking, less easily controlled or influenced by the first state than if they were private or club actors.

Secondly, and again broadly speaking, this matters so much precisely because other states have a greater capacity for action, and so a greater propensity not only to produce security-based public goods, but also to prejudice the first state's capacity to do likewise, than do other individual or club actors. These prejudicial effects may register within the classic matrix of external security – through aggressive acts of war or their threat by other states directed against the first state, or through a shift in the strategies of self-defence of these other states (e.g. the development of new weapons systems or the forming of new alliances) so as to leave the first state more exposed in terms of *its* actual and perceived capacity for self-defence (Waltz 1993). Increasingly, however, the power of other states to prejudice the internal security of the first state operates through a logic that is more recognizably one of 'internal security'; that is to say, through those actual or perceived negative externalities affecting the first state that are consequential upon both the effective and ineffective development and pursuit of whichever domestic policy agendas of these other states are directed towards their own internal security. For example, these externalities might arise or might at least be perceived to arise for the first state through the displacement effect of the *successful* repression by other states of certain criminal possibilities in areas such as drugs or organized crime, or of their restrictive approach to asylum applications or other supposedly 'security-destabilizing' migratory movements. Conversely, externalities for the first state might arise through the *failure* of other states to 'contain' their own security problems, whether through an ineffective regime of monitoring the international movement of indigenous criminals or inadequate control of cross-border transactions in illicit goods and services, or, more broadly, through social and political policies which lead to the flight or export of persons and groups capable of posing a threat to the internal security of the first state.

Yet, thirdly, the introduction of other states into the internal security equation invites commonalities as well as differences. Also being states, these other states share with the first state the same general *raison d'état*, the same broad set of priorities and incentives – and importantly, underlying this, the same deep cultural orientation or sense of the political imaginary – to be the dominant provider of public goods for their respective populations. Their relationship with the first state, in other words, including those aspects of the relationship which are potentially antagonistic or competitive, is structured not by their efforts to provide the benefits associated with public goods from *different motivations* and by *different means*, as with private agents or clubs, but by their aspirations in an interdependent world to bring the same motives to bear, and to use the same means, for the primary benefit of *different populations*.

We will return to some of these more detailed points in due course, and in particular will have more to say about the cultural dimension of the state's production of public goods. For now, it is important simply to register the conclusion of Kaul and her collaborators that in the present institutional configuration of global politics the dangers in the shift from a national to a global context of optimal provision of public goods seem to overshadow the opportunities. They convincingly claim that there is in the world today a 'serious under-provision of global public goods' (Kaul *et al.* 1999a: xxi), a condition they attribute in very general terms to 'the absence of a global sovereign' able to assume a central coordinating role (Kaul *et al.* 1999b: 15) and which on closer enquiry they locate in the combined effect of three crucial gaps. First, there is a jurisdiction gap between global problems that span national frontiers and demand transnational attention and discrete national units and regulatory structures of policy-making. We find, in other words, a mismatch between national policy-makers concerned about losing sovereignty to the market and civil society and the imperatives of an international policy environment, creating chronic difficulties with regard to who is responsible for global issues, particularly externalities. Second, there is a participation gap between those state actors involved in fora of national policy-making and international cooperation and non-state actors in the market and civil society who are likely to be affected by or to represent those affected by relevant decisions but who have little or no hand in their authorship or in holding their authors to account. There has developed, in short, a serious lack of symmetry and congruence between transnational 'decision-makers' and 'decision-takers' (Held 2004: 13). There exists, thirdly, an incentive gap between the substance of stated national commitments and international agreements and the realities of implementation on-the-ground. The absence of effective supranational authority, coupled with weak or imbalanced incentive structures, means that states and non-state actors will seek to free-ride, or lack the necessary motivation to 'do their bit' in tackling global problems (Kaul *et al.* 1999a: xxvi–xxvii).

If we examine these gaps in the round, we can plainly see the outline of a dynamic of mutual impoverishment of the ordering and the cultural dimensions – the instrumental and the affective – in the transnational and global domains, and we can observe how this produces the linked problems of legitimacy and effectiveness to which we earlier alluded. The combination of a jurisdiction gap with regard to the development of an adequately empowered and regulated institutional apparatus, the participation gap with regard to an adequately and inclusively deliberated-upon policy agenda, and a gap in reliable incentives to comply with or cooperate in whatever policies and with and through whatever cooperative structures and implementation agencies do exist, creates a series of linked problems. Foremost among them are the lack of proper authorization of and support for policing capacity and the failed or selective and unaccountable mobilization of that capacity – problems that patently bear upon both the public acceptability of transnational policing and the quality of its output. Yet we cannot assume that the pathological potential of these 'gap effects' will have a positive effect in encouraging the closing of the gaps in question. Rather, the danger is that the problems become exacerbated just because, as seems likely, attempts to produce global public goods in the presence of these gaps may fail to provide the experience of successful common commitment and to fertilize the grounds of increased trust and confidence apt to overcome the motivation problem responsible for the gaps in the first place.

A simple – too simple – response to the difficulties that Kaul and her collaborators pinpoint is that they are a function of the very instrumental conception of public goods they work with. As we saw in chapter 6, the instrumental conception always has a problem in identifying the proper boundaries of political community, in locating the optimal level at which the undoubted collective action problems which attend the provision of any non-excludable or difficult-to-exclude goods should be addressed. To explain why people in general should be motivated to put things in common in terms of their individual and sometimes convergent security interests does not explain why *any particular combination of people* should be sufficiently more motivated than any other overlapping particular combination of people so as to make *their* common motivation count decisively. The missing *explanans*, moreover, means that the instrumental conception encounters special problems in accounting for transnational or global cooperation. Faced with the massive datum of state formation, the instrumental conception, notwithstanding its lack of adequate theorization, can take for granted or is bound to acknowledge that, for whatever reason and under whatever constraints, people have already laid their collective action bets with this or that state, which in cumulative consequence becomes the increasingly credible and dominant source of public security solutions. It then becomes all the more puzzling how and why they might make and respect additional commitments to collective security provision at wider levels of political community other than those commitments which are parasitic on and articulated through the states themselves. On this analysis, the fact that the state and its security interests remain so central to the solution of transnational and global security begins to look like part of the problem – a straitjacket on the prospects of better global security management. But since it is precisely the dead weight of analytical dependence on the building-blocks of the state as the default site for addressing collective action problems that suggests the jurisdiction, participation and incentive-based impediments to moving to wider conceptions of security as a public good in the first place, the instrumental argument lies open to the accusation that it has boxed itself into this particular Westphalian corner through the circularity of its reasoning. The basic assumption underscoring the economistic conception of public goods employed by Kaul and her associates, in short, may seem persuasively to suggest just the state-centred and state-limited conclusion they seek to move beyond.

Why this would be too simple a critique, however, is because it depends upon our interpreting as conceptual blindness or prejudice, and dismissing as mere tautology, what may instead and more challengingly be viewed as considered sociologically grounded judgement. If the answer to an unduly 'thin' conception of public goods that is unable to account for any of its particular sites of articulations – in this case transnational or global sites – is to replace it with a thicker sense, we still need to demonstrate why and how the ingredients of that thicker mix might become available at any particular transnational or global site. How, in other words, does a more socially grounded sense of security as a public good akin to that which we have sought to locate at the state level begin to 'catch on' in the transnational context? How, if at all, do we conceive of security provision at the transnational level, like the statist template, as a platform for the achievement of other goods of (transnational) political community? How, if at all, do we conceive of security as an education in transnational society, just as it has this tutorial role in national society? And how, if at all, do security concerns and their treatment help constitute transnational publics alongside similarly constituted national publics? For if we cannot imagine that, and how at least some of these things in at least some measure are happening or might happen at the transnational or global level, then we cannot escape the limits of the instrumental conception at the transnational and global level.

The very posing of these questions alerts us to just how difficult it is to answer them with any degree of affirmation. In particular, we cannot simply assume that the problem is one of time-lag, that in due course transnational public sentiment and the structures which feed off and refuel that common feeling will emerge alongside the brave new practice of international security. There is a wealth of literature that indicates that despite the deepening of global interdependence, the growth of institutions of global governance, and an arguably greater public consciousness of both of these developments, sentiments of trust, loyalty and abstract solidarity remain somewhat 'stuck' at national or subnational levels – a stubborn tendency that continues to condition the development of even a relatively mature post-national political order such as the EU (see, e.g., Grimm 1995; Weiler 1999; Haltern 2003). There appears not to exist, in other words, the common store of memories, myths, symbols and language, or any equivalent basis of affinity, around which forms of identification and belonging can coalesce and take shape at a regional or global level (Held and McGrew 2002: 30). It may appear, then, that the cultural bar for imagining and giving institutional expression to the public interest in this cultural sense remains set at the level of the nation state.[3] Indeed, it is precisely the imbalance between strong national cultures and weak post-national solidarity that in part explains why the development of such new security institutions as have emerged has often been driven by professional and bureaucratic interests (Deflem 2003; N. Walker 2003), and why such interests have been able to pursue technocratic security agendas in ways that are remote from popular sentiment and demands, and insulated from any effective form of democratic scrutiny. What is more, to the extent that the development of transnational security does nevertheless register in a deeper cultural sense, it may do so in ways that reinforce rather than supplement nationalist sentiments. Under the combined influence of professional and bureaucratic interests and of the performative effects of a discourse of existential threat, the definition of public interest within the transnational security configuration tends to be presented in terms of narrowly drawn security registers. A strong, exclusionary and threatened sense of we-feeling that trades in xenophobic stereotypes of the criminal tends to develop in consequence, as a key form of corroboration of a police-centred and militaristic politics of security.

But we should of course be careful not to replace conceptual fiat with sociological essentialism. There may be something embedded, but there is certainly nothing inevitable about the present constellation of identities and institutional architecture – nothing that says that they are the only possible medium and outcome of a transnational security politics. It is our task in the remainder of the chapter to explore how other possibilities might be imagined and pursued.

---

[3] Consider, as an instance of this, the following conundrum. Which constituencies – beyond the immediate victims and their families or representatives – are likely to be outraged or moved to action by an abuse or atrocity involving, say, Europol officers or members of a UN peacekeeping mission? Possible answers appear to include: (i) hardly anyone at all; (ii) co-nationals of the victims; (iii) members of transnational human rights organizations; (iv) co-nationals of the officers concerned; (v) European or globally conscious citizens ashamed that 'our' police have acted in such a way. Our point here is that the answer is currently unlikely to be (v). This does, however, cut two ways. The lack of affective attachment to transnational police organizations makes it less likely that public audiences will seek to deny that 'our' police could ever do such a thing, thereby laying the potential ground for a less prejudiced politics of security (N. Walker 2002b).

Models of transnational security

In this section, we begin to explore the wider frontiers of the transnational security imaginary by bringing this initial problematization of what a transnational public interest might entail into 'conversation' with various models of transnational security. These different models – namely, the state-centric approach, unilateralism, security regimes or communities, global civil society and cosmopolitanism – are drawn from the current literature on international relations and globalization and from the practical circumstances of transnational politics. They have explanatory and normative dimensions – seeking to account both for how the world of transnational relations is presently configured and for what it ought and is likely to become. We can identify the key assumptions underlying these explanatory and normative differences and so usefully situate the various models in relation to one another – and also to our preferred alternative – by reference to the thinness or thickness of their conception of policing and security as public goods at both domestic and transnational levels. This give rises to the range of permutations depicted in figure 1. Security can (1) be produced as a thin public good at both the state and at the transnational level (as proposed by the UNDP authors, and, as we shall see, by many cosmopolitans). It can (2) be thick at the state level and thin at transnational level (as in various state-centric models and under unilateralism), or else (3) thick at the transnational and thin at the domestic levels (a possibility implicit in some cosmopolitan writing). Or, finally, security can (4) be understood in thick, social and cultural, terms at both the state and transnational levels (a possibility implicit in some security regimes and global civil society models, and more fully developed in our own approach). The models overlap and are not necessarily mutually incompatible, yet

	State	*Transnational*
1	Thin	Thin
2	Thick	Thin
3	Thin	Thick
4	Thick	Thick

Figure 1. Dimensions of trans/national security

each continues to offer a distinctive range of perspectives on the current practice, possibilities and prospects of political arrangements beyond the state, and so of the current practice, problems and prospects of transnational security. Let us consider each in turn.

The state-centric approach

This describes a wide umbrella of positions within the international relations literature, and a still dominant set of attitudes within international relations practice, that have in common an enduring attachment to the state as the sole or main actor in global politics. Such an orientation covers all the main variants of the realist and liberal internationalist schools, and the various hybrids that incorporate elements of both.[4] Traditionally, the distinguishing feature of the realist approach has been its emphasis on the self-interest of state actors, the prevalence of power politics and the consequent 'anarchy' of the international system (Bull 1977) – similar to the Hobbesian state of nature but with no credible Leviathan to impose international order.[5] Accordingly, realists see international cooperation as hard to achieve, difficult to maintain and always ultimately dependent upon the balance of state powers and interests. In this picture international institutions and regimes can do little to mitigate the anarchic impulses of the international order. Whereas realism is commonly regarded as the dominant theory – and even more dominant practice – in the history of international relations, liberalism by contrast has been described as the 'tradition of optimism' (Clark 1989: 49–66). Unlike realists, liberal internationalists have

---

[4] See, in particular, the so-called 'neo-neo debate' in which neo-realist and neo-liberal institutionalists over the course of the 1980s and 1990s gradually converged on a common agenda of debate and priorities, and even began to share some founding premises (see Baldwin 1993).

[5] The major difference within this school is between the classic realism typified in the writings of Hans Morgenthau (e.g. 1948) and the structural realism of Kenneth Waltz (e.g. 1959, 1993) and his followers. Whereas the former stresses the self-interested character of the states themselves, the latter is more interested in the instability of an international order defined by the absence of an overarching authority and asymmetry of power. However, whether the Hobbesian problem of international relations is due mainly to the intrinsic 'nature' of states or to their coordination problems, the same basically pessimistic conclusions are drawn about the possibility of any framework of international cooperation in which these initial state preferences are qualitatively transformed and deepened by the very process of such cooperation.

tended to believe in the possibility of international peace and order being stably achieved through some harmony or concurrence of interests, or even through the sharing or development of certain ideals concerning the proper conduct of international relations and its proper respect for individual and collective values. For the liberal, the tendency is not to see the interests of states as being purely homogeneous and selfish, but as reflecting more fluid domestic coalitions of interest and preferences and in turn as being more responsive to the fluid coalitions of interests and preferences of other states. Self-interest, then, is always mitigated by an enlightened view about the value of cooperation, and perhaps about other more substantive values which different domestic coalitions or segments of domestic coalitions find in common, and peace and order may be stabilized or nurtured through a transnational institutional framework in which success is defined not in terms of the absolute interests of states – even the most powerful states – but in terms of the prospect of 'positive-sum' gains for all.

For all of their sometimes stark differences of orientation as regards the motivations of actors and the viability of transnational institutions, realists and liberals, as already noted, continue to agree that the dominant actors – in the first and last analyses – remain the states. States are the main source of capacity, the main reference point of legitimacy – thus consigning international institutions to a kind of delegated legitimacy at best – and the main source of both the definition of purposes of security cooperation and the wherewithal to guarantee its effectiveness. But whatever their merits under the traditional Westphalian model of the international system, in conditions of exponentially increased transnational exchange there is an inherent instability in both these solutions. Such is the range and volume of interdependence and transnational externalities involved in global security decision-making, and such is the range of decision-making required to address this, that the adequacy of each approach is acutely challenged. The realists have severe problems in locating a stable balance of power to cope with the increasing scope for an anarchy of colliding interests emanating not only from state but also from non-state entities, while the liberal internationalists find it difficult to locate an institutional framework with sufficiently stable state support, and, in the face of disagreement over ends and the limits of delegated power, with sufficient decision-making economy and implementation capacity to cope with the multifarious problems of interdependence.

This state-centred logic might, for example, help us make sense of the chequered history of Interpol – the most venerable of the extant international policing institutions. Born in 1923 and revived in 1946, Interpol's enduring record is as an organization of uncertain constitutional status in international law, and, being perennially vulnerable to the indifference and neglect or self-interested exploitation of the states whose expedient resource it is (realism) or who are its contracting principals (liberalism), as an entity that reflects the influence as well as the restrictions and instability in both positions (see, e.g., M. Anderson 1989). The actual or predicted limitations of each position – realist and liberal – can of course reinforce the claim of the other, and certainly the political history of Interpol has remained resolutely state-centred. But the common limitations of realism and liberalism can also lead in the direction of a number of other, less state-centred approaches to be discussed below.

The new unilateralism

Before we turn to these other approaches, however, we should consider one other possibility – one that is also state-centred, but in the singular rather than the plural. What we are referring to is the new unilateralism registered or advocated by those who see in the demise of Cold War bi-polarity and the rise of the United States as by far the world's most powerful military actor, the empirical preconditions – and, perhaps, the normative hope – of a new kind of empire. Again, there are a number of variants on a position which sees the United States as having the capacity and the legitimacy to be the 'world's policeman' (perhaps *the* most telling active metaphor for the gradual merging of internal and external security concerns). At one end of the continuum there is an ultra-realist perspective, which holds the United States entitled to assert and defend its interests wherever they fall, and treats the fate of all other interests as dependent upon non-interference with, or even support for, American priorities (The White House 2002). At the other end of the spectrum is the 'empire-lite' brand (Ignatieff 2003), wherein the United States provides a vehicle for spreading certain 'civilized' values around the globe. In this second kind of approach, the United States might indeed be projected and viewed as a kind of surrogate for failed or faltering liberal international institutions from the UN downwards, perhaps simply holding the fort until the structures damaged by Iraq and its aftermath are repaired or replaced.[6]

What is true of all variants of the new unilateralism, however, is the aggressively proactive approach of the USA in pursuit of its conception of its interest or of the common good. Sometimes the suggestion is made in the context of the new unilateralism or indeed the post-9/11 approach to terror more generally (e.g. Ignatieff, 2003, 2004) that while aggressive assertiveness may indeed be the price of a militaristic approach, a policing-centred approach tends by its nature to be less monocular and more cooperative. But this must be treated with great caution. To begin with, as already noted, there is an increased blurring of internal and external security mentalities, practices and personnel. Secondly, this is entirely consistent with a logic of empire – or at least of an asymmetrically centred world order – in which external policy tends to be treated simply as the pursuit of the internal policy *of* the centre in another arena, and, reciprocally, internal policy *at* the centre is pursued with a view to securing domestic interests against external challenge and threat (Andreas and Price 2001). As regards the foreign arm of domestic security policy, whether it be the overseas activities of the FBI, the DEA (Drugs Enforcement Administration) or the myriad other forms of agency and liaison through which the USA establishes a police presence abroad – and by no means only in its Latin American and Caribbean 'neighbourhood' – there is much evidence of the direct pursuit through widely dispersed security institutions and networks of domestic US policy agendas in areas such as drugs control, organized crime and illegal immigration (N. Walker 2003). And, likewise, as regards the domestic arm of foreign policy, the consolidation of previously discrete specialist security capabilities and concerns (Immigration and Naturalization, the Coast Guard, Customs, Federal Emergency Management, etc.,) after 9/11 in the Department of Homeland Security, alongside the development of a more integrated and robust approach to the legislation of US security interests in compact with the EU and other security areas

---

[6] The post-9/11 (and post-Hardt and Negri 2000) literature on American empire is voluminous indeed. It ranges not only from the realist to the idealist, but also – and often cross-cutting the realist–idealist division – from the celebratory to the denunciatory, and differs greatly on the degree of central control and unity of purpose which the conduct of empire is claimed to entail. See, for example, Ikenberry (2002), Barber (2003), Mann (2003), Todd (2003), Johnson (2004) and Ferguson (2004).

(Bunyan 2004) on matters such as data on airline passengers, mutual extradition, exchange of evidence and anti-terrorist cooperation, both reflects and facilitates a much more concerted awareness of, and prosecution of, external interests in internal policy domains.

In this new hybridized world of security there are significant problems with both realist and liberal variants of unilateralism, and indeed with the (more common) perspectives which involve some kind of combination of the two. First, in terms of capacity, this position tends to take a myopic approach towards the nature of power. 'Hard' military power and, to a lesser extent, other types of internal security capacity tend to be seen as the key to *all* power, and there is little or no recognition of other 'soft' forms of power – economic, regulatory and cultural – which continue to be dispersed across other sites, and which may indeed be reinforced at these other sites by American security activism and the opposition which this generates (Nye 2002). Secondly, even if military power had not – once again – proved itself to be non-fungible in Iraq, the idea of a single state imposing solutions to the problem of global goods is profoundly lacking in legitimacy. This is most nakedly the case from an ultra-realist position, where the 'specific order' of the United States is treated as pre-emptive of, or at best co-terminous with, the 'general order' associated with a global conception of the public interest (Marenin 1982). Yet it is also true of a more value-based approach – perhaps even more dangerously so to the extent that this lends messianic support to a greater interventionism. At worst this is merely the export of one set of understandings of how to resolve the problem of global peace and security without any sensitivity to other strategies, models and background cultural propensities. At best it is a kind of *ersatz* liberal internationalism, with the United States, like the crudest type of hypothetical social contractualist, assuming what the diversity of states and peoples would decide was in the general interest if only they could overcome their collective action problems – a stance that allows little or no scope for genuine dialogue in order to test and validate, still less generate, that sense of a global public interest (Habermas 2006; N. Walker forthcoming a).

Security regimes or communities

The distinctiveness of the regime approach lies in its identification of the ways in which states either with certain common *interests* or

common *values* – again depending upon whether the underlying theoretical orientation is realist or liberal – come together in certain policy
areas – such as security, environment, economy or communication – or
in certain regional groupings – such as the EU or NAFTA – to provide
a framework of common rules of action and decision-making procedures. There is an inherently optimistic flavour to regime theory to the
extent that it seeks to move beyond the vast problems of legitimacy and
effectiveness when the possibility of developing transnational politics
from and beyond national building-blocks is considered in the abstract,
and instead concentrates on more concrete and more discriminating
possibilities and achievements of collaboration and common cause-
making (Buzan 1991: chs. 4–5; Little 1997; Adler and Barnett 1998).

However, the strength of the regime approach is also its limitation.
Even if it could be assumed that there is some kind of equality of representation and influence, and some level of general consideration of
the common good as opposed to mere strategic collaboration, *within*
particular regimes the regime approach is always left with a profound
problem of the 'outside'. We return below to these positive assumptions about regimes, which are surely more valid in more broadly inte-
grationist and more deeply historically embedded regional regimes (in
particular the EU) than in many global policy-specific regimes, and
more plausible in areas where resources are more evenly distributed
than where there is a significant underlying asymmetry (as with military capacity inside NATO). On the debit side, regimes can act and
understand themselves as universal nations or decentred empires
exporting a particular conception of the good (liberal) or certain 'externalities' as the cost of the internal preservation of the good (realist) to
those who have no voice and little capacity to influence that conception of the good. For example, in its 'conditionality' approach to east-
ward Enlargement and in its 'neighbourhood' policy generally in the
context of its Justice and Home Affairs policy engine, the EU is vulnerable to the charge that in making secure borders, the suppression of
certain kinds of criminality, and the exclusion or return of certain types
of undesirable ethnic groups its first priority, it tends to export insecurity as the price of protecting its own security (Anderson and Apap
2002; Guild and Bigo 2002; Pastore 2002; Lindahl 2005, Melossi
2005). More generally, as with the famous 'democratic peace' thesis
(Doyle 1995; Brown *et al.* 1996), by which the 'separate peace' established by democratic states is celebrated and preserved, the regime

approach can reinforce a process of global ghettoization and a myopic or unreflectively superior approach to the needs of others.

Moreover, just as there are limitations to the effectiveness of modern empires, there are limitations to the effectiveness and legitimacy of regimes even on their own security terms, something that is exacerbated by two additional features of the context within which regimes have emerged. First, regimes may have significant coordination problems or clashes of interest or values with other regimes in adjacent policy areas or other regions – or indeed with other powerful states. One need think only of the deterioration of US–EU relations – at least at the level of 'high politics' – in recent years to see how regimes can contribute to a new kind of instability in the balance of power following the Cold War (Kagan 2003). Secondly, given that the success of even the best-embedded 'post-sovereign' regional or functional regimes in transcending the particular interests of the states within these regimes remains limited and precarious (Morgan 2005), not only can this lead to internal division and asymmetry of influence, but also to under-capacity (Barcelona Report 2004), indiscriminate securitization (Bigo 1996; Huysmans 2006) and the maintenance of an obstinate gap between the development and diversification of supranational internal security practice and its regulation. Notwithstanding the expansion of the EU's capability in policing and related matters – since the introduction of the Europol office and various flanking forms of cooperation in the Third Pillar of the EU Treaty at Maastricht in 1992; through the embracing of new and more penetrative policy instruments and fewer national decision-making vetoes in the Area of Freedom, Security and Justice baptized at Amsterdam in 1997; to the attempt (so far unsuccessful) at the overall constitutionalization of the European supranational regime in the early years of the new century (N. Walker 2004; Guild and Carrera 2005; Kostakopolou forthcoming) – many observers would testify to the resilience of these problems. For the continuing deep ambivalence of member states towards putting internal security matters in common over and above purely domestic security imperatives and priorities not only produces a recurrent problem of internal trust and of credible commitments at the political and the professional level. It also, and partly in response to default national parochialism, leads to the accentuation of certain narrow and potentially illiberal and exclusionary frames, whether organized crime, illegal immigration, or, now, terrorism, as a means of mobilizing transnational bias – a trend that favours the prioritization of a narrowly instrumental conception of concurrent security concerns.[7] Here, more than anywhere else in the field of transnational security politics, and precisely *because* it is more developed than any other area of transnational security politics, we see the re-enactment of the deep struggle, transposed from its original state context, to develop the four Rs of civilizing security practice – resources, recognition, rights and reasons – in the face of and against the pathological tendencies of paternalism, consumerism, authoritarianism and fragmentation.

Global civil society

One further, though partial, response to the capacity, legitimacy and effectiveness problems of the traditional state-centred approach and the unilateralist and regime alternatives to, or outgrowths of, that approach lies in the emergence of transnational civil society (Kaldor 2003; Keane 2003). It is now well documented that there has been a huge and spiralling increase both in the quantity and in the quality of influence of international NGOs and other movements of 'disorganized civil society' in recent decades (de Burca and Walker 2003; Anheier *et al.* 2004). Global civil society responds to the democratic or participation deficit in transnational politics in at least four ways. First, it provides forms of representation of interests and values that are not state-centred, but which track and help to generate common or convergent preferences across states. Secondly, international NGOs in particular offer a vital means of monitoring abuses of individual and group rights in the operation of international politics, a function that is especially important in the area of policing and security – as the activities of groups as diverse as Amnesty International, Statewatch

---

[7] One consequence of this is a continuing propensity to reconceive of security within the EU as a 'club good' – something more appropriate to particular groups of closely aligned, integration-friendly countries than to the EU as a whole. This was evident, for instance, in the initial Schengen initiative in 1985, undertaken by a small group of countries who wanted to anticipate the general dismantling of border controls within the EU and the new security measures required to deal with a borderless regime. It has very recently resurfaced in the form of the 2005 Prum Convention – an initiative by substantially the same group of 'core' EU countries to push ahead with new and potentially wide-reaching forms of cross-border police cooperation and common operations outside the framework of the constitutive treaties of the EU (Balzacq *et al.* 2006).

and Interrights indicate. Thirdly, global civil society provides a key means for developing the idea of a global 'public sphere', a space of communication and interaction within which notions of a global interest may be framed, debated and generated. It thus aspires to remedy the underlying cultural base of the democratic deficit in international relations, the lack of a genuine consciousness and articulation of common interest on which transnational institutions can feed and to which they must respond. Fourthly, global civil society, and the 'anti-globalization movement' in particular, claims to offer a prefiguration of an alternative paradigm of world politics – one in which states are no longer the dominant institutions, violence is no longer power's 'final analysis', and/or capital is no longer the dominant transactional logic and policy motor.

Clearly, any serious attempt to think through the possibility of developing a conception of a transnational public interest dedicated to the articulation and implementation of global public goods must take seriously the aspirations and achievements of global civil society. Yet global civil society can only ever be one part of the jigsaw, and indeed unless the other parts are also in place some of the effects of global civil society can be perverse, acting to undermine as much as to advance the best aspirations on which it is based. In the first place, global civil society cannot *replace* the policy capacity of the present configuration of state and transnational institutions, but only supplement and complement it. And in so doing, it must avoid two opposite dangers. One is of co-option, a danger well documented in the world of both national and international NGO politics. The other is that of negative capacity, the legitimate oppositional role of civil society threatening to descend into a form of critique which cannot articulate a positive counterfactual, or can only do so in the most vaguely utopian terms. This kind of negative capacity, ironically, can lead to a kind of default statism, with all attempts to put transnational interests or values institutionally in common condemned *a priori* for their lack of democratic credentials. In the second place, transnational civil society must attend to its own legitimacy problems. Direct global democracy is of course not an option, both on account of the scale and the diversity of policy areas and the need for coordination between them, in which case global civil society movements must be as attentive to their own deliberative procedures and representational capacity as the institutions they monitor and criticize. Thirdly, and cumulatively, global civil society must be concerned with questions of effective implementation. In security politics, as elsewhere, an opposition culture must be seriously engaged with the implementation gap – with the consideration that the 'evil' of global politics in the face of unrealized global public goods lies as much in false negatives as it does in false positives; as much in *inaction* – the failure to translate concerns into policy and policy into normative regulation and normative regulation into effective application – as it does in illegitimate *action*. This requires an approach that is at once critical and constructive, as willing to support institutions for what they might achieve as pillory them for what they have not, or hold them to account for what they have wrongly pursued and accomplished.

Cosmopolitanism

Cosmopolitanism has, since Kant, enjoyed a richly diverse development (Kleingeld 1999) and been associated at its outer limits with ideas of 'federal' global government and citizenship. But most contemporary cosmopolitans do not pitch their ambitions in such terms. Instead, many of today's cosmopolitans want to emphasize and give precedence to two sorts of developments (Archibugi *et al.* 1998; Held 2004; cf. Waldron 2000, 2003b; Vertovec and Cohen 2002). First, at the level of social ontology and normative theory, they want to stress, against communitarian positions, that an appropriate focus of our attempts to improve the world should be, and increasingly can be, either humanity as a whole or indeed any section of humanity regardless of whether it is bound together by any special ties of affinity. In turn, this is based on a conception of human nature which questions the dominance, and in some cases even the continued relevance, of affective ties rooted in the traditions and practices of particular state and substate political communities.[8] Rather, as global circuits of communication and interdependence spread, and as institutions develop to articulate and track these new circuits, this provides a practical context within which transnational ties of trust, loyalty and common cause can be fostered. And it is this new range of transnational institutions that provides a

---

[8] A distinction may be drawn here between strict and moderate cosmopolitans, with only the (less common) former category holding that the community of all human beings is the *exclusive* reference point for moral community. See, e.g., Kleingeld and Brown (2002).

second focus of emphasis: not, as said, some rigid and utopian notion of universal order framed by a world government, but a strengthening and democratization of the existing mosaic of institutions at global and regional level, with regions such as the EU given great emphasis as much for their role as a prototype of the 'civilian-power'-based possibilities of 'post-national' collective action as for their specific contribution to current transnational politics (see, e.g., Zielonka 1998; Cooper 2003). Cosmopolitanism tends, furthermore, to emphasize the strengths of global civil society movements and their role, in symbiosis with the new institutions, in forging new forms of transnational collective identity and solidarity.

There is much that is attractive in the cosmopolitan vision. On the one hand, its emphasis on the needs and aspirations of common humanity – its insistence on regarding 'nothing human as alien' (Waldron 2000: 243) – puts the question of global public goods squarely in focus, and does so within a basically optimistic intellectual and political framework, one that rejects the sterile dichotomies and stalled understanding associated with a certain type of conceptual or sociological essentialism. On the other hand, the rejection of any simple institutional solutions, or of any complacent sense that new forms of political community will inevitably emerge around these institutions after a decent time-lag, and the stress on the need to nurture forms of popular consciousness in conjunction with institutional development sit well with the insight that effectiveness and legitimacy are intimately related aspirations, and that effective implementation of global policy – including global security policy – depends on both.

Yet cosmopolitanism remains somewhat predisposed to underplaying the continuing relevance – and value – of national and other local norms of political community, and so to making the opposite error to the kind of preoccupation with national political community that we find in the different variants of the state-centred approach to international relations (Fine and Smith 2003: 484). Certainly, modern cosmopolitans do not want to phase out national institutions. But this seems to be a pragmatic concession – a recognition of their embedded influence over and thus indispensability to the development of more robust transnational institutions – rather than an acknowledgement and appreciation of any irreducible value in local political community and the goods which they can articulate and provide. The danger, here, is that it is assumed that because global public goods transcend domestic public goods in scope and jurisdiction, they also eclipse them in intrinsic value, and that the appropriate model is one in which domestic public goods are simply nested within and finally subordinate to the demands of global public goods.

Such an approach would seem to rest upon one or both of two mistakes. In the first place, it may be that, as noted, cosmopolitans simply fail to acknowledge any irreducible value in local community. And in our immediate terms, this translates into a failure to view public goods, including the good of security, as thick socially constitutive and socially vindicatory goods rather than, as we see for instance in the case of Held (2004: ch. 6), as merely convergent or instrumental public goods. Alternatively or additionally – and returning finally to the zero-sum thinking whose challenge we highlighted at the beginning of the chapter – even if the thickness of the domestic good of security is acknowledged, this may be seen as something to regret and to suppress inasmuch as it is thereby concluded or assumed that a parallel conception of cosmopolitan solidarity sufficiently robust to address the common security needs of wider levels of community is automatically ruled out. On this view, the preferred options are either – much as with the UNDP – the promotion of a 'thin–thin' conception of security at the state *and* transnational levels (see figure 1 above), or else a politics that seeks to build a thick ideal of the public interest at and only at the global level precisely because it is the level that knows no boundaries other than common humanity. Such a conclusion, we would argue, is flawed both as a theoretical understanding of how and why people come to place and retain matters in common and as a practical strategy to draw upon the sources of social capacity and popular legitimacy in building an effective framework for the development of global public goods – including those of policing and security.

Security as a global public good

In the above section, we presented the attempt to cope with increasing interdependence in global politics in general, and in global security politics in particular, in terms of a continuum marked at either end by solutions which collapse their vision of a viable and legitimate politics into a state-centred approach or into a universalist cosmopolitanism which trumps particular ties and obligations. Each of these positions continues to gives insufficient recognition to one of the two key coordinates in any viable and legitimate global politics of security. The other alternatives are also unsatisfactory, though for different reasons. The unilateralist approach merely compounds the problems of the state-centred approach. The regime approach and the civil society suggest important institutional and cultural parts of the jigsaw respectively, but do not solve the whole puzzle.

The way ahead, in our view, and the focus of our closing remarks, is to provide a principled basis, grounded in a proper understanding of the plural structure of public goods, on which to give proper recognition to both levels simultaneously – the universal and the domestic – and from that starting point to begin to imagine the institutional and social developments which would give best effect to that plural structure in terms of the maximization of the net overall state of security. Such a principled basis starts with a reassertion not just of the virtue of the state, but, as we discussed at length in chapter 7, of the *necessity* of that virtue. Just because the public good of security, unlike some public goods, is about more than the convergence of discrete individual interests but has in addition an inherently social dimension, and just because, in consequence, this social dimension is woven into deep cultural understandings of what it is to constitute a social group *as* a public, we cannot ignore this deeper sociological dynamic in forging a comprehensive framework. Objective security depends on the social environment, subjective security depends on the quality of social relations, and our basic sense of preparedness to put things in common is partly understood through a security sensibility and vernacular on account of these thick social properties. This, in turn, reinforces the very sense of trust and confidence, and of rootedness in the social world, which is the stuff of (subjective) security as a public good. This is a tightly enmeshed and self-reinforcing set of relations. It both presupposes and consolidates the idea of a resilient unit of political community, and of a sense of location within that political community, the paradigm form and basic level of which, as we saw in chapter 7, remains the state. At this basic level of political community, therefore, the social dimension of security simply cannot be wished away. It may be a matter of regret if, building on the meddling, partisan, imperialist or idiotic tendencies of the state, that social dimension develops in accordance with a dynamic that encourages paternalistic, authoritarian, consumerist or fragmentary trends, but it cannot be a matter of regret that the inevitable exists *in some form or other.*

However, and this is our second point of principle, the fact that there remains a strong reinforcing dynamic in support of national political community and national conceptions of security does not mean, as we have said, that we need despair at the possibility of the parallel realization of a global conception of the public good, or that we need conceive of that higher level merely in 'thin' convergent terms. We need not, in other words, especially if we are to develop the idea and practice of axiomatic security in the transnational arena, conceive of security between different and overlapping levels of political community in zero- or negative-sum terms, and so we need not be resigned as a matter of sociological default to a state-centred conception of security. Indeed, the prevalence of such zero-sum thinking is a sign of how the pervasive view of security we summarized at the end of chapter 6 currently structures world politics, either in the form of an introverted, fear-laden, reactive superficiality and its attendant police and militarized mindsets (its shallow and wide form), or because of the operation in the international arena of states seeking to defend their particular homogenous and securitized conception of ontological security (its deep and wide form).

There are a number of reasons why we need not accept this state of affairs and on the basis of which we can transcend such zero-sum calculations. The first takes as its point of departure the purely convergent conception of global public goods. As the ceaseless preoccupation with international security of even the most state-centred realist scholars eloquently indicates, the fact that states have such a strong self-interest in security means that they are, and will always remain, willing participants in collaborative strategies, notwithstanding the difficulties involved in stabilizing these strategies in institutional terms. Indeed, the problems of stabilization do not arise from a lack of awareness of the interdependence, but rather, from an *acute and constant* awareness of interdependence coupled with a sometimes unbridled determination to assert one's own national interest in the light of the factors of interdependence. Secondly, as the content of the internal security imperative of states is in all cases strikingly similar, states may be encouraged nevertheless to think of the global public good as something more than the optimal convergence of presumptively diverse individual state interests. As we were reminded in chapter 4, perhaps more so than in any other policy domain all states adhere to the same broad conception of general order – the same appreciation of (and appreciation of their need to respond to) their populations' desire to live in a state of tranquillity and in a context of predictable social relations. Thirdly and relatedly, states may also find common cause in their very understanding of the social quality of the public good of security. Earlier, when discussing alternative ways of providing security, we contrasted the rivalry between states and clubs and private actors, on the one hand, and the rivalry between different states, on the other. For all that their particular interests may differ, states also have a common understanding of the social and public quality of that which they seek to defend, which in turn allows, however unevenly and intermittently, for a greater imaginative openness to the possibility of *other* sites and levels of social or public 'added value' in the accomplishment of security.[9]

The constancy and priority of international security needs (and the urgency that arises from them) and the 'mirror effect' of regarding other states in the process of pursuing these needs (and the empathy which this entails) are clearly important ingredients of being able to configure global security in positive-sum terms. But a crucial final reason why we can begin to imagine a thicker transnational conception of security alongside thick individual national conceptions can also be added to the mix and has to do with the very dynamic through which the relationship between sociality and security is produced. In the main part of the book, with its concern to think through the civilizing of security first and foremost at the state level, we have tended to view that relationship as something *always already accomplished*, and to concentrate instead on avoiding the pathologies and pursuing the promise of its self-reinforcement. What this tends to overlook, and what is by contrast much more apparent and pertinent in the 'unfinished' world of international society, is that in the making of political community security possesses a *chronological* as well as a *logical* priority. When we summed up our discussion of axiomatic security at the

---

[9] To return to the EU example, it is easier to think of 'European security' as a holistic social good – as something whose value may increase just by the fact of its being held in common – if one already has a sense of the same process at work in the nurturing of domestic security. Indeed, the very fact that European security 'makes sense' in these experiential terms is one of the reasons that the Area of Freedom, Security and Justice has been pushed so strongly as a catalyst of EU integration in recent years. Public goods which do not possess that strong social element, such as the provision of utilities, carry less intuitive appeal when relocated at new sites, although, by the same token, the fact that they do not possess a thick resonance anywhere else means they are also less likely to provoke strong resistance from those affected by them anywhere else.

end of chapter 6 by referring to its dual catalytic role – as a platform for and an education in society – we were alluding to just that dual sense of priority. In turn, this helps us to think about how central the practices of transnational security are to the very constitution of international society, however immature or frustrated such a project might be. It is difficult for us to imagine, and, more importantly, difficult for global decision-makers to imagine, the effective supply of other global public goods without the stable platform supplied by the global public good of security. Furthermore, it is difficult for us to imagine, and, more importantly, difficult for global decision-makers to imagine, the very idea of transnational *society* rather than merely relations between discrete national *societies* in the absence of the salutary education a common concern for security can provide in bringing together instrumental and affective registers of common action. What is more, the 'social' here is always more-or-less rather than either/or. Not only is security necessarily 'in at the beginning' of new levels and points of social relations, but just because of its catalytic role, its initial and continuing viability does not depend upon some prior standard of 'sociality' or 'demos' or 'culture' or whatever other basis of affinity or measure of 'we-feeling' already having been reached, still less upon these *not* having been reached or having been relinquished elsewhere. Rather than in terms of absolute and mutually exclusive thresholds of viability or success, therefore, the platform-building and societally generative work of security, if successfully initiated, can operate in accordance with an incremental dynamic and with a different momentum in various different sites – national and post-national – simultaneously.

Yet, of course, it would be naïve to assume that even democratic states, if left to their own devices, will find their way to an optimal conception of the global public good of security in addition to an optimal conception of their own public good. We are claiming something much more modest than that: namely, that states have a multiple and in some measure mutually reinforcing structure of incentives to consider collaboration in protection of their security interests. Moreover, after a century which has seen such defining state-transcending security events as Hiroshima, the Holocaust, the nuclear arms race and, now, the rise of network terror (Robertson 1992; Kaldor 2003: 112), they possess some of the common vulnerabilities, value predilections and imaginative tools to think at the same time about the possibility of a thicker global model of security too – one in which they understand themselves at least some of the time as representing not just national citizens but also potential 'citizens of the world', and where to share a concern for common humanity is both a necessary assumption and a constituent part of a sense of regional or global security.

So we must start with states in building the institutional and social framework necessary for the realization of some thicker notion of the transnational public interest to parallel and complement state public interests. But equally we must not and we need not finish with states. Alongside states, and the bargaining structures and institutions set up between states, we need some kind of influential regional and global fora in which those who are not fettered by state interests, and whose voice and 'citizenship' are not defined in exclusively statist terms, can give fuller rein to their political imaginations and think through the ways in which security may be achieved as a thick public good at the global level. The reasons for this are not just ones of political morality – concerning the increasing demands for a meta-democratic 'reframing' of the global order in recognition of these new and old constituencies who are not well represented by states (Fraser 2005). They are also intensely practical. States, we believe, are like any actors who have much invested individually in a particular framework of collective action, but who can nevertheless imagine another or additional framework of collective action that might better serve the interests *they hold in common*. That is to say, they may lack the individual will to seek, or the collective negotiating dynamic to find, the optimal sense of these common interests within the existing framework, yet just because of their awareness of this, they will not necessarily or consistently be averse to the construction or evolution of alternative frameworks which *do* emphasize common rather than merely concurrent interests, and which may provide both the cultural momentum and the adjusted incentive structures to realize these common interests. Indeed, if this were not true in principle, then it would be very hard to understand and explain *existing* developments of international and supranational legal and political regimes that move beyond the thin and unstable logic of realism or other predominantly state-centred structures of control.

We must, even at this very late stage, remain vigilant in keeping the promise made in the last chapter *not* to issue institutional wish lists – an activity still more presumptuous and elusive in the volatile and precarious world of contemporary transnational security than in the internal structure of the state itself. In the most general terms, however, we would envisage an extension of our conception of *anchored pluralism*, now looking upwards to transnational society as well as outwards to civil and market society and downwards to substate society. The institutional matrix should, and for the foreseeable future inevitably will, remain anchored in states as the primary motors of common action and sources of institutional initiative both within and beyond their boundaries. But it should be pluralist in its principled and non-negotiable recognition, not least by states themselves, that there are two levels of abstract political community at which we can think of security as a thicker public good that are not reducible to one another but which need different registers of debate and institutional fora for their articulation. At the second level, transnational civil society and regional regimes would be important additional sources of initiative and key participants, as they are already defined in part in terms of their transcendence of national interests. Professional and administrative corps who have become distant from national political contexts but, at their best, not from the security-maximizing occupational ethics which drive situational decision-making in these national contexts, would also, inevitably and potentially productively, be significant players at this level.[10] This, of course, would still leave open the large 'reframing' question of how to address and resolve the possible tensions between the 'aggregative' or convergent tendencies of proposals or approaches arrived at in the purely national and international discourse and fora, on the one hand, and the more transcendent proposals and approaches arrived at in regional and global fora, on the other. But at least the tension, and the need for its negotiation, should be institutionally recognized on the basis of a principled understanding of the pluralism of levels of the public good of security, none of which can hold a monopoly on ensuring or expressing security's civilizing virtue, if ever such virtue is to be optimized.

---

[10] In particular, the work and research programme of Sheptycki (forthcoming) on the idea of a transnational 'constabulary ethic' is suggestive here. This is partly driven by the desire to turn the inevitability of high levels of police discretion in transnational theatres into a virtue. But it is also partly based on a sense that the idea of a common constabulary ethic is part of the constitutive self-understanding of security operatives in many different contexts, and that this is driven not just by professional self-interest or self-regard (of the type discussed under the paternalism syndrome in chapter 8), but by a genuine structural continuity between the dynamics of security-threatening situations across a broad range of national and transnational contexts and a real sense of the value of a common policecraft in repairing these situations.

References

Abrahamsen, R. and M. C. Williams 2006. 'Security Sector Reform: Bringing the Private in', *Conflict, Security and Development* 6: 1–23.

Ackerman, B. 2004. 'The Emergency Constitution', *Yale Law Journal* 113: 1029–91.

Ackerman, B. and J. Fishkin 2002. 'Deliberation Day', *Journal of Political Philosophy* 10: 129–52.

Adler, E. and M. Barnett (eds.) 1998. *Security Communities*. Cambridge: Cambridge University Press.

Adorno, T. W., E. Frenkel-Brunswik, D. J. Levinson and R. N. Sanford 1950. *The Authoritarian Personality*. New York: Harper.

Agamben, G. 1993. 'Sovereign Police', in B. Massumi (ed.), *The Politics of Everyday Fear*. Minneapolis: University of Minnesota Press, pp. 55–63.

Agamben, G. 1998. *Homo Sacer: Sovereign Power and Bare Life*. Stanford: Stanford University Press.

Agamben, G. 2004a. *State of Exception*. Chicago: Chicago University Press.

Agamben, G. 2004b. 'An Interview with Giorgio Agamben', *German Law Journal* 5/5: 609–14.

Ahire, P. 1991. *Imperial Policing: The Emergence and Role of the Police in Colonial Nigeria 1860–1960*. Milton Keynes: Open University Press.

Albrow, M. 1996. *The Global Age*. Cambridge: Polity.

Alderson, J. 1979. *Policing Freedom*. Plymouth: McDonald & Evans.

Alexander, G. 1997. 'Civic Property', *Social & Legal Studies* 6/2: 217–34.

Althusser, L. 1971. 'Ideology and Ideological State Apparatus', in *Lenin and Philosophy and Other Essays*. London: New Left Books, pp. 128–76.

Anderson, B. 1991. *Imagined Communities: Reflections on the Origins and Spread of Nationalism*. London: Verso.

Anderson, D. and D. Killingray (eds.) 1991. *Policing the Empire*. Manchester: Manchester University Press.

Anderson, D. and D. Killingray (eds.) 1992. *Policing and Decolonisation*. Manchester: Manchester University Press.

Anderson, M. 1989. *Policing the World*. Oxford: Oxford University Press.

Anderson, M. and J. Apap 2002. *Striking a Balance Between Freedom, Security and Justice in an Enlarged European Union*. Brussels: Centre for European Policy Studies.

Anderson, M., M. den Boer, P. Cullen, W. Gilmore, C. Raab and N. Walker 1995. *Policing the European Union: Theory, Law and Practice*. Oxford: Clarendon.

Andreas, P. and R. Price 2001. 'From War Fighting to Crime Fighting: Transforming the American National Security State', *International Studies* 4: 31–52.

Anheier, H., M. Kaldor and M. Glasius (eds.) 2004. *Global Civil Society 2004/5*. London: Sage.

Aradau, C. 2004. 'Security and the Democratic Scene: Desecuritization and Emancipation', *Journal of International Relations and Development* 7: 388–413.

Arato, A. 2002. 'The Bush Tribunals and the Spectre of Dictatorship', *Constellations* 9/4: 457–76.

Archibugi, D., D. Held and M. Köhler (eds.) 1998. *Re-Imagining Political Community: Studies in Cosmopolitan Democracy*. Cambridge: Polity.

Audit Commission 1993. *Helping with Enquiries: Tackling Crime Effectively*. London: Audit Commission.

Avant, D. 2005. *The Market for Force: The Consequences of Privatising Security*. Cambridge: Cambridge University Press.

Ayres, I. and J. Braithwaite 1992. *Responsive Regulation: Transcending the Deregulation Debate*. Oxford: Oxford University Press.

Baldwin, D. (ed.) 1993. *Neorealism and Neoliberalism: The Contemporary Debate*. New York: Columbia University Press.

Balzacq, T., D. Bigo, S. Carrera and E. Guild 2006. *Security and the Two-Level Game: The Treaty of Prum, the EU and the Management of Threats* (CEPS Working Document 234). Brussels: Centre for European Policy Studies.

Barber, B. 2003. *Fear's Empire: War, Terrorism and Democracy*. New York: Norton.

Barcelona Report 2004. *A Human Security Doctrine for Europe: The Barcelona Report of the Study Group on Europe's Security Capabilities*. Barcelona: Caixa de Catalunya. Available at: www.lse.ac.uk/depts/global/studygroup/studygroup.htm

Baudrillard, J. 1983. *Simulations*. London: Semiotext(e).

Bauman, Z. 1992. *Intimations of Postmodernity*. London: Routledge.

Bauman, Z. 1998. *Globalization: The Human Consequences*. Cambridge: Polity.

Bauman, Z. 2004. *Wasted Lives: Modernity and its Outcasts*. Cambridge: Polity.

Bauman, Z. and K. Tester 2001. *Conversations with Zygmunt Bauman*. Cambridge: Polity.

Bayley, D. 1985. *Patterns of Policing*. New Brunswick, NJ: Princeton University Press.

Bayley, D. 1994. *Police for the Future*. Oxford: Oxford University Press.

Bayley, D. 2001. 'Security and Justice for All', in H. Strang and J. Braithwaite (eds.), *Restorative Justice and Civil Society*. Cambridge: Cambridge University Press, pp. 211–21.

Bayley, D. 2006. *Changing the Guard: Developing Democratic Police Abroad*, Oxford: Oxford University Press.

Bayley, D. and C. Shearing 1996. 'The Future of Policing', *Law and Society Review* 30/3: 585–606.

Bayley, D. and C. Shearing 2001. *The New Structure of Policing: Description, Conceptualization and Research Agenda*. Washington, DC: National Institute of Justice.

Beck, U. 2000. *What Is Globalization?* Cambridge: Polity.

Becker, H. 1967. 'Whose Side Are We on?', *Social Problems*, 14/3: 239–47.

Bellamy, A., P. Williams and S. Griffin 2004. *Understanding Peacekeeping*. Cambridge: Polity.

Benhabib, S. 2004. *The Rights of Others: Aliens, Residents and Citizens*. Cambridge: Cambridge University Press

Benjamin, W. 1921/1985. 'Critique of Violence', in *One-Way Street and Other Essays*. London: Verso, pp. 132–54.

Benson, B. 1990. *The Enterprise of Law: Justice Without the State*. San Francisco, CA: Pacific Research Institute for Public Policy.

Berki, R. N. 1986. *Security and Society: Reflections on Law, Order and Politics*. London: Dent.

Bernstein, S., T. Platt, J. Frappier, G. Ray, R. Shauffler, L. Trujillo, L. Cooper, E. Currie and S. Harring 1982. *The Iron Fist and the Velvet Glove: An Analysis of the US Police*, 3rd edn. Berkeley, CA: Center for Research on Criminal Justice.

Bigo, D. 1996. *Police en réseaux: l'expérience européenne*. Paris: Presse de Sciences Po.

Bigo, D. 2000a. 'When Two Become One: Internal and External Securitisations in Europe', in M. Kelstrup and M. Williams (eds.), *International Relations Theory and the Politics of European Integration: Power, Security and Community*. London: Routledge, pp. 171–204.

Bigo, D. 2000b. 'Liaison Officers in Europe: New Officers in the European Security Field', in J. Sheptycki (ed.), *Issues in Transnational Policing*. London: Routledge, pp. 67–100.

Bigo, D. 2002. 'Security and Immigration: Towards a Critique of the Governmentality of Unease', *Alternatives* 27: 63–92.

Bigo, D. (ed.) 2006. *Illiberal Practices in Liberal Regimes*. Paris: L'Harmattan.

Bigo, D. and E. Guild (eds.) 2005. *Controlling Frontiers: Free Movement into and within Europe*. Aldershot: Ashgate.

Bittner, E. 1967. 'The Police on "Skid Row": A Study in Peacekeeping', *American Sociological Review* 32: 699–715.

Bittner, E. 1970. *The Functions of Police in Modern Society*. Chevy Chase, MD: National Institute of Mental Health.

Bittner, E. 1983. 'Legality and Workmanship', in M. Punch (ed.), *Control in the Police Organization*. Cambridge, MA: MIT Press, pp. 1–12.

Bittner, E. 1990. *Aspects of Police Work*. Boston, MA: Northeastern University Press.

Blagg, H. 1997. 'A Just Measure of Shame? Aboriginal Youth Conferencing in Australia', *British Journal of Criminology* 37: 481–501.

Blair, I. 2002. 'The Policing Revolution: Back to the Beat', *New Statesman* 23 September, 21–3.

Blakely, E. and M. Snyder 1997. *Fortress America: Gated Communities in the USA*. Washington, DC: Brookings Institute Press.

Bobbitt, P. 2002. *The Shield of Achilles: War, Peace and the Course of History*. Harmondsworth: Penguin.

Boer, M. den and J. Monar 2002. '11 September and the Challenge of Global Terrorism to the EU as a Security Actor', *Journal of Common Market Studies* 40: 11–28.

Boer, M. den and A. Peters 2005. 'Urban Security: A View from the European Balcony', in K. van der Vijver and J. Terpstra (eds.), *Urban Safety: Problems, Governance and Strategies*. Enschede: IPIT, pp. 145–63.

Bohman, J. and W. Rehg (eds.) 1997. *Deliberative Democracy*. Cambridge, MA: MIT Press.

Bottoms, A. 1995. 'The Philosophy and Politics of Punishment and Sentencing', in C. Clark and R. Morgan (eds.), *The Politics of Sentencing Reform*. Oxford: Clarendon, pp. 17–49.

Bourdieu, P. 1987. 'The Force of Law: Toward a Sociology of the Juridical Field', *Hastings Law Journal* 38: 805–57.

Bourdieu, P. 1990. *The Logic of Practice*. Cambridge: Polity.

Bourdieu, P. 1996. *The State Nobility: Elite Schools in the Field of Power*. Stanford, CA: Stanford University Press.

Bourdieu, P. and others 1999. *The Weight of the World: Social Suffering in Contemporary Society*. Cambridge : Polity.

Braithwaite, J. 1992. 'Good and Bad Police Services and How to Pick Them', in P. Moir and H. Eijkman (eds.), *Policing Australia*. Sydney: Macmillan, pp. 11–29.

Braithwaite, J. and P. Pettit 1990. *Not Just Deserts: A Republican Theory of Criminal Justice*. Oxford: Oxford University Press.

Bratton, W. 1998. *Turnaround: How America's Top Cop Reversed the Crime Epidemic*. New York: Random House.

Brewer, J. 1991. 'Policing in Divided Societies', *Policing and Society* 1/3: 179–91.

Brodeur, J.-P. 1983. 'High Policing and Low Policing: Remarks About the Policing of Political Activities', *Social Problems* 30/5: 507–20.

Brogden, M. 1982. *The Police: Autonomy and Consent*. London: Academic Press.

Brogden, M. 1987. 'The Emergence of the Police: The Colonial Dimension', *British Journal of Criminology* 27: 4–14.

Brogden, M. and P. Nijhar 2005. *Community Policing: National and International Models and Approaches*. Cullompton: Willan.

Brogden, M. and C. Shearing 1993. *Policing for a New South Africa*. London: Routledge.

Brooks, T. R. 1965. 'New York's Finest', *Commentary* 40/August.

Brown, J. and F. Heidensohn 2000. *Gender and Policing*. Basingstoke: Macmillan

Brown, M., S. Lynn-Jones and S. Miller (eds.) 1996. *Debating the Democratic Peace*. Cambridge, MA: MIT Press.

Brunckhorst, H. 2005. *Solidarity: From Civic Friendship to a Global Legal Community*. Cambridge, MA: MIT Press.

Buchanan, K. 1978. 'From Private Preferences to Public Philosophy: The Development of Public Choice', in J. Buchanan *et al.*, *The Economics of Politics*. London: Institute of Economic Affairs, pp. 1–20.

Bull, H. 1977. *The Anarchical Society: A Study of Order in World Politics*. Basingstoke: Macmillan.

Bullock, K. and N. Tilley (eds.) 2003. *Crime Reduction and Problem-Oriented Policing*. Cullompton: Willan.

Bunyan, T. 2002. *The War on Freedom and Democracy*. London: Statewatch.

Bunyan, T. 2004. *While Europe Sleeps*. Available at: www.spectrezine.org/europe/

Burca, G. de and N. Walker 2003. 'Law and Transnational Civil Society: Upsetting the Agenda?', *European Law Journal* 9: 387–400.

Burke, A. 2002. 'Aporias of Security', *Alternatives* 27/1: 1–27.

Burke, J. 2004. *Al Qaeda: The True Story of Radical Islam*. Harmondsworth: Penguin.

Burris, S. 2004. 'Governance, Microgovernance and Health', *Temple Law Review* 77: 335–62.

Burris, S. 2006. 'From Security to Health', in J. Wood and B. Dupont (eds.), *Democracy, Society and the Governance of Security*. Cambridge: Cambridge University Press, pp. 196–216.

Butler, A. 1984. *Police Management*. London: Gower.

Buzan, B. 1991. *People, States and Fear: An Agenda for International Security Studies in the Post Cold War Era*, 2nd edn. Brighton: Harvester.

Buzan, B. 2004. *The United States and the Great Powers: World Politics in the Twenty-First Century*. Cambridge: Polity.

Buzan, B., O. Wæver and J. de Wilde 1998. *Security: A New Framework for Analysis*. London: Lynne Rienner.

Cain, M. 2000. 'Orientalism, Occidentalism and the Sociology of Crime', in D. Garland and R. Sparks (eds.), *Criminology and Social Theory*. Oxford: Oxford University Press, pp. 71–102.

Caldeira, T. 2001. *City of Walls: Crime, Segregation and Citizenship in São Paulo*. Berkeley: University of California Press.

Campbell, D. and M. Dillon (eds.) 1993. *The Political Subject of Violence*. Manchester: Manchester University Press.

Canovan, M. 1996. *Nationhood and Political Theory*. London: Edward Elgar.

Canovan, M. 2005. *The People*. Cambridge: Polity.

Cashmore, E. and E. McLaughlin (eds.) 1991. *Out of Order? Policing Black People*. London: Routledge.

Castells, M. 1997. *The Information Age: Economy, Society and Culture*, vol. 1. Oxford: Basil Blackwell.

Castoriadis, C. 1987. *The Imaginary Institution of Society*. Cambridge, MA: MIT Press.

Caygill, H. 2001. 'Perpetual Police?: Kosovo and the Elision of Police and Military Violence', *European Journal of Social Theory* 4/1: 73–80.

Chalmers, D. 2004. *Constitutional Reason in an Age of Terror* (*Global Law Working Paper* 06/04). New York: New York University Law School.

Cherney, A. 2005. 'Contingency and Resistance: Studying Developments in the Governance of Security'. Unpublished ms., School of Social Science, University of Queensland.

Clark, I. 1989. *The Hierarchy of States: Reform and Resistance in the International Order*. Cambridge: Cambridge University Press.

Cohen, H. 1985. 'Authority: The Limits of Discretion', in F. A. Elliston and M. Feldberg (eds.), *Moral Issues in Police Work*. New York: Rowan & Allanheld, pp. 27–42.

Cohen, J. and C. Sabel 1997. 'Directly-Deliberative Polyarchy', *European Law Journal* 3/4: 313–40.

Cohen, P. 1979. 'Policing the Working Class City', in B. Fine, R. Kinsey, J. Lea, S. Picciotto and J. Young (eds.), *Capitalism and the Rule of Law*. London: Hutchinson, pp. 118–36.

Cohen, S. 2001. *States of Denial: Knowing About Atrocities and Suffering.* Cambridge: Polity.

Commission on Global Governance 1995. *Our Global Neighbourhood.* Oxford: Oxford University Press.

Commission on Human Security 2003. *Human Security Now: Protecting and Empowering People.* New York: United Nations.

Cooper, R. 2003. *The Breaking of Nations: Order and Chaos in the Twenty-First Century.* London: Atlantic Books.

Cowell, D., T. Jones and J. Young (eds.) 1982. *Policing the Riots.* London: Junction Books.

Cox, R. W. 1987. *Production, Power and World Order: Social Forces in the Making of History.* New York: Columbia University Press.

Crawford, A. 1997. *The Local Governance of Crime: Appeals to Partnerships and Community.* Oxford: Clarendon.

Crawford, A. 1998. *Crime Prevention and Community Safety: Politics, Policies and Practices.* Harlow: Longman.

Crawford, A. 2003. 'The Pattern of Policing in the UK: Policing Beyond the Police' in T. Newburn (ed.), *Handbook of Policing.* Cullompton: Willan, pp. 136–68.

Crawford, A. 2006. 'Policing and Security as "Club Goods": The New Enclosures', in J. Wood and B. Dupont (eds.), *Democracy, Society and the Governance of Security.* Cambridge: Cambridge University Press, pp. 111–38.

Crawford, A. and S. Lister 2005. *The Extended Police Family: Visible Patrols in Residential Areas.* Bristol: Policy Press.

Creveld, M. van 1999. *The Rise and Decline of the State.* Cambridge: Cambridge University Press.

Dalby, S. 1997. 'Contesting an Essential Concept: Reading the Dilemmas in Contemporary Security Discourse', in K. Krause and M. Williams (eds.), *Critical Security Studies.* London: University College London Press, pp. 3–32.

Deflem, M. 2003. *Policing World Society: Historical Foundations of International Police Cooperation.* Oxford: Oxford University Press.

De Lint, W. 1997. 'The Constable Generalist as Exemplary Citizen, Networker and Problem-Solver: Some Implications', *Policing and Society* 6: 247–64.

De Lint, W. and S. Virta 2004. 'Security in Ambiguity: Towards a Radical Security Politics', *Theoretical Criminology* 8/4: 465–90.

Della Porta, D. and H. Reiter (eds.) 1998. *Policing Protest: The Control of Mass Demonstrations in Western Democracies.* Minneapolis, MN: University of Minnesota Press.

Della Porta, D. and H. Reiter 2004. 'The Policing of Global Protest: The G8 at Genoa and its Aftermath', paper presented at the International

Conference on Protest Policing and Globalization, Gothenburg, 1–4 May.

Dennis, N. (ed.), 1997. *Zero Tolerance: Policing a Free Society*. London: Institute of Economic Affairs.

Derrida, J. 1992. 'Force of Law: The "Mystical Foundations of Authority" ', in D. Cornell, M. Rosenfeld and D. G. Carlson (eds.), *Deconstruction and the Possibility of Justice*. London: Routledge, pp. 3–67.

Dillon, M. 1996. *Politics of Security: Towards a Political Philosophy of Continental Thought*. London: Routledge.

Dixon, B. 2004. 'In Search of Interactive Globalisation: Critical Criminology in South Africa's Transition', *Crime, Law and Social Change* 41: 359–84.

Dixon, B. and E. van der Spuy (eds.) 2004. *Justice Gained? Crime and Crime Control in South Africa's Transition*. Cullompton: Willan.

Dixon, D. 1997. *Law in Policing: Legal Regulation and Police Practices*. Oxford: Oxford University Press.

Dorf, M. and C. Sabel 1998. 'A Constitution of Democratic Experimentalism', *Columbia Law Review* 98: 367–473.

Douzinas, C. 2003. 'Humanity, Military Humanism and the New Moral Order', *Economy and Society* 32/2: 159–83.

Doyle, M. 1995. 'On the Democratic Peace', *International Security* 19/4: 180–4.

Dryzek, J. 2000. *Deliberative Democracy and Beyond*. Oxford: Oxford University Press.

Dubber, M. D. 2004. ' "The Power to Govern Men and Things": Patriarchal Origins of the Police Power in American Law', *Buffalo Law Review* 52/4: 1277–1346.

Dubber, M. D. 2005. *The Police Power: Patriarchy and the Foundations of American Government*. New York: Columbia University Press.

Dunn, J. 1993. *Western Political Theory in the Face of the Future*. London: Canto.

Dunn, J. 2000. *The Cunning of Unreason: Making Sense of Politics*. London: HarperCollins.

Dunn, J. 2005. *Setting the People Free: The Story of Democracy*. London: Atlantic Books.

Dupont, B. 2004. 'Security in an Age of Networks', *Policing and Society* 14/1: 76–91.

Dupont, B., P. Grabosky and C. Shearing 2003. 'The Governance of Security in Weak and Failing States', *Criminal Justice* 3: 331–49.

Dyzenhaus, D. and M. Hunt forthcoming. 'Deference, Security and Human Rights', in B. Goold and L. Lazarus (eds.), *Security and Human Rights*. Oxford: Hart.

Elias, N. 1939/1978. *The Civilizing Process*, vol. 1: *The History of Manners*. New York: Pantheon Books.

Elias, N. 1939/1982. *The Civilizing Process*, Vol. 2: *State Formation and Civilization*. New York: Pantheon Books.

Elliot, N. 1989. *Streets Ahead*. London: Adam Smith Institute.

Ellison, G. forthcoming. 'Fostering a Dependency Culture: The Commodification of Community Policing in a Global Marketplace', in A. Goldsmith and J. Sheptycki (eds.), *Crafting Global Policing*. Oxford: Hart.

Ellison, G. and A. Mulcahy (eds.) 2001. Special issue of *Policing and Society* on 'Policing in Northern Ireland' 11: 3–4.

Ellison, G. and J. Smyth 2000. *The Crowned Harp: Policing in Northern Ireland*. London: Pluto Press.

Elster, J., C. Offe and U. K. Preuss 1998. *Institutional Design in Post-Communist Societies: Rebuilding the Ship at Sea*. Cambridge: Cambridge University Press.

Emsley, C. 1992. 'The English Bobby: An Indulgent Tradition', in R. Porter (ed.), *Myths of the English*. Cambridge: Polity, pp. 114–35.

Emsley, C. 1993. 'Peasants, Gendarmes and State Formation', in M. Fulbrook (ed.), *National Histories and European History*. London: University College Press.

Emsley, C. 1996. *The English Police: A Political and Social History*, 2nd edn. Harlow: Longman, pp. 69–93.

Emsley, C. 2000. *Gendarmes and the State in Nineteenth Century Europe*. Oxford: Oxford University Press.

Ericson, R. 1982. *Reproducing Order: A Study of Police Patrol Work*. Toronto: University of Toronto Press.

Ericson, R. 1994. 'The Division of Expert Knowledge in Policing and Security', *British Journal of Sociology*, 45/2: 149–75.

Ericson, R. and K. Haggerty 1997. *Policing the Risk Society*. Oxford: Oxford University Press.

Estlund, D. 1999. 'Beyond Fairness and Deliberation: The Epistemic Dimension of Democratic Authority', in J. Bohman and W. Rehg (eds.), *Deliberative Democracy*. Cambridge, MA: MIT Press, pp. 173–204.

Etzioni, A. 2004. *The Common Good*. Cambridge: Polity.

Falk, R. 1995. *On Humane Governance: Toward a New Global Politics (The World Order Models Project Report of the Global Civilization Initiative)*. Cambridge: Polity.

Feldman, N. 2002. 'Choices of Law, Choices of War', *Harvard Journal of Law and Public Policy* 25: 457–85.

Ferguson, N. 2004. *Colossus: The Price of America's Empire*. New York: Penguin.

Ferret, J. 2004. 'The State, Policing and "Old Continental Europe": Managing the Local/National Tension', *Policing and Society* 14/1: 49–65.

Fielding, N. 1984. 'Police Socialisation and Police Competence', *British Journal of Sociology* 35/4: 568–90.

Fine, R. 1999. 'Benign Nationalism? The Limits of the Civic Ideal', in E. Mortimer (ed.), *People, Nation and State: The Meaning of Ethnicity and Nationalism*. London: I. B. Tauris, pp. 149–61.

Fine, R. and D. Millar (eds.) 1984. *Policing the Miners' Strike*. London: Lawrence & Wishart.

Fine, R. and W. Smith 2003. 'Jürgen Habermas's Theory of Cosmopolitanism', *Constellations* 10: 469–87.

Finer, S. 1997. *The History of Government*, vol. 3: *Empires, Monarchies and the Modern State*. Oxford: Oxford University Press.

Fishkin, J. 1991. *Democracy and Deliberation: New Directions for Democratic Reform*. New Haven: Yale University Press.

Foucault, M. 1978. *A History of Sexuality: An Introduction*. Harmondsworth: Penguin.

Foucault, M. 1981. 'Omnes et Singulatim: Towards a Criticism of "Political Reason"', in S. McMurrin (ed.), *The Tanner Lectures on Human Values*, vol. 2. Salt Lake City: University of Utah Press, pp. 225–54.

Foucault, M. 1984. *A History of Sexuality*, vol. 3: *The Care of the Self*. Harmondsworth: Penguin.

Fraser, N. 2003. 'Social Justice in an Age of Identity Politics: Redistribution, Recognition and Participation', in N. Fraser and A. Honneth, *Redistribution or Recognition?: A Political-Philosophical Exchange*. London: Verso, pp. 7–109.

Fraser, N. 2005. 'Reframing Justice in a Globalizing World', *New Left Review* 36 (Nov.–Dec.): 69–88.

Fredman, S. forthcoming. 'Security as Equality: Security from Poverty, Illness and Degradation', in B. Goold and L. Lazarus (eds.), *Security and Human Rights*. Oxford: Hart.

Freeden, M. 1996. *Ideologies and Political Theory: A Conceptual Approach*. Oxford: Oxford University Press.

Friedman, M. 1962. *Capitalism and Freedom*. Chicago: University of Chicago Press.

Friedrich, C. J. 1963. *Man and Government*. New York: McGraw-Hill.

Fukuyama, F. 1992. *The End of History and the Last Man*. Harmondsworth: Penguin.

Gambetta, D. 1993. *The Sicilian Mafia: The Business of Private Protection*. Cambridge, MA: Harvard University Press.

Gamble, A. 1988. *The Free Economy and the Strong State: The Politics of Thatcherism*. Basingstoke: Macmillan.

Gans, J. 2000. 'Privately Paid Public Policing: Law and Practice', *Policing and Society*, 10/2: 183–206.

Garland, D. 2001. *The Culture of Control: Crime and Social Order in Contemporary Society*. Oxford: Oxford University Press.

Gerstenberg, O. and C. Sabel 2002. 'Directly Deliberative Polyarchy: An Ideal for Europe', in C. Joerges and R. Dehousse (eds.), *Good Governance in Europe's Integrated Market*. Oxford: Oxford University Press, pp. 289–392.

Geuss, R. 2003. *Public Goods, Private Goods*. Princeton: Princeton University Press.

Giddens, A. 1984. *The Constitution of Society*. Cambridge: Polity.

Giddens, A. 1991. *Modernity and Self-Identity*. Cambridge: Polity.

Gilmore, B. 2002. *The Twin Towers and the Third Pillar: Some Security Agenda Developments*. Florence: European University Institute Working Paper.

Gilroy, P. 2004. *After Empire: Melancholia or Convivial Culture?* London: Routledge.

Girling, E., I. Loader and R. Sparks 2000. *Crime and Social Change in Middle England: Questions of Order in an English Town*. London: Routledge.

Glaeser, A. 2000. *Divided in Unity: Identity, Germany and the Berlin Police*. Chicago: Chicago University Press.

Goldberg, D. T. 2001. *The Racial State*. Oxford: Basil Blackwell.

Goldsmith, A. 1990. 'Taking Police Culture Seriously: Police Discretion and the Limits of Law', *Policing and Society* 1: 2–20.

Goldsmith, A. 2003. 'Policing Weak States: Citizen Safety and State Responsibility', *Policing and Society* 13: 3–21.

Goldsmith, A. and C. Lewis (eds.) 2000. *Civilian Oversight of Policing: Governance, Democracy and Human Rights*. Oxford: Hart.

Goldsmith, A., M. V. Llorente and A. Rivas forthcoming. 'Foreign Assistance in Colombian Policing', in A. Goldsmith and J. Sheptycki (eds.), *Crafting Global Policing*. Oxford: Hart.

Goldsmith, A. and J. Sheptycki (eds.) forthcoming. *Crafting Global Policing*. Oxford: Hart.

Goldstein, H. 1990. *Problem-Oriented Policing*. London: McGraw-Hill.

Golove, D. and S. Holmes 2004. 'Terrorism and Accountability: Why Checks and Balances Apply Even in "The War on Terrorism"', *The NYU Review of Law and Security* 2/April: 2–7.

Goold, B. and L. Lazarus (eds.) forthcoming. *Security and Human Rights*. Oxford: Hart.

Gordon, P. 1984. 'Community Policing: Towards the Local Police State', *Critical Social Policy* 10/Summer.

Gorer, G. 1955. *Exploring English Character*. London: Cresset.

Gouldner, A. 1976. *The Dialectic of Ideology and Technology*. London: Macmillan.

Grabosky, P. 1995. 'Using Non-Governmental Resources to Foster Regulatory Compliance', *Governance* 8: 527–50.

Gray, J. 2003. *Al Qaeda and What it Means to be Modern*. London: Faber.

Grimm, D. 1995. 'Does Europe Need a Constitution?', *European Law Journal* 1: 282–96.

Grimm, D. 2005. 'The Constitution in the Process of Denationalization', *Constellations* 12: 447–63.

Grimshaw, R. and T. Jefferson 1987. *Interpreting Policework*. London: Allen & Unwin.

Guild, E. and D. Bigo 2002. 'The Legal Mechanisms – Collectively Specifying the Individual: The Schengen Border System and Enlargement', in M. Anderson and J. Apap (eds.), *Police and Justice Co-operation and the New European Borders*. The Hague: Kluwer, pp. 121–38.

Guild, E. and S. Carrera 2005. *No Constitutional Treaty? Implications for the Area of Freedom, Security and Justice* (CEPS Working Document 231). Brussels: Centre for European Policy Studies.

Günther, K. 2005. 'World Citizens between Freedom and Security', *Constellations* 12: 379–91.

Gutmann, A. and D. Thompson 2004. *Why Deliberative Democracy?* Princeton, NJ: Princeton University Press.

Habermas, J. 1974. *Knowledge and Human Interests*. London: Heinemann.

Habermas, J. 1996. *Between Facts and Norms*. Cambridge: Polity.

Habermas, J. 2001. 'Constitutional Democracy: A Paradoxical Union of Contradictory Principles?', *Political Theory* 29: 770–81.

Habermas, J. 2006. *The Divided West*. Cambridge: Polity.

Hale, C. 1996. 'Fear of Crime: A Review of the Literature', *International Review of Victimology* 4/1: 79–150.

Hall, S. 1980. *Drifting into a Law and Order Society*. London: Cobden Trust.

Hall, S., J. Clarke, C. Critcher, T. Jefferson and B. Roberts 1978. *Policing the Crisis*. Basingstoke: Macmillan/Palgrave.

Haltern, U. 2003. 'Pathos and Patina: The Failure and Promise of Constitutionalism in the European Imagination', *European Law Journal* 9: 14–44.

Harcourt, B. 2001. *Illusion of Order: The False Promise of Broken Windows Policing*. Cambridge, MA: Harvard University Press.

Harcourt, B. 2006. *Against Prediction: Profiling, Policing, and Punishing in an Actuarial Age*. Chicago: Chicago University Press.

Hardin, R. 1999. 'Democracy and Collective Bads', in I. Shapiro and C. Hacker-Cordon (eds.), *Democracy's Edges*. Cambridge: Cambridge University Press, pp. 63–83.

Hardt, M. and A. Negri 2000. *Empire*. Cambridge, MA: Harvard University Press.

Harvey, D. 2003. *The New Imperialism*. Oxford: Oxford University Press.

Hayek, F. von 1948. *Individualism and Economic Order*. Chicago: University of Chicago Press.

Hayek, F. von 1978. 'Why I Am Not a Conservative', in *The Constitution of Liberty*. Chicago: University of Chicago Press, pp. 397–413.

Hayek, F. von 1979. *Law, Legislation and Liberty*, vol. 3: *The Political Order of a Free People*. London: Routledge & Kegan Paul.

Hayes, B. 2002. *The Activities and Development of Europol: Towards an Unaccountable 'FBI' in Europe*. London: Statewatch.

Held, D. 2004. *Global Covenant: The Social Democratic Alternative to the Washington Consensus*. Cambridge: Polity.

Held, D. and A. McGrew 2002. *Globalization/Anti-Globalization*. Cambridge: Polity.

Held, D., A. McGrew, D. Goldblatt and J. Perraton 1999. *Global Transformations: Politics, Economics and Culture*. Cambridge: Polity.

Herbert, S. 2006. *Citizens, Cops, and Power: Recognizing the Limits of Community*. Chicago: University of Chicago Press.

Herbst, J. 2003. 'Let Them Fail: State Failure in Theory and Practice. Implications for Policy', in R. I. Rotberg (ed.), *When States Fail: Causes and Consequences*. Princeton, NJ: Princeton University Press, pp. 302–18.

Heritier, A. 2002. 'Introduction', in A. Heritier (ed.), *Common Goods: Reinventing European and International Governance*. Lanham, MD: Rowman & Littlefield, pp. 1–27.

Hirschman, A. 1970. *Exit, Voice and Loyalty: Responses to Decline in Firms, Organisations and States*. Cambridge, MA: Harvard University Press.

Hirst, P. 2000. 'Democracy and Governance', in J. Pierre (ed.), *Debating Governance: Authority, Steering and Democracy*. Oxford: Oxford University Press, pp. 13–35.

Hirst, P. and G. Thompson 1996. *Globalization in Question*. Cambridge: Polity.

Hobbes, T. 1946. *Leviathan*. Oxford: Blackwell.

Holmes, S. 1993. *The Anatomy of Anti-Liberalism*. Cambridge, MA: Harvard University Press.

Holmes, S. 1995. *Passions and Constraint: On the Theory of Liberal Democracy.* Chicago: University of Chicago Press.

Home Office 1994. *Partners Against Crime.* London: Home Office.

Home Office 2001. *Policing a New Century: A Blueprint for Reform.* London: Home Office. Cm. 5326.

Home Office 2004. *Building Communities, Beating Crime: A Better Police Service for the 21st Century.* London: Home Office. Cm. 6360.

Honneth, A. 2003. 'Redistribution as Recognition', in N. Fraser and A. Honneth, *Redistribution or Recognition? A Political-Philosophical Exchange.* London: Verso, pp. 110–97.

Hope, T. 1997. 'Inequality and the Future of Community Crime Prevention', in S. P. Lab (ed.), *Crime Prevention at a Crossroads.* Cincinnati, OH: Anderson Publishing, pp. 143–60.

Hope, T. 2000. 'Inequality and the Clubbing of Private Security', in T. Hope and R. Sparks (eds.), *Crime, Risk and Insecurity: Law and Order in Everyday Life and Political Discourse.* London: Routledge, pp. 83–106.

Hope, T. and S. Karstedt 2003. 'Towards a New Social Crime Prevention', in H. Kury and J. Obergfell-Fuchs (eds.), *Crime Prevention: New Approaches.* Mainz, Germany: Weisse Ring, pp. 461–89.

Hope, T., S. Karstedt and S. Farrall 2001. *The Relationship between Calls and Crimes.* London: Home Office.

Huggins, M. 1998. *Political Policing: United States and South America.* Durham, NC: Duke University Press.

Hughes, G. 2007. *The Politics of Crime and Community.* Basingstoke: Palgrave.

Hughes, G. and A. Edwards (eds.) 2002. *Crime Control and Community: The New Politics of Public Safety.* Cullompton: Willan.

Hume, D. 1951. *A Treatise of Human Nature.* Oxford: Oxford University Press.

Huysmans, J. 2002. 'Defining Social Constructivism in Security Studies: The Normative Dilemma of Writing Security', *Alternatives* 27: 41–62.

Huysmans, J. 2004. 'Minding Exceptions: The Politics of Insecurity and Liberal Democracy', *Contemporary Political Theory* 3: 321–41.

Huysmans, J. 2006. *The Politics of Insecurity: Fear, Migration and Asylum in the EU.* London: Routledge.

Ignatieff, M. 2001. *Human Rights as Politics and Idolatry.* Princeton, NJ: Princeton University Press.

Ignatieff, M. 1993. *Blood and Belonging.* London: BBC Books.

Ignatieff, M. 2003. *Empire Lite: Nation-Building in Bosnia, Kosovo and Afghanistan.* London: Vintage.

Ignatieff, M. 2004. *The Lesser Evil: Political Ethics in an Age of Terror.* Edinburgh: Edinburgh University Press.

Ikenberry, G. J. (ed.) 2002. *America Unrivalled: The Future of the Balance of Power*. Ithaca, NY: Cornell University Press.

Innes, M. 2004. 'Reinventing Tradition: Reassurance, Neighbourhood Security and Policing', *Criminal Justice* 4/2: 151–71.

James, C. L. R. 1963. *Beyond a Boundary*. London: Yellow Jersey Press.

Jefferson, T. and R. Grimshaw 1984. *Controlling the Constable: Police Accountability in England and Wales*. London: Muller.

Jessop, B. 1990. *State Theory: Putting the Capitalist State in its Place*. Cambridge: Polity.

Johnson, C. 2004. *The Sorrows of Empire: Militarism, Secrecy and the End of the Republic*. New York: Metropolitan Books.

Johnston, L. 1992. *The Rebirth of Private Policing*. London: Routledge.

Johnston, L. 1999. *Policing Britain: Risk, Security and Governance*. Harlow: Longman.

Johnston, L. 2000. 'Transnational Private Security', in J. Sheptycki (ed.), *Issues in Transnational Policing*. London: Routledge, pp. 21–42.

Johnston, L. 2003. 'From "Pluralisation" to "the Extended Police Family": Discourses on the Governance of Community Policing in Britain', *International Journal of the Sociology of Law* 31: 185–204.

Johnston, L. 2006. 'Transnational Security Governance', in J. Wood and B. Dupont (eds.), *Democracy, Society and the Governance of Security*. Cambridge: Cambridge University Press, pp. 33–51.

Johnston, L. and C. Shearing 2003. *Governing Security: Explorations in Policing and Justice*. London: Routledge.

Jones, T. 2003. 'The Governance and Accountability of Policing', in T. Newburn (ed.), *Handbook of Policing*. Cullompton: Willan, pp. 603–27.

Jones, T. and T. Newburn 1998. *Private Security and Public Policing*. Oxford: Oxford University Press.

Jones, T. and T. Newburn 2001. *Widening Access: Improving Police Relations with Hard to Reach Groups* (Police Research Series Paper 138). London: Home Office.

Jones, T. and T. Newburn 2002. 'The Transformation of Policing?: Understanding Current Trends in Policing Systems', *British Journal of Criminology* 42: 129–46.

Jones, T. and T. Newburn 2004. 'The Convergence of US and UK Crime Control Policy: Exploring Substance and Process', in T. Newburn and R. Sparks (eds.), *Criminal Justice and Political Cultures: National and International Dimensions of Crime Control*. Cullompton: Willan, pp. 123–51.

Jones, T. and T. Newburn (eds.) 2006. *Plural Policing in Comparative Perspective*. London: Routledge.

Jordan, B. 1996. *A Theory of Poverty and Social Exclusion*. Cambridge: Polity.

Jordana, J. and D. Levi-Faur (eds.) 2004. *The Politics of Regulation: Institutional and Regulatory Reform for the Age of Governance*. Cheltenham: Edward Elgar.

Kádár, A. (ed.) 2001. *Police in Transition*. Budapest: Central European University Press.

Kagan, R. 2003. *Of Paradise and Power: America and Europe in the New World Order*. New York: Alfred A. Knopf.

Kagan, R. 2004. 'America's Crisis of Legitimacy', *Foreign Affairs* 83/2: 65–87.

Kaldor, M. 1999. *New and Old Wars: Organized Violence in a Global Era*. Cambridge: Polity.

Kaldor, M. 2003. *Global Civil Society: An Answer to War*. Cambridge: Polity.

Kantorowicz, E. H. 1957. *The King's Two Bodies: A Study in Mediaeval Political Theology*. Princeton, NJ: Princeton University Press.

Karn, J. 2007. *Narratives of Neglect: Community, Exclusion and the Local Governance of Security*. Cullompton: Willan.

Kaul, I., P. Conceição, K. Le Goulven and R. U. Mendoza 2003a. 'Why do Global Public Goods Matter Today?', in I. Kaul, P. Conceição, K. Le Goulven and R. U. Mendoza (eds.), *Providing Global Public Goods: Managing Globalization*. Oxford: Oxford University Press, pp. 2–20.

Kaul, I., P. Conceição, K. Le Goulven and R. U. Mendoza 2003b. 'How to Improve the Provision of Global Public Goods', in I. Kaul, P. Conceição, K. Le Goulven and R. U. Mendoza (eds.), *Providing Global Public Goods: Managing Globalization*. Oxford: Oxford University Press, pp. 21–58.

Kaul, I., P. Conceição, K. Le Goulven and R. U. Mendoza (eds.) 2003c. *Providing Global Public Goods: Managing Globalization*. Oxford: Oxford University Press.

Kaul, I., I. Grunberg and M. A. Stern 1999a. 'Introduction', in I. Kaul, I. Grunberg and M. A. Stern (eds.), *Global Public Goods: International Cooperation in the 21st Century*. Oxford: Oxford University Press, pp. xix–xxxviii.

Kaul, I., I. Grunberg and M. A. Stern 1999b. 'Defining Global Public Goods', in I. Kaul, I. Grunberg and M. A. Stern (eds.), *Global Public Goods: International Cooperation in the 21st Century*. Oxford: Oxford University Press, pp. 2–19.

Kaul, I., I. Grunberg and M. A. Stern (eds.) 1999c. *Global Public Goods: International Cooperation in the 21st Century*. Oxford: Oxford University Press.

Keane, J. 2003. *Global Civil Society?* Cambridge: Cambridge University Press.

Keane, J. 2004. *Violence and Democracy*. Cambridge: Cambridge University Press.

Keenan, A. 2003. *Democracy in Question: Democratic Openness in a Time of Political Closure*. Stanford: Stanford University Press.

Keith, M. 1993. *Race, Riots and Policing*. London: University College London Press.

Kelling, G. and C. Coles 1996. *Fixing Broken Windows: Restoring Order and Reducing Crime in Our Communities*. New York: Free Press.

Kempa, M., R. Carrier, J. Wood and C. Shearing 1999. 'Reflections on the Evolving Concept of "Private Policing" ', *European Journal of Criminal Policy and Research* 7: 197–223.

Kempa, M., P. Stenning and J. Wood 2004. 'Policing Communal Spaces: A Reconfiguration of the "Mass Private Property" Hypothesis', *British Journal of Criminology* 44/4: 562–81.

Kinsey, R., J. Lea and J. Young 1986. *Losing the Fight Against Crime*. Oxford: Basil Blackwell.

Kjaer, A. M. 2004. *Governance*. Cambridge: Polity.

Kleingeld, P. 1999. 'Six Varieties of Cosmopolitanism in Late Eighteenth-Century Germany', *Journal of the History of Ideas* 60: 505–24.

Kleingeld, P. and E. Brown 2002. 'Cosmopolitanism', in E. N. Zalta (ed.), *The Stanford Encyclopaedia of Philosophy*. Available at: http://plato. stanford.edu/archives/fall2002/entries/cosmopolitanism/

Klockars, C. 1985 *The Idea of Police*. Beverly Hills, CA: Sage.

Knemeyer, F. 1980. 'Polizei', *Economy and Society*, 9/2: 172–96.

Kostakopolou, D. forthcoming. 'The Area of Freedom, Security and Justice and the European Union's Constitutional Dialogue', in C. Barnard (ed.), *EU Law: Revisiting the Fundamentals in Light of the Constitutional Debate*. Oxford: Oxford University Press.

Krahmann, E. (ed.) 2005. *New Threats and New Actors in International Security*. Basingtoke: Palgrave.

Krause, K. and M. Williams (eds.) 1997. *Critical Security Studies*. London: University College London Press.

Kymlicka, W. 2005. 'Justice and Security in the Accommodation of Minority Nationalism', unpublished ms. (on file with the authors).

Laclau, E. and C. Mouffe 1985. *Hegemony and Socialist Strategy: Towards a Radical Democratic Politics*. London: Verso.

Laurie, P. 1972. *Scotland Yard*. Harmondsworth: Penguin.

Lawrence, P. 2005. *Nationalism: History and Theory*. Harlow: Pearson.

Lazarus, L. forthcoming. 'Mapping the Right to Security', in B. Goold and L. Lazarus (eds.), *Security and Human Rights*. Oxford: Hart.

Leander, A. 2006. 'Privatizing the Politics of Protection: Military Companies and the Definition of Security Concerns', in J. Huysmans, A. Dobson and R. Prokhovnik (eds.), *The Politics of Protection: Sites of Security and Political Agency*. London: Routledge, pp. 19–33.

Lee, J. 1981. 'Some Structural Aspects of Police Deviance in Relations with Minority Groups', in C. Shearing (ed.), *Organizational Police Deviance*. Toronto: Butterworth, pp. 51–82.

Lee, S. Y. 1990. 'Morning Calm, Rising Sun: National Character and Policing in South Korea and Japan', *Police Studies* 13: 91–110.

Levy, J. 2000. *The Multiculturalism of Fear*. Oxford: Oxford University Press.

Liang, H.-H. 1992. *The Rise of the Modern Police and the European State System from Metternich to the Second World War*. Cambridge: Cambridge University Press.

Lindahl, H. 2005. '*Jus Includendi et Excludendi*: Europe and the Borders of Freedom, Security and Justice', *King's College Law Journal* 16: 234–47.

Linden, R., D. Last and C. Murphy forthcoming. 'Obstacles on the Road to Peace and Justice: The Role of Civilian Police in Peacekeeping', in A. Goldsmith and J. Sheptycki (eds.), *Crafting Global Policing*. Oxford: Hart.

Lindseth, P. forthcoming. 'Agents without Principals? Delegation in an Age of Diffuse and Fragmented Governance', in F. Cafaggi (ed.), *Reframing Self-Regulation*. Dordrecht: Kluwer.

Little, R. 1997. 'International Regimes', in J. Baylis and S. Smith (eds.) *The Globalization of World Politics*. Oxford: Oxford University Press., pp. 299–316.

Loader, I. 1996. *Youth, Policing and Democracy*. Basingstoke: Macmillan/Palgrave.

Loader, I. 1997a. 'Thinking Normatively About Private Security', *Journal of Law and Society* 24/3: 377–94.

Loader, I. 1997b. 'Private Security and the Demand for Protection in Contemporary Britain', *Policing and Society* 7/3: 143–62.

Loader, I. 1997c. 'Policing and the Social: Questions of Symbolic Power', *British Journal of Sociology* 48/1: 1–18.

Loader, I. 1999. 'Consumer Culture and the Commodification of Policing and Security', *Sociology* 33/2: 373–92.

Loader, I. 2000. 'Plural Policing and Democratic Governance', *Social and Legal Studies* 9/3: 323–45.

Loader, I. 2002. 'Policing, Securitization and Democratization in Europe', *Criminal Justice* 2/2: 125–53.

Loader, I. 2006a. 'Fall of the "Platonic Guardians": Liberalism, Criminology and Political Responses to Crime in England and Wales', *British Journal of Criminology* 46/4: 561–86.

Loader, I. 2006b. 'Policing, Recognition and Belonging', *The Annals of the American Academy of Political and Social Science* 605/1: 202–21.

Loader, I. forthcoming a. 'The Cultural Lives of Security and Rights', in B. Goold and L. Lazarus (eds.) *Security and Human Rights*. Oxford: Hart.

Loader, I. forthcoming b. 'Playing with Fire?: Democracy and the Emotions of Crime and Punishment', in S. Karstedt, I. Loader and H. Strang (eds.), *Emotions, Crime and Justice*. Oxford: Hart.

Loader, I. and A. Mulcahy 2003. *Policing and the Condition of England: Memory, Politics and Culture*. Oxford: Oxford University Press.

Loader, I. and N. Walker 2001. 'Policing as a Public Good: Reconstituting the Connections Between Policing and the State', *Theoretical Criminology* 51: 9–35.

Loader, I. and N. Walker 2004. 'State of Denial?: Rethinking the Governance of Security', *Punishment and Society* 6/2: 221–8.

Loader, I. and N. Walker 2006. 'Necessary Virtues: The Legitimate Place of the State in the Production of Security', in J. Wood and B. Dupont (eds.), *Democracy, Society and the Governance of Security*. Cambridge: Cambridge University Press, pp. 165–95.

Loader, I. and L. Zedner 2007. 'Police Beyond Law?', *New Criminal Law Review* (formerly *Buffalo Criminal Law Review*) 10/1: 142–52.

Łoś, M. 2002. 'Post-Communist Fear of Crime and the Commercialization of Security', *Theoretical Criminology* 6/2: 165–88.

Łoś, M. and A. Zybertowicz 2000. *Privatizing the Police State: The Case of Poland*. New York: St Martin's Press.

Loughlin, M. 2003. *The Idea of Public Law*. Oxford: Oxford University Press.

Low, S. 2003. *Behind the Gates: Life, Security and the Pursuit of Happiness in Fortress America*. London: Routledge.

Luhmann, N. 1979. *Trust and Power*. Chichester and New York: Wiley.

Lyon, D. 2003. *Surveillance after September 11*. Cambridge: Polity.

Maanen, J. van 1983. 'The Boss', in M. Punch (ed.), *Control in the Police Organisation*. Cambridge, MA: MIT Press, pp. 275–317.

MacKinnon, C. 1989. *Toward a Feminist Theory of the State*. Cambridge, MA: Harvard University Press.

Maguire, M. 2000. 'Policing by Risks and Targets: Some Dimensions and Implications of Intelligence-Led Social Control', *Policing and Society* 9/4: 315–37.

Mair, P. 2005. *Democracy Beyond Parties (Paper 05–06)*. Center for the Study of Democracy, University of California, Irvine. Available at: http://repositories.cdlib.org/csd/05–06

Mann, M. 1986. *The Sources of Social Power*, Vol. 1. Cambridge: Cambridge University Press.

Mann, M. 2003. *Incoherent Empire*. London: Verso.

Manning, P. 1979. 'The Social Control of Police Work', in S. Holdaway (ed.), *The British Police*. London: Edward Arnold, pp. 41–65.

Manning, P. 2001. 'Theorizing Policing: The Drama and Myth of Crime Control in the NYPD', *Theoretical Criminology* 5/3: 315–44.

Marenin, O. 1982. 'Parking Tickets and Class Repression: The Concept of Policing in Critical Theories of Criminal Justice', *Contemporary Crises* 6/2: 241–6.

Marenin, O. 1996a. 'Policing Change, Changing Police: Some Thematic Questions', in O. Marenin (ed.), *Policing Change, Changing Police: International Perspectives*. New York: Garland, pp. 3–22.

Marenin, O. 1996b. 'Changing Police, Policing Change: Towards More Questions', in O. Marenin (ed.), *Policing Change, Changing Police: International Perspectives*. New York: Garland, pp. 309–30.

Marenin, O. (ed.) 1996c. *Policing Change, Changing Police: International Perspectives*. New York: Garland.

Marenin, O. forthcoming. 'Implementing Police Reforms: The Roles of the Transnational Condition', in A. Goldsmith and J. Sheptycki (eds.), *Crafting Global Policing*. Oxford: Hart.

Margalit, A. and J. Raz 1990. 'National Self-Determination', *The Journal of Philosophy* 87: 439–61.

Markell, P. 2003. *Bound by Recognition*. Princeton, NJ: Princeton University Press.

Marks, G., L. Hooghe and K. Blank 1996. 'European Integration from the 1980s: State-centric v. Multi-level Governance', *Journal of Common Market Studies* 34: 341–78.

Marquand, D. 2004. *Decline of the Public: The Hollowing out of Citizenship*. Cambridge: Polity.

Matthews, R. 2005. 'The Myth of Punitiveness', *Theoretical Criminology* 9/2: 175–202.

Mawby, R. I. 1990. *Comparative Policing Issues: The British and American Experience in International Perspective*. London: Routledge.

Mawby, R. I. (ed.) 1999. *Policing Across the World: Issues for the Twenty-First Century*. London: University College London Press.

Mawby, R. I. 2003. 'Models of Policing', in T. Newburn (ed.), *Handbook of Policing*. Cullompton: Willan, pp. 15–40.

Maynor, J. 2003. *Republicanism in the Modern World*. Cambridge: Polity.

Mayntz, R. 2002. 'Common Goods and Governance' in A. Heritier (ed.), *Common Goods: Reinventing European and International Governance*. Lanham, MD: Rowman & Littlefield, pp. 15–28.

Mazerolle, L. and J. Ransley 2006. *Third Party Policing*. Cambridge: Cambridge University Press.

McBride, C. 2005. 'Deliberative Democracy and the Politics of Recognition', *Political Studies* 53: 497–515.

McCabe, S., P. Wallington, J. Alderson, L. Gostin and C. Mason 1988. *The Police, Public Order and Civil Liberties*. London: Routledge.

McConville, M., A. Sanders and R. Young 1991. *The Case for the Prosecution*. London: Routledge.

McCormick, J. 1997. *Carl Schmitt's Critique of Liberalism: Against Politics as Technology*. Cambridge: Cambridge University Press.

McEvoy, K. and T. Newburn (eds.) 2003. *Criminology, Conflict Resolution and Restorative Justice*. Basingstoke: Palgrave.

McLaughlin, E. and K. Murji 1997. 'The Future Lasts a Long Time: Public Policework and the Managerialist Paradox', in P. Francis, P. Davis and V. Jupp (eds.), *Policing Futures*. London: Macmillan/Palgrave, pp. 80–103.

McLaughlin, E. and K. Murji 2001. 'Lost Connections and New Directions: Neo-Liberalism, New Public Managerialism and the "Modernization" of the British Police', in K. Stenson and R. Sullivan (eds.), *Crime, Risk and Justice*. Cullompton: Willan, pp. 104–22.

McSweeney, B. 1998. *Security, Identity and Interests: A Sociology of International Relations*. Cambridge: Cambridge University Press.

Melossi, D. 2005. 'Security, Social Control, Democracy and Migration within the "Constitution" of the EU', *European Law Journal* 11: 5–21.

Melossi, D. and R. Selmini 2000. 'Social Conflict and the Micro-Physics of Crime: The Experience of the Emilia Romagna Citta Sicure Project', in T. Hope and R. Sparks (eds.), *Crime, Risk and Insecurity*. London: Routledge, pp. 146–65.

Melossi, D., R. Sparks and M. Sozzo (eds.) forthcoming. *Travels of the Criminal Question*. Oxford: Hart.

Michalowski, R. 1992. 'Crime and Justice in Socialist Cuba: What Can Realists Learn?', in B. Maclean and J. Lowman (eds.), *Realist Criminology: Crime Control and Policing in the 1990s*. Toronto: University of Toronto Press, pp. 115–38.

Michnik, A. 1998. *Letters from Freedom: Post-Cold War Realities and Perspectives*. Berkeley: University of California Press.

Miliband, R. 1969. *The State in Capitalist Society*. London: Weidenfeld & Nicolson.

Miller, D. 1995. *On Nationality*. Oxford: Oxford University Press.

Morgan, G. 2005. *The Idea of a European Superstate: Public Justification and European Integration*. Princeton, NJ: Princeton University Press.

Morganthau, H. 1928. *Politics Among Nations: The Struggle for Power and Peace*. New York: Knopf.

Mouffe, C. (ed.) 1999. *The Challenge of Carl Schmitt*. London: Verso.

Mouffe, C. 2000. *The Democratic Paradox*. London: Verso.

Muir, W. K. 1977. *Police: Streetcorner Politicians*. Chicago: University of Chicago Press.

Mulcahy, A. 2005. *Policing Northern Ireland: Conflict, Legitimacy and Reform*. Cullompton: Willan.

Murphy, L. and T. Nagel 2002. *The Myth of Ownership: Taxes and Justice*. New York: Oxford University Press.

Muthien, J. and I. Taylor 2002. 'The Return of the Dogs of War?: The Privatization of Security in Africa', in R. Bruce Hall and T. J. Bierstaker (eds.), *The Emergence of Private Authority in Global Governance*. Cambridge: Cambridge University Press.

Nadelman, E. 1993. *Cops Across Borders: The Internationalization of US Criminal Law Enforcement*. Philadelphia: Pennsylvania State University Press.

Neocleous, M. 1998. 'Policing and Pin-Making: Adam Smith, Police and the State of Prosperity', *Policing and Society*, 8/4: 425–49.

Neocleous, M. 2000. *The Fabrication of Social Order: A Critical Theory of Police Power*. London: Pluto.

Neumann, F. 1957. 'Anxiety and Politics', in H. Marcuse (ed.), *The Democratic and Authoritarian State: Essays in Political and Legal Theory*. New York: Free Press, pp. 270–300.

Newburn, T. 2003. 'Community Safety and Policing: Some Implications of the Crime and Disorder Act 1998', in G. Hughes, E. McLaughlin and J. Muncie (eds.), *Crime Prevention and Community Safety: New Directions*. London: Sage, pp. 12–122.

Newburn, T. and R. Sparks (eds.) 2004. *Criminal Justice and Political Cultures: National and International Dimensions of Crime Control*. Cullompton: Willan.

Newman, S. 2004. 'Terror, Sovereignty and Law: On the Politics of Violence', *German Law Journal* 5/5: 569–84.

Nordstrom, C. 2002. 'Shadow Sovereigns', *Theory, Culture and Society* 17/4: 35–54.

North, D. C. 1993. *Institutions, Institutional Change and Economic Performance*. Cambridge: Cambridge University Press.

Nozick, R. 1974. *Anarchy, State and Utopia*. Oxford: Basil Blackwell.

Nussbaum, M. 2002. 'Patriotism and Cosmopolitanism', in J. Cohen (ed.), *For Love of Country?* Boston: Beacon Press, pp. 131–44.

Nye, J. S. 2002. *The Paradox of American Power: Why the World's Only Superpower Can't Go It Alone*. Oxford: Oxford University Press.

Oakley, R., M. Dziedzic and E. Goldberg (eds.) 2002. *Policing the New World Disorder: Peace Operations and Public Security*. Honolulu: University Press of the Pacific.

Oakshott, M. 1949/1991. *Rationalism in Politics and Other Essays*. Indianapolis: Liberty Press.

Ocqueteau, F. 2004. 'Public Security as "Everyone's Concern"?: Beginnings and Developments of a Useful Misunderstanding', *Policing and Society* 14/1: 66–75.

Offe, C. 2003. 'The European Model of "Social" Capitalism: Can It Survive European Integration?', *The Journal of Political Philosophy* 11/4: 437–69.

Olsen, M. 1971. *The Logic of Collective Action*. Cambridge, MA: Harvard University Press.

O'Malley, P. 1992. 'Risk, Power and Crime Prevention', *Economy and Society* 21/3: 251–68.

O'Malley, P. 1999. 'Volatile and Contradictory Punishment', *Theoretical Criminology* 3/2: 175–96.

O'Malley, P. and D. Palmer 1996. 'Post-Keynesian Policing', *Economy and Society* 25/2: 137–55.

Osborne, D. and T. Gaebler 1992. *Reinventing Government*. Harmondsworth: Penguin.

Parenti, C. 1999. *Lockdown America*. London: Verso.

Paris, R. 2001. 'Human Security: Paradigm Shift or Hot Air?', *International Security* 26/2: 87–102.

Parker, C. and J. Braithwaite, 2003. 'Regulation', in P. Cane and M. Tushnet (eds.), *The Oxford Handbook of Legal Studies*. Oxford: Oxford University Press, pp. 119–45.

Pasquino, P. 1991. 'Theatricum Politicum: The Genealogy of Capital-Police and the State of Prosperity', in G. Burchell, C. Gordon and P. Miller (eds.), *The Foucault Effect*. Brighton: Harvester, pp. 115–18.

Pastore, F. 2002. 'The Asymmetrical Fortress: The Problem of Relations between Internal and External Security Policies in the European Union', in M. Anderson and J. Apap (eds.), *Police and Justice Co-operation and the New European Borders*. The Hague: Kluwer, pp. 59–80.

Patten, C. 1999. *A New Beginning for Policing in Northern Ireland: The Report of the Independent Commission on Policing for Northern Ireland*. Belfast: HMSO.

Pettit, P. 1997. *Republicanism: A Theory of Freedom and Government*. Oxford: Oxford University Press.

Pettit, P. 2001a. *A Theory of Freedom: From the Psychology to the Politics of Agency*. Cambridge: Polity.

Pettit, P. 2001b. 'Is Criminal Justice Politically Feasible?', *Buffalo Criminal Law Review* 5: 427–50.

Pettit, P. 2004. 'Depoliticizing Democracy', *Ratio Juris* 17/1: 52–65.

Pfaff, W. 2006. 'France: The Children's Hour', *The New York Review of Books* 23/8: 40–3.

Pierre, J. (ed.) 2000. *Debating Governance: Authority, Steering and Democracy*. Oxford: Oxford University Press.

Poulantzas, N. 1978. *State, Power, Socialism*. London: New Left Books.

Power, M. 1997. *The Audit Society: Rituals of Verification*. Oxford: Oxford University Press.

Pyle, D. 1995. *Cutting the Costs of Crime*. London: Institute of Economic Affairs.

Rawls, J. 1971. *A Theory of Justice*. Oxford: Oxford University Press.

Rawls, J. 1993. *Political Liberalism*. New York: Columbia University Press.

Rawls, J. 1999. 'The Idea of Public Reason Revisited', in *The Law of Peoples*. Harvard: Harvard University Press, pp. 131–80.

Raz, J. 1986. *The Morality of Freedom*. Oxford: Oxford University Press.

Reiner, R. 1980. 'Fuzzy Thoughts: The Police and Law-and-Order Politics', *Sociological Review* 28/2: 377–413.

Reiner, R. 1995. 'Myth vs. Modernity: Reality and Unreality in the English Model of Policing', in J.-P. Brodeur (ed.), *Comparisons in Policing: An International Perspective*. Aldershot: Avebury.

Reiner, R. 2000. *The Politics of the Police*, 3rd edn. Brighton: Harvester, pp. 16–48.

Rigakos, G. 2002. *The New Parapolice: Risk Markets and Commodified Social Control*. Toronto: University of Toronto Press.

Roach, K. (ed.) 2001. *The Security of Freedom: Essays on Canada's Anti-Terrorism Bill*. Toronto: University of Toronto Press.

Robertson, R. 1992. *Globalization, Social Theory and Global Culture*. London: Sage.

Robin, C. 2004. *Fear: The History of a Political Idea*. Oxford: Oxford University Press.

Roche, D. 2002. 'Restorative Justice and the Regulatory State in South African Townships', *British Journal of Criminology* 42/3: 514–32.

Roche, D. 2003. *Accountability and Restorative Justice*. Oxford: Oxford University Press.

Roermund, B. van 2003. 'Sovereignty: Popular and Unpopular', in N. Walker (ed.), *Sovereignty in Transition*. Oxford: Hart, pp. 33–54.

Rorty, R. 2004. 'Post-Democracy', *London Review of Books*, 1 April, pp. 10–11.

Rose, D. 2004. *Guantanamo: America's War on Human Rights*. New York: The New Press.

Rotberg, R. 2003. 'Failed States, Collapsed States, Weak States: Causes and Indicators', in R. Rotberg (ed.), *State Failure and State Weakness in a Time of Terror*. Cambridge, MA: World Peace Foundation, pp. 1–26.

Rothbard, M. 1985. *For a New Liberty: The Libertarian Manifesto*. New York: Libertarian Review Foundation.

Rothschild, E. 1995. 'What is Security?', *Daedalus* 124/3: 53–98.

Royal Commission into Aboriginal Deaths in Custody 1991. *Final Report*. Sydney: Royal Commission.

Runciman, D. 1997. *Pluralism and the Personality of the State*. Cambridge: Cambridge University Press.

Sandel, M. 1996. *Democracy's Discontent: America in Search of a Public Philosophy*. Cambridge, MA: Harvard University Press.

Sands, P. 2005. *Lawless World: Making and Breaking Global Rules*. Harmondsworth: Penguin.

Santos, B. de Sousa 1995. *Toward a New Common Sense*. London: Routledge.

Scharpf, F. 1999. *Governing in Europe: Effective and Democratic?* Oxford: Oxford University Press.

Scheuerman, W. 2002. 'Rethinking Crisis Government', *Constellations* 9/4: 492–505.

Schmitt, C. 1922/1985. *Political Theology: Four Chapters on the Concept of Sovereignty*. Cambridge, MA: MIT Press.

Schmitt, C. 1933/1996. *The Concept of the Political*. Chicago: University of Chicago Press.

Schulze, H. 1996. *Nations and Nationalism: From the Middle Ages to the Present*. Oxford: Basil Blackwell.

Scott, C. 2002. 'Private Regulation of the Public Sector: A Neglected Facet of Contemporary Governance', *Journal of Law and Society* 29: 56–76.

Scott, C. 2004. 'Regulation in an Age of Governance: The Rise of the Post-Regulatory State', in J. Jordana and D. Levi-Faur (eds.), *The Politics of Regulation: Institutional and Regulatory Reform for the Age of Governance*. Cheltenham: Edward Elgar, pp. 145–74.

Scott, J. C. 1998. *Seeing Like a State: How Certain Schemes to Improve the Human Condition Have Failed*. New Haven: Yale University Press.

Scraton, P. (ed.) 1987. *Law, Order and the Authoritarian State*. Milton Keynes: Open University Press.

Seldon, A. 1990. *Capitalism*. Oxford: Basil Blackwell.

Sennett, R. 2003. *Respect in a World of Inequality*. New York: W. W. Norton.

Shapiro, I. 2003. *The State of Democratic Theory*. Princeton, NJ: Princeton University Press.

Shearing, C. 1981. 'Subterranean Process in the Maintenance of Power', *Canadian Review of Sociology and Anthropology* 18/3: 283–98.

Shearing, C. 1996. 'Reinventing Policing: Policing as Governance', in

O. Marenin (ed.), *Policing Change, Changing Police: International Perspectives*. New York: Garland, pp. 285–307.

Shearing, C. 2001. 'Punishment and the Changing Face of Governance', *Punishment & Society* 3: 203–20.

Shearing, C. 2006. 'Reflections on the Refusal to Acknowledge Private Governments', in J. Wood and B. Dupont (eds.), *Democracy, Society and the Governance of Security*. Cambridge: Cambridge University Press, pp. 11–32.

Shearing, C. and L. Johnston 2005. 'Justice in the Risk Society', *Australian and New Zealand Journal of Criminology* 38: 25–38.

Shearing, C. and M. Kempa 2000. 'The Role of "Private Security" in Transitional Democracies', in M. Shaw (ed.), *Crime and Policing in Transitional Societies*. Johannesburg: Konrad Adenauer Stifting, pp. 205–13.

Shearing, C. and P. Stenning 1983. 'Private Security: Its Implications for Social Control', *Social Problems* 30: 125–38.

Shearing, C. and P. Stenning (eds.) 1987. *Private Policing*. Beverly Hills, CA: Sage.

Shearing, C. and J. Wood 2003a. 'Governing Security for Common Goods', *International Journal for the Sociology of Law* 31: 205–25.

Shearing, C. and J. Wood 2003b. 'Nodal Governance, Democracy, and the New "Denizen"', *Journal of Law and Society* 30/3: 400–19.

Shelley, L. 1997. *Policing Soviet Society: The Evolution of State Control*. London: Routledge.

Sheptycki, J. (ed.) 2000. *Issues in Transnational Policing*. London: Routledge.

Sheptycki, J. 2002. 'Accountability Across the Policing Field: Towards a General Cartography of Accountability for Post-Modern Policing', *Policing and Society* 12/4: 323–38.

Sheptycki, J. forthcoming. 'The Constabulary Ethic and the Transnational Condition', in A. Goldsmith and J. Sheptycki (eds.), *Crafting Global Policing*. Oxford: Hart.

Silver, A. 1967. 'The Demand for Order in Civil Society', in D. J. Bordua (ed.), *The Police: Six Sociological Essays*. New York: Wiley, pp. 1–24.

Simon, J. 2001. 'Megan's Law: Crime and Democracy in Late Modern America', *Law and Social Inquiry* 25/4: 1111–49.

Simon, J. 2006. *Governing Through Crime*. New York: Oxford University Press.

Singer, P. W. 2003. *Corporate Warriors: The Rise of the Privatized Military Industry*. Ithaca: Cornell University Press.

Skinner, Q. 1989. 'The State', in T. Ball, J. Farr and R. L. Hanson (eds.), *Political Innovation and Conceptual Change*. Cambridge: Cambridge University Press, pp. 90–131.

Skinner, Q. 1996. *Reason and Rhetoric in the Philosophy of Hobbes.* Cambridge: Cambridge University Press.

Sklar, J. 1989. 'The Liberalism of Fear', in N. Rosenblum (ed.), *Liberalism and the Moral Life.* Cambridge, MA: Harvard University Press, pp. 21–38.

Skolnick, J. 1966. *Justice Without Trial.* New York: Wiley.

Skolnick, J. 1969. *The Politics of Protest.* New York: Bantam.

Skolnick, J. and D. Bayley 1988. 'Theme and Variation in Community Policing', in M. Tonry and N. Morris (eds.), *Crime and Justice: An Annual Review of Research*, vol. 10. Chicago: University of Chicago Press, pp. 1–37.

Smith, A. D. 2001. *Nationalism.* Cambridge: Polity.

Smith, M. and N. Tilley (eds.) 2005. *Crime Science: New Approaches to Preventing and Detecting Crime.* Cullompton: Willan.

Sorensen, G. 2004. *The Transformation of the State: Beyond the Myth of Retreat.* Basingstoke: Macmillan/Palgrave.

Spitzer, S. 1981. 'The Political Economy of Policing', in D. Greenberg (ed.), *Crime and Capitalism: Readings in Marxist Criminology.* Palo Alto: Mayfield, pp. 314–40.

Stanley, W. 1996. 'International Tutelage and Domestic Political Will: Building a New Civilian Police Force in El Salvador', in O. Marenin (ed.), *Policing Change, Changing Police: International Perspectives.* New York: Garland, pp. 37–78.

Stenning, P. and LaPrairie 2003. ' "Politics by Other Means": The Role of Commission of Inquiry in Establishing the "Truth" about "Aboriginal" Justice in Canada', in G. Gilligan and J. Pratt (eds.), *Crime, Truth and Justice: Official Inquiry, Discourse, Knowledge.* Cullompton: Willan, pp. 138–60.

Taussig, M. 1997. *The Magic of the State.* London: Routledge.

Taussig, M. 2003. *Law in a Lawless Land: Diary of a Limpieza.* New York: New Press.

Taylor, C. 1991. *The Ethics of Authenticity.* Cambridge, MA: Harvard University Press.

Taylor, C. 1994. 'The Politics of Recognition', in A. Guttmann (ed.), *Multiculturalism.* Princeton, NJ: Princeton University Press, pp. 25–74.

Taylor, C. 1995. *Philosophical Arguments.* Cambridge, MA: Harvard University Press.

Taylor, C. 2004. *Modern Social Imaginaries.* Durham, NC: Duke University Press.

Taylor, I. 1999. *Crime in Context: A Critical Criminology of Market Societies.* Cambridge: Polity.

Terriff, T., S. Croft, L. James and P. M. Morgan 1999. *Security Studies Today*. Cambridge: Polity.

Thompson, G. 2003. *Between Hierarchies and Markets: The Logic and Limits of Network Forms of Organization*. Oxford: Oxford University Press.

Tilley, N. 2003. 'Community Policing, Problem-Oriented Policing and Intelligence-Led Policing', in T. Newburn (ed.), *Handbook of Policing*. Cullompton: Willan, pp. 311–39.

Tilly, C. (ed.) 1975. *The Formation of National States in Western Europe*. Princeton, NJ: Princeton University Press.

Tilly, C. 1985. 'War Making and State Making as Organized Crime', in P. Evans, D. Rueschemeyer and T. Skocpol (eds.), *Bringing the State Back In*. Cambridge: Cambridge University Press, pp. 169–91.

Todd, E. 2003. *After the Empire: The Breakdown of American Order*. New York: Columbia University Press.

Tshehla, B. 2002. 'Non-State Justice in Post Apartheid South Africa: A Scan of Khaylelistsha', *African Sociological Review* 6: 47–70.

Tully, J. 1995. *Strange Multiplicity: Constitutionalism in an Age of Diversity*. Cambridge: Cambridge University Press.

Tully, J. 2002. 'The Unfreedom of the Moderns in Comparison to Their Ideals of Constitutional Democracy', *Modern Law Review* 65/2: 204–28.

Turner, V. 1974. *Dramas, Fields and Metaphors: Symbolic Action in Human Society*. Ithaca: Cornell University Press.

Tyler, T. 2004. 'Enhancing Police Legitimacy', *Annals of the American Academy of Social and Political Science* 593/1: 84–99.

Uildriks, N. and P. van Reenan 2003. *Policing Post-Communist Societies: Police–Public Violence, Democratic Policing and Human Rights*. Antwerp: Intersentia.

United Nations 2000. *Report of the Panel on United Nations Peace Operations*. United Nations: New York.

Varese, F. 2001. *The Russian Mafia: Private Protection in a New Market Economy*. Oxford: Oxford University Press.

Vertovec, S. and R. Cohen (eds.) 2002. *Conceiving Cosmopolitanism: Theory, Context and Practice*. Oxford: Oxford University Press.

Vijver, K. van der and J. Terpstra (eds.) 2005. *Urban Safety: Problems, Governance and Strategies*. Enschede: IPIT.

Vincent, A. 2002. *Nationalism and Particularity*. Cambridge: Cambridge University Press.

Wacquant, L. 2003. 'How Penal Common Sense Comes to Europeans: Notes on the Transatlantic Diffusion of the Neoliberal *Doxa*', *European Societies* 1/3: 319–52.

Waddington, P. A. J. 1986. 'The Objectives Debate', *Policing* 2/2: 223–35.

Wæver, O. 1995. 'Securitization and Desecuritization', in R. Lipschutz (ed.), *On Security*. New York: Columbia University Press, pp. 46–86.

Wæver, O. 1996. 'European Security Identities', *Journal of Common Market Studies* 34: 103–23.

Wakefield, A. 2003. *Selling Security: The Private Policing of Public Space*. Cullompton: Willan.

Walden, K. 1982. *Visions of Order: The Canadian Mounties in Symbol and Myth*. Toronto: Butterworths.

Waldron, J. 1993. *Liberal Rights: Collected Papers 1981–1991*. Cambridge: Cambridge University Press.

Waldron, J. 2000. 'What Is Cosmopolitan?', *Journal of Political Philosophy* 8: 227–43.

Waldron, J. 2003a. 'Security and Liberty: The Image of Balance', *Journal of Political Philosophy* 2: 191–210.

Waldron, J. 2003b. 'Who Is my Neighbor? Humanity and Proximity', *The Monist* 86: 333–46.

Waldron, J. 2004. 'Liberty and Security: Security as a Public Good', paper presented at Conference on Political Thought, St Catherine's College, Oxford (on file with the authors).

Walker, N. 2000. *Policing in a Changing Constitutional Order*. London: Sweet & Maxwell.

Walker, N. 2002a. 'The Problem of Trust in an Enlarged Area of Freedom, Security and Justice: A Conceptual Analysis', in M. Anderson and J. Apap (eds.), *Police and Justice Co-operation and the New European Borders*. Dordrecht: Kluwer, pp. 19–34.

Walker, N. 2002b. 'Policing and the Supranational', *Policing and Society* 12/4: 307–22.

Walker, N. 2003. 'The Pattern of Transnational Policing', in T. Newburn (ed.), *Handbook of Policing*. Cullompton: Willan, pp. 111–35.

Walker, N. 2004. 'In Search of the Area of Freedom, Security and Justice: A Constitutional Odyssey', in N. Walker (ed.), *Europe's Area of Freedom, Security and Justice*. Oxford: Oxford University Press, pp. 3–40.

Walker, N. 2006a. 'Sovereignty, Global Security and the Regulation of Armed Conflict: The Possibilities of Political Agency', in J. Huysmans, A. Dobson and R. Prokhovnik (eds.), *The Politics of Protection: Sites of Security and Political Agency*. London: Routledge, pp. 154–74.

Walker, N. 2006b. 'EU Constitutionalism and New Governance', in G. de Burca and J. Scott (eds.), *Law and New Governance in the EU and the US*. Oxford: Hart, pp. 15–36.

Walker, N. 2006c. 'EU Constitutionalism in the State Constitutional Tradition', *Current Legal Problems* 59: 51–90.

Walker, N. forthcoming a. 'Making a World of Difference? Habermas, Cosmopolitanism and the Constitutionalization of International Law', in O. Shabani (ed.), *The Practice of Law-Making and the Problem of Difference*. Aldershot: Dartmouth.

Walker, N. forthcoming b. 'On Regulating the Regulation of Regulation', in F. Cafaggi (ed.), *Reframing Self-Regulation*. Dordrecht: Kluwer.

Walker, N. and M. Telford 2000. *Designing Criminal Justice: The Northern Ireland System in Comparative Perspective*. Belfast: The Northern Ireland Office.

Walker, R. B. J. 1997. 'The Subject of Security', in K. Krause and M. Williams (eds.), *Critical Security Studies*. London: University College London Press, pp. 61–82.

Walker, R. B. J. 2004. 'Conclusion: Sovereignties, Exceptions, Worlds', in J. Edkins, V. Pin-Fat and M. J. Shapiro (eds.), *Sovereign Lives: Power in Global Politics*. London: Routledge, pp. 239–50.

Walt, S. 1991. 'The Renaissance of Security Studies', *International Studies Quarterly*, 35: 211–39.

Walters, R. 2003. *Deviant Knowledge: Criminology, Politics and Public Policy*. Collumpton: Willan.

Waltz, K. 1959. *Man, the State and War*. New York: Columbia University Press.

Waltz, K. 1993. 'The Emerging Structure of International Politics', *International Security* 18: 50–78.

Warren, M. 1996. 'What Should We Expect from More Democracy? Radically Democratic Responses to Politics', *Political Theory* 24/2: 241–70.

Weber, M. 1948. *From Max Weber*, ed. and trans. H. Gerth and C. Wright Mills. London: Routledge & Kegan Paul.

Weiler, J. H. H. 1999. *The Constitution of Europe*. Cambridge: Cambridge University Press.

Weisburd, D., S. Mastroski, A. McNally, R. Greenspan and J. Willis 2003. 'Reforming to Preserve: Compstat and Strategic Problem Solving in American Policing', *Criminology and Public Policy* 2: 421–56.

Weitzer, R. 1995. *Policing Under Fire: Ethnic Conflict and Police–Community Relations in Northern Ireland*. New York: State University of New York Press.

Westley, W. 1970. *Violence and the Police*. Cambridge, MA: MIT Press.

Westmarland, L. 2001. *Gender and Policing*. Cullompton: Willan.

White House, The. 2002. *The National Security Strategy of the United States of America*. Washington: The White House. Available at: www.cdi.org/national-security-strategy/washington.cfm.

Whitman, J. Q. 2003. *Harsh Justice: Criminal Punishment and the Widening Divide Between America and Europe*. Oxford: Oxford University Press.

Williams, R. 1964. *The Long Revolution*. Harmondsworth: Penguin.

Wilson, J. M. 2006. 'Law and Order in an Emerging Democracy: Lessons from the Reconstruction of Kosovo's Police and Judicial Systems', *Annals of the American Academy of Social and Political Science* 605/1: 152–77.

Wilson, J. Q. and G. Kelling 1982. 'Broken Windows', *Atlantic Monthly*, March: 29–38.

Wong, K. 2002. 'Policing in the People's Republic of China: The Road to Reform in the 1990s', *British Journal of Criminology* 42: 281–316.

Wood, J. 2004. 'Cultural Change in the Governance of Security', *Policing and Society* 14/1: 31–48.

Wood, J. 2006. 'Research and Innovation in the Field of Security: A Nodal Governance View', in J. Wood and B. Dupont (eds.), *Democracy, Society and the Governance of Security*. Cambridge: Cambridge University Press, pp. 217–40.

Wood, J. and B. Dupont 2006a. 'Introduction: Understanding the Governance of Security', in J. Wood and B. Dupont (eds.), *Democracy, Society and the Governance of Security*. Cambridge: Cambridge University Press, pp. 1–10.

Wood, J. and B. Dupont (eds.) 2006b. *Democracy, Society and the Governance of Security*. Cambridge: Cambridge University Press.

Wood, J. and E. Font forthcoming. 'Crafting the Goverance of Security in Argentina: Engaging with Global Trends', in A. Goldsmith and J. Sheptycki (eds.), *Crafting Global Policing*. Oxford: Hart.

Wood, J. and C. Shearing 2006. *Imagining Security*. Cullompton: Willan.

Wright, A. 2002. *Policing: An Introduction to Concepts and Practice*. Cullompton: Willan.

Yack, B. 2003. 'Nationalism, Popular Sovereignty and the Liberal Democratic State', in T. V. Paul, G. J. Ikenberry and J. A. Hall (eds.), *The Nation-State in Question*. Princeton, NJ: Princeton University Press, pp. 29–50.

Young, I. M. 2000. *Inclusion and Democracy*. Oxford: Oxford University Press.

Young, J. 1971. 'The Role of the Police as Amplifiers of Deviance', in S. Cohen (ed.), *Images of Deviance*. Harmondsworth: Penguin, pp. 27–61.

Young, J. 1999. *The Exclusive Society: Social Exclusion, Crime and Difference in Late Modernity*. London: Sage.

Zedner, L. 2003. 'Too Much Security?', *International Journal of the Sociology of Law* 31: 155–84.

Zedner, L. forthcoming. *Security*. London: Routledge.

Zielonka, J. 1998. *Explaining Euro-paralysis: Why Europe is Unable to Act in International Politics*. New York: St Martin's Press.

Zimring, F. E. and D. T. Johnson 2006. 'Public Opinion and the Governance of Punishment in Democratic Political Systems', *Annals of the American Academy of Social and Political Science* 605/1: 265–80.

Index